D0801846

THE SECRET LIFE OF MONEY

THE
SECRET LIFE
OF MONEY

*Teaching Tales of Spending,
Receiving, Saving, and Owing*

TAD CRAWFORD

A JEREMY P. TARCHER/PUTNAM BOOK
Published by G. P. PUTNAM'S SONS
New York

A Jeremy P. Tarcher/Putnam Book
Published by G. P. Putnam's Sons
Publishers Since 1838
200 Madison Avenue
New York, NY 10016

Library of Congress Cataloging-in-Publication Data

Crawford, Tad, date.
    The secret life of money : Teaching Tales of Spending, Receiving, Saving, and Owing / by Tad Crawford.
        p.   cm.
    Includes bibliographical references and index.
    ISBN 0-87477-786-0
    1. Money.   2. Finance, Personal.   I. Title.
HG255.C676   1995
332.4—dc20   94-15320 CIP

Design by Irving Perkins Associates

Printed in the United States of America

1   2   3   4   5   6   7   8   9   10

This book is printed on acid-free paper.

For Susan

ACKNOWLEDGMENTS

I deeply appreciate my friends, family, and colleagues whose encouragement and insights helped bring this book to fruition. I would like to thank the staff at Jeremy P. Tarcher, Inc., especially Connie Zweig for her perceptive editorial suggestions. I am also thankful to have been aided in so many ways by the excellent staff at Allworth Press. Finally, I appreciate my agent of nearly two decades, Jean Naggar, who offered exemplary guidance for *The Secret Life of Money* as it entered the world of commerce.

CONTENTS

INTRODUCTION

ONCE UPON A TIME there was a man who prayed to a wooden idol, which he had enshrined in his home. He beseeched the idol to give him money and make him prosper in the world. But even if he had knelt until his knees ached and his muscles cramped, the idol would have given him no reward. In fact, with each passing day, the winds blew ill for this man's fortunes. He had less money; prosperity eluded him.

At last, the man was awakened by a terrible rage to have prayed so long and so hard to so little purpose. He seized the wooden idol and smashed its head to pieces against the wall. Suddenly, as if a magic key had turned in a lock, a fortune in shining gold poured from the idol's broken head.

This ancient tale captures the paradox of money. To pray for money brings frustration and despair. Our fervent petition gives life to the wooden idol, as if the idol knows the secret way to make us prosper. But if we can shatter our ideas about how money has the power to be our salvation, often we will find wealth in places and forms that we would never have imagined, even hidden in what seems most familiar to us.

The Secret Life of Money is an exploration of why

money is so much more than the useful tool we think it is. To understand money we must see its symbolic value. This book gathers together stories and myths from around the world, from the present and the past, that reveal money as a marker of issues of the human heart and soul. The subjects of the stories revolve around money, or sometimes gold or even food, but the themes are about our nature, our inner richness, and our connection to other people and to community.

This is not a book about finance. It does not tell how to earn more, balance a budget, play the stock market, or hide money in foreign bank accounts. Many books give practical advice about money; this book does not cover that familiar territory. And, emphatically, this is not a book about how certain spiritual practices might enable one to "manifest" divine favor in the form of money.

In this book the quest for money is not a quest for acquisition, but for understanding. We have to seek the origins of money if we want to know why it has the power to captivate our minds. When we understand these origins, we see that money speaks to us of life and death, of the fertility of the natural world, and of our own natures.

We deal constantly with money in our daily lives, so much so that money may seem too familiar to merit our curiosity. What can we learn from money? Its rules look so simple. If you have it, you can buy what you want. If you don't have it, you must either get it or suffer deprivation.

If we are literal-minded when we approach money, we may love money and want to possess it whatever the cost. It is this love, or attachment, rather than money itself, that is corrupting to us. But if we see money as a symbol, we may feel a deepening connection to others and a desire to express and share an ever-increasing inner richness.

Keeping the symbolic value of money firmly in mind, we can understand how inheritance may raise emotional issues that have little to do with the money and property we receive. We can gain a new view of debt, seeing it not merely as an obligation that must be repaid but also as a statement about how our inner richness will be expressed in the future. We become able to contrast the symbolism of money with the seductive symbolism of bank credit cards that rely on the creation of debt for profits. We can better comprehend why in the last hundred years we have seen the invention and widespread use of credit cards, changes in bank architecture, the growth of debt, and a dramatic transformation in the very nature of United States money.

We refer so frequently to money in our everyday lives that we forget how taboo a subject money truly is. Of course, we feel comfortable chatting about prices, bargains, and news stories about the wealthy. But how often do we dare ask how much someone else earns, has in the bank, has inherited, or owes? Inquiries like these violate boundaries of privacy about which we feel strongly. But we can only understand why we feel so strongly if we understand money's secret life and symbolic value.

This book is titled *The Secret Life of Money* because it seeks to see beyond and beneath the usefulness of money and understand the ways in which money lives in our imaginations. It seeks to present money as a challenge, a door to a path on which we journey in search of greater knowledge of ourselves. If we do not go through this door, we risk losing our inner richness and our vital connection to family and community. Knowing the secret life of money—why, for example, "In God We Trust" appears on our bills and coins—may help us find an inner richness that is certainly wealth, but not the wealth that money can measure.

CHAPTER ONE

THE MANY FORMS OF MONEY

Understanding Its Symbolic Value

In THIS ERA of extraordinary inventions, many of our grandparents knew a world where horses reared at the first glimpse of an automobile, recordings of sound were a new marvel, airplanes realized the dream of flight, and radio, television, nuclear bombs, computers, and genetic engineering were obscured in the mysteries of the future.

But who, even among the eldest of us, can remember a time without money? Many believe that in an era of immense change, money is our North Star, the one reference we can trust to be stable and unchanging. We may have to worry about inflation, debt, and where the interest rate is pegged, but few people question whether we should have money. Checks, credit cards, electronic fund transfers, and automatic teller machines merely enhance the ease with which money is used. Money feels to us like language, a great invention whose date of origin is lost in prehistory. And like language, money can be translated and exchanged from one currency to another.

The ubiquity of money, its easy flow through our hands and the world around us, allows us to link our identity to money. We allow our self-worth to depend, at least in part, on whether we succeed in gaining money. In this chapter, we will take a step back from the everyday pursuit of money. We will see how dreams of having more money can be symbolic and serve us whether or not we in fact get the money. By looking at the innumerable forms that money has taken in different societies and at different times, we will see that the value of money rests, for the most part, in its power over our minds. Money is a potent symbol, but of what? To answer that question, we will meet a goddess named Moneta and see how money is rooted in challenges to each of us and our society to be fertile and productive.

THE POWER OF MONEY AS A SYMBOL

"If only I had more money, I would . . ."

We can find an infinite variety of ways to complete that sentence: Take a trip. Buy clothing. Have a nicer home. Help the poor. Continue our education. The list flows on and on, as endless as the needs and dreams of human beings.

When we fantasize about what more money would bring us, we rarely distance ourselves so that we can see the fantasy as distinct from the money that would be needed to realize the fantasy. But which is more important—the money or the fantasy? The fantasy is within us, the money outside us. Because of this, the fantasy tells us what we desire. The money is neutral, silent as to who we are or what we desire.

An examination of money fantasies reveals our minds to us, the inmost workings of ourselves. For example, a man of thirty-five yearns to leave his work and go to live on a tropical island. If only he had the money, he would go. If he forgets about the absence of money and welcomes the opportunity to explore his own thoughts, he may discover any number of truths: He fears the duties that he will have to perform if he is promoted; he is worried about his marriage but feels unable to confront his spouse; or even the banal possibility that he needs a vacation.

If the man stalls this self-examination by saying that he doesn't have enough money, he loses the opportunity to see into himself. He goes through his days dreaming of another life, an unlived life filled with equatorial passion and spent on the sandy shores of exotic islands. He does not recognize that this other life, this island life, is illusory, a flight from his reality. He sees money as an adversary and chooses to live with his feelings of deprivation. However, his deprivation is not of money but of self-exploration.

We seldom think of the power that we mentally give to money. We are aware that we feel limited by the absence of money, or that we feel strengthened by possessing it. Yet money is truly powerless until we vivify it through the power of our minds. Money itself has never built a building, manufactured a product, performed an operation to save a life, or given sound investment advice. Especially in today's world, money is valueless paper—valueless except for the consensual value that we give it.

THE STONE MONEY OF YAP

To illustrate the power our minds give to money—and then money's power over our minds—let us take an example that seems far away in time and place. In the nineteenth century, the islanders on Yap (one of the Caroline Islands in the Pacific) used money in the form of quarried stones. These stones were one foot to twelve feet in diameter with a hole drilled in the center of each stone. The hole allowed this very heavy money to be slung on poles and carried.

The money, called *fei*, was quarried on an island four hundred miles to the south of Yap. The stone had to be a close-grained, white limestone. Assuming the stone was of the proper quality, size was the most important factor in determining value. After the sea voyage to transport the money to Yap, many of the pieces of currency were too large to be moved easily around the island. This led to transactions in which the ownership of the fei would be transferred, but the actual stone would not be moved. The old owner would merely give a verbal acknowledgment of the change of ownership without even a mark of any kind being put on the stone. The stone itself might remain on the property of the old owner, but everyone understood that the ownership of the fei had changed hands. (Even the term "changing hands" is so much better suited to our contemporary bills and coins than to this majestic stone money which, when moved, had to be "shouldered" by many men.) To serve as "coins" with the fei, the islanders used coconuts, tobacco, and strings of beads.

If ownership of the fei could change simply by agreement, a meeting of minds and nothing more, why was it necessary to move it from one island to another? If everyone agreed that someone owned a certain stone, it shouldn't matter where the stone rested. This supposition is borne out by a fascinating story about a stone of immense proportions.

This stone endowed the wealth of a certain family on Yap, yet the stone had not been seen for several generations. Everyone agreed that the family was indeed wealthy, but this particular stone had been lost at sea on the long voyage home from the island where it was quarried. In the face of a violent storm, the raft bearing the stone was cut free and the stone slipped into the depths. It certainly could not be recovered. However, when the adventurers told of the size and beauty of the stone and the fact that its owner could not be faulted for its loss, everyone agreed that its value should not be affected by its position on the bottom of the sea. Nor did the passage of several generations diminish the value of this legendary stone. It might as well have been in the family's front yard as lost at sea, since its value as money remained undiminished in the minds of living men and women.

This is a remarkable illustration of the connection between mind and money. In essence, the islanders decided that the money did not have to be in their immediate possession, or even visible, to have value and be owned. By this communal assent, the life of money was conferred on inanimate (and invisible) stone. By giving life to stone, the islanders also gave it power. And, like the sculptor whose beautiful statue became a living woman, the islanders found that stone transformed to life can be the source of great anguish.

In 1898, the German government acquired the Caroline Islands from Spain. Since Yap had no roads and the paths were in poor condition, the islanders were ordered to improve the condition of the paths. However, the islanders had walked these paths for generations with fei hanging from their shoulder poles. They neither needed nor wanted to improve the paths.

Faced with the passive resistance of the people of Yap, the German authorities pondered how to force compliance. The wealth of the islanders dotted the landscape in the form of fei, but it would require far too much work to confiscate this money. And if it could be moved, where would it be stored? At last the Germans came up with a diabolic plan. A single man was dispatched around the island with a can of black paint. On the most valuable pieces of fei he painted a small black cross. That was all.

The Germans then announced that the black crosses symbolized the fact that the stones were no longer money. The people of Yap, who had floated tons of stone on unruly seas, were impoverished by a paintbrush. Immediately the islanders set to work improving the paths. When their work had been completed to the satisfaction of the authorities, the Germans sent another man to remove the black crosses from the fei. The islanders rejoiced to have their wealth restored.

Of course, nothing had changed on the island except for paint being applied and removed and the thoughts in people's minds changing. The brilliant stratagem of the German authorities placed the fei under the power of the German mind. This led directly to their gaining power over the islanders, since they gave the fei itself power over their own minds.

We may feel that the minds of the islanders of Yap are nothing like our own minds, but, for a moment, let us imagine a science fiction scenario somewhat like *War of the Worlds* by H. G. Wells. Alien spacecraft begin landing all over the Earth. The aliens' technology is far more advanced than ours. Fortunately, the aliens are benevolent. Their only demand is that we improve our highway system.

We are happy with our highway system as it is and do nothing. The aliens then issue an ultimatum. If we do not repair the highway system within thirty days, all the currencies of Earth will lose their status as money. To demonstrate their power, the aliens use an electromagnetic pulse to void all credit cards, making reliance on cash all the more necessary.

Suddenly we seem far more like the people of Yap than we might have imagined (or wanted). Most of our money is simply paper and obviously valueless except for the value we give it. If the aliens are to void our money, surely we can change to some new system. Isn't it merely a matter of agreeing to call something else money? All things considered, however, who can doubt that we would immediately improve our highways and hope for an early departure by the aliens?

Life is never the same after the aliens visit. On Yap, fei remained in use until the outbreak of World War II. Although the islanders changed to using American and Japanese money, they did so with reluctance. The white spheres of stone that had once been money became ornaments, their value as currency a memory.

THE MANY FORMS OF MONEY

Economists usually define money by its functions: (1) Money must serve as a means of exchange and be freely accepted for goods and services; (2) Money must offer a measuring device, like a ruler, so that goods and services can be evaluated in relation to one another; and (3) Money must be in a form in which wealth can be stored.

How dry this definition is compared to the variety of money itself! For money can take almost any form and still meet these functions. Stones, coconuts, tobacco, and strings of beads only suggest how money, like the god Proteus, can assume innumerable forms.

One haunting example is of Chinese skin money. First used in the reign of Wu-ti (circa 140 B.C.), skin money was made of white stag skin. Each piece was square and represented significant wealth. In the white deer the Chinese had money with a life of its own and a propensity to breed more! The Chinese solution to inflation was to limit the imperial herds of white deer.

This process of limitation had unforeseen and unfortunate consequences. In their zeal to control inflation, the Chinese authorities restricted the herds too greatly. Ultimately, the white deer became extinct. Now the powerful white stag, leaping through ancient forests, is simply an image that flickers in our minds. It has no reality, for the stag and much of the forest have been consumed. It is as if money can be vampiric and take the beauty, and the very life, of nature.

This sacrifice of life for money has been reenacted in numerous societies. Porpoise teeth served as money for the islanders of Malaita (in the Solomons). A school of porpoises would be driven into the shallows, slaughtered, and their teeth extracted for use as money. On Fiji, whale's teeth served as currency, with the rarer red teeth worth twenty times the value of the white teeth. On the island of San Cristobel, thousands of dogs were reared and killed so that their teeth could be harvested as money. In parts of New Guinea, the tusks of boar were used as money. In the Santa Cruz Islands, the young men made money from the red feathers that crested the head of a tiny jungle bird. By filling a shell with sticky sap and imitating the bird's call, they would lure the bird to its death. In the Pacific Northwest, beaver skins were commonly used as currency along with the shells of snails and abalone, blankets, other skins, and even human slaves. These slaves were fortunate, however, to remain alive, when compared to the money of Borneo that was made of human skulls. This skull money is certainly the most literal (and gruesome) example of the triumph of money over mind.

Money often evolved from what was either nourishing or beautiful. The ancient Egyptians used grain as money, while cattle were the prevalent form of money in the Mediterranean countries. Many coastal and island peoples made beautiful strings of shells, especially cowrie shells, which are about an inch long and white or straw colored. These shells may have been the first money. They circulated for thousands of years before Christ in India, China, and the Middle East, and were later used in Africa, Asia, and throughout the Pacific Islands. In fact, when the Japanese military handed out large quantities of cowrie shells in New Guinea in 1942, the value of the cowries tumbled and the financial system of the island was threatened.

Settlers in the New World found that the Indians made wampum from seashells. Wampum became the first local currency of New Netherland. In a 1648 law, Connecticut set a standard that wampum should be "strung suitable and not small and great uncomely and disorderly mixt as formerly it hath been." This has the ring of a law against counterfeiting, which indeed was a serious problem with wampum. The white beads, four to eight of which equalled a penny, were often dyed to simulate the more valuable black beads. Massachusetts allowed the payment of small debts with wampum, but would not allow it to be used in payment of taxes.

The first money in the modern sense, that is, a currency minted for the specific purpose of serving as money, was created in China, where agricultural tools had been used as money over a long period of time. In about the twelfth century B.C., the Tchou rulers substituted miniatures of tools to act as currency in place of the actual tools. Over nearly a thousand years, one of these "coins"—the knife—evolved so that its blade disappeared and only its round handle with a hole in it remained. The hole had originally allowed the knives to be strung together.

The first coins in the West were minted by the Greeks in about 750 B.C. and were made from electrum, an alloy of gold and silver. Because this alloy was easily debased, Croesus, the sixth-century king of Lydia, minted coins of pure gold and silver. His legendary wealth is why we still say today, "As rich as Croesus."

What we receive for our employment, which determines the use of so much of our energy and time, is not only money but salary. The word salary comes from the Roman word *salarium*, which means salt, and reflects the Romans' use of salt to pay the wages of workers.

TOBACCO AS MONEY IN THE COLONIES

The colonial governments fixed the values of various farm products for use as currency. Taxes could be paid in such produce, and the taxing authorities struggled to avoid taking lean cattle (since the best cattle were "hoarded" and not used to pay taxes) and to dispose of surpluses. It was only in 1670 that Massachusetts repealed the law that fixed a value for the use of corn and cattle as money. South Carolina's legislature fixed a value for rice as money as late as 1720.

Tobacco, in particular, offers a fascinating history of the power of money over the minds of its inventors. By 1619, tobacco was already a local currency in Virginia, and the legislature declared tobacco to be money with a pound of the best tobacco equal to three shillings. Production increased very rapidly, so that by 1631 the value of tobacco had tumbled in relation to minted money. To raise the value of tobacco, laws were enacted forbidding certain people (such as carpenters and other crafts workers) from growing tobacco, restricting the amount that could be grown by those allowed to grow it, and raising standards for the quality of the crop. In 1640 and 1641, the legislature set the value of tobacco as currency, but fixed it at about five times the value in the marketplace. Growers were forbidden to sell their tobacco for less than the official rate. Not only were these laws ineffective, but they created serious inequities between debtors and creditors.

When these laws failed to halt the increasing cultivation of tobacco and its decline in value in relation to money, in 1642 the legislature took the remarkable step of enacting a law requiring that contracts be payable in tobacco. This virtually made tobacco the sole currency, so, of course, people wanted all the more to grow money. By 1666, Maryland, Virginia, and Carolina had to enter into a treaty in which they agreed to grow no tobacco during that year. By 1683, the falling price of tobacco caused vigilante groups to go about burning the tobacco crops. The legislature viewed this destruction of currency as subversion and made it punishable by the death penalty.

Once given the magical designation of money, tobacco

became far more than a crop. Its seeds were no longer rooted in the earth alone but in the minds of the people as well. Its power as money caused far more tobacco to be planted than the price of tobacco could have justified. The authorities refused to accept the prices set in the marketplace, but instead believed they could legislate the value that tobacco as money should have. Crops were not planted and fields were burned, but the powerful lure of money was such that the supplies of tobacco/money increased nonetheless.

MONEY AS AN ARCHETYPE

We have seen the innumerable, often surprising, forms that money has taken. If we *believe* in money, it doesn't matter whether the money is shaped as minted coins, printed paper, giant wheels of stone, grain, tobacco, the teeth of dogs and porpoises, or the feathers of exotic birds.

The key point is that money must have power over us inwardly in order to have power in the world. We must believe in its value before we will change our conduct based on whether or not we will receive it. In the broadest sense, money becomes a vehicle of relationship. It enables us to make choices and cooperate with one another; it signals what we will do with our energy.

It is this flow of our energy into the world that demands exchange, whether of conversation, love, bartered goods, or money. In fact, another definition of money is simply that it is energy, the potential for action.

The life of money comes mainly from its hidden nature.

Money is not only about the financial transactions of individuals, corporations, or even nations. It is also about the deeper questions of how life energy will be spent, how people live in relation to one another, and how culture and community survive and grow. Our daily striving for our salt obscures the deeper meanings of money and the way in which, whether we realize it or not, money confronts us with the meaning of our existence and our actions.

Because money is about relationship and exchange, which are fundamental issues of the human condition, it is archetypal. An archetype is a pattern inherited from ancient human experiences and present in each of us. Often we are not aware of these patterns, but they exist in us nonetheless. So these patterns are unconscious, living in the part of us that is separate from our everyday awareness and identity. Yet we are influenced by these patterns. And we may have a desire to understand the archetypes so that we can better understand ourselves.

This realm of the archetypes is timeless and transcends the individual. It is truly the realm of the gods. Our contemporary fascination with ancient gods is largely because they express archetypes. To use some of the Greek gods for examples: Zeus is the chief god who integrates and organizes all the aspects of life; Hera, the wife of Zeus, is concerned with marriage and the family; Hermes plays many roles, including the god of commerce who helps us to exchange among ourselves.

When a corporate president reorganizes a company to increase profits, he or she is operating with the archetypal energy of Zeus. A husband or wife's concern that there be enough money for the family to prosper comes from the archetypal pattern of Hera. Every step that brings a product to the consumer is influenced by the archetype of Hermes who governs commerce: the market research, the product design, the packaging, the advertising campaign, and the determination of the price to charge. The study of gods lets us see the larger patterns that operate within us. We learn of the forces that shape the destiny of the human race and sometimes make the individual feel overwhelmed and at a loss to understand his or her experiences.

THE GODDESS MONETA

What are the origins of the word *money*? If we search in this direction, we meet a goddess. She lives in the world of archetypes, the larger patterns that shape us and await our discovery. Often such a goddess can help us in our efforts to become aware of these patterns.

The word "money" derives from the Roman goddess named Moneta. Coins minted in her temples were issued to the far reaches of the empire. In fact, the Latin word *moneta* (meaning mint or coins) evolved into the Old English word *mynet* (meaning coins or money), which became the English word "mint."

To understand Moneta, we have to speak of Juno, the mother goddess of Rome. Juno is a fertility goddess whose origins are with the Mother Goddesses who imbue fertility and make harvests abundant. June, the month named for Juno, is a favored month in which to marry. In her role as the preeminent goddess, Juno is the protectress of the city of Rome, her favorite city and the capital of the empire. In a more personal role, Juno is the protectress of women and so presides over marriage (as Juno *Jugalis*), childbirth (as Juno *Lucina*), and motherhood (as Juno *Matronalia*).

Ancient gods and goddesses often had more than a single name. Each name revealed an aspect of their nature. Like Juno, a goddess might preside over marriage, childbirth, and motherhood, and possess a different name for each of these roles. If she made the earth fertile, she would have a name to match that role. Moneta is the name of Juno in her role as the mother of money. She is Juno Moneta from whom money plentifully issues forth.

It will help us to have an image of a fertility goddess like Juno, because such fertility goddesses will play an important role in our exploration of money. Let us imagine Juno Moneta standing before us as a radiant, tall, and full-figured woman. She is mature, no longer a girl and not yet old. Her face is powerful and serene. She wears a flowing gown not from modesty but to protect us from being blinded by her overpowering radiance. On her head she carries a basket filled to overflowing with wheat, corn, and all the foods which nourish humanity. She holds an infant in each arm, a girl and a boy, and has lowered the top of her gown to let them suckle at her full breasts. Wild and domesticated animals rub against her flanks to gain her gift of fertility. At her feet are measureless piles of gold and silver coins that flow from her like water from an unending spring. In everything she is abundant, cornucopic, rich beyond measure or imagining.

Let us fix this image of Moneta in our minds. She symbolizes the pattern or archetype to which we will return as we examine the meaning of money. It would be natural to assume such a goddess is wise. In the case of Moneta, wisdom is rooted in her very name.

The Latin word *moneta* derives from the Indo-European root *men-*, which meant to use one's mind or think. The goddess Moneta is modelled on the Greek goddess of memory, Mnemosyne. Contained in the power to remember is the ability to warn, so Moneta is also considered to be a goddess who can give warnings. To suggest how money can affect us in different ways, we might remember that the Greek words *menos* (which means spirit, courage, purpose) and *mania* (which means madness) come from the same root as memory and Moneta. Measurement, from the Indo-European root *me-*, also relates to mental abilities and is a crucial aspect of money.

Measurement, memory, and warning are important concepts that will figure in our explorations, but the theme of this chapter has been the power of money over our minds. In one form or another, we all worship wooden idols. Moneta draws our attention to this fact. Because the derivation of her name reveals the deep connections between money and mind, she alerts us to the likelihood of confusion and illusion. Even more, she suggests the necessity of using our minds to bring light to the subject of money, to remove the obscurity and mystery which surrounds what we do not think about and do not understand.

THE RABBI'S ADVICE

A folktale from the Jewish tradition tells of a poor man who comes to his rabbi for advice. It is a few days before Passover and the man complains bitterly that he hasn't any money for matzos, meat, and sacramental wine. He feels that he and his family cannot come to the synagogue in their tattered clothes.

The rabbi tries to relieve the man's fears by saying, "God will help you. Don't worry."

The poor man cannot let go of his fears. Finally the rabbi asks him to list the items that he needs and what each would cost. The total for the matzos, meat, wine, and new clothing is fifty-two rubles.

"So you need fifty-two rubles," the rabbi says. "Now there's no need to worry about matzos, meat, wine, or clothing. You'll have only one worry: How to get fifty-two rubles."

Is this rabbi cruel or wise? He has offered this poor man the solace of God. If the man cannot trust that God will help him, then, in a sense, he is not ready to enter the synagogue and worship. He has a task to perform. He must worry about money. If he worries deeply enough and long enough, perhaps his worries will transform his understanding of money. He may see money in a new and brilliant light, transfigured, something quite other than he might ever have imagined.

The story doesn't tell us whether the poor man finally worshipped in the synagogue. But for Christian, Hindu, Moslem, Buddhist, polytheist, animist, atheist, or agnostic, money holds the same mysteries, the same secret life. Why do we so frequently set up wooden idols? Why are we so seldom awakened by a rage that allows us to smash their heads to smithereens? Why do people of goodwill lament that we worship money or accuse us for losing ourselves in pursuit of the almighty dollar?

If we had the memory of Moneta, we might answer these questions and more. One image of Moneta shows her head tilted to one side and a hand cupped to her listening ear. What she hears, she remembers. When she speaks to us, she is like a woman we meet in a dream. Our task, our challenge, is not only to hear her, but to remember her words when we wake.

CHAPTER TWO

THE ALMIGHTY DOLLAR

Why Money Is So Easily Worshipped

WE OFTEN HEAR condemnations of the worship of money. These critics—whether of a society driven by consumption, of the inordinate millions made by stock market manipulators, or of the crass ostentation of certain of the wealthy—miss a fundamental point. The reason that so many people worship money is because money, in its origins, was divine. It is no accident that the Roman mint was in a temple sacred to Moneta.

If we simply complain of the evils of money, we miss the opportunity to explore its symbolic richness. Certainly the Bible does not condemn money, but warns: "The love of money is the root of all evils." Not money, but the love of money, is the root of evil. If we love money, we are likely to lose sight of its deeper significance. If we literalize money as our goal, we fail to see it as a symbol of life forces that could connect us more deeply to ourselves, our families, and our communities. So the evil that flows from an attachment to money is done not only to ourselves but also to those we most hope to love. In a sense, money challenges us to learn what is truly worthy of our love. If we understand the origins of money, we can direct our love away from money as we develop the potentials that it symbolizes.

This chapter will explore how, thousands of years ago, the divine origins of money were lost to sight, lost to consciousness. We are left only with the device of money and its practical applications in the world. Of its sources and first purposes, we know nothing. Yet the initial religious fervor which forged money remains within us. It animates us and gives money a mystical allure. Mystical because we are unaware that in our imaginal world the touch of money can be experienced as contact with the divine.

Hints and vestiges of money's divine origins are present on money today—in some cases quite visible, in other cases more hidden. The coins and bills of the United States firmly pledge "In God We Trust." This is remarkable in a country whose Constitution guarantees the separation of Church and State. The First Amendment states that "Congress shall make no law respecting the establishment of religion, or prohibit the free exercise thereof. . . ." The Supreme Court has interpreted this clause to forbid the federal government, states, and agencies of the states (such as school boards) from enforcing regulations or "laws which aid one religion, aid all religions, or prefer one religion over another." So no one can be punished for going to church or refusing to go to church, and prayers in schools, even interdenominational prayers, violate this Constitutional safeguard.

If a school board required students in public school to say "In God We Trust" each morning, the board would transgress the First Amendment. But the Treasury, as required by federal law, must place the phrase "In God We

Trust" on all coins and bills. Each day hundreds of millions of people hand this phrase back and forth when they exchange money. If the phrase means nothing, perhaps it should be changed to "In the Federal Reserve We Trust." Of course, that wouldn't have the same ring or the same profound meaning. The reason that we accept "In God We Trust" on our coins but not in our schools probably has to do with the most ancient origins of money.

To delve into these ancient origins, we will look first at societies that had no money. Money did not suddenly appear, fully imagined and realized, in the world. Rather, it came gradually and in response to the evolution of human needs. To understand the origins of money, we must imagine worlds without money. We have to see how cycles of exchange came to connect both hunting and agricultural societies to their gods, and how money and markets evolved from these cycles of exchanges.

HOW HUNTERS INFLUENCED THE SPIRIT WORLD

Early tribal peoples attempted to influence nature by entering into a proper relationship with it. This proper relationship is, fundamentally, a relationship of exchange. If nature gives its abundance today, what will make it willing to give its abundance tomorrow? Early peoples found the answers to this question in numerous rituals of prayer and sacrifice. These rituals forged a bond of spirit between the people and the world in which they lived. The very word "sacrifice" derives from the Latin *sacrum facere*, which means to make sacred, to perform a sacred ceremony. So a sacrifice is a sacred giving to the gods. The rationale offered for sacrifice was *do ut des:* I give to you so that you will give to me. Nor was this a crass exchange, like merchants bickering in a bazaar. Because the power of nature could not be contested, the sacrifice had to be made with reverence, humility, and, at most, hope for an auspicious outcome.

For example, the American Indians sought to honor the spirits of the game that nourished them. In the Pacific Northwest, the Tlingit, Haida, Tsimsyan, and other tribes lived off their stocks of dried and smoked salmon through the long winters. The annual migratory return of the salmon was eagerly awaited, and a tale was told of how a young boy went to the land of the salmon people. There he learned of the rituals that would cause the salmon consumed by the tribe to be given flesh again in the spirit world and return with the annual migration. From the boy's experience, the Indians came to show their respect for the spirits of the salmon by burning any parts that were not eaten. These offerings restored the salmon, who in turn nourished the Indian tribes.

Even inland tribes held great feasts to honor the first salmon. At these feasts the chief, or shaman, would ask for the continued blessings of the Sky Chief. Then each person present would be given a small piece of the salmon to eat, so that the first fruits of the salmon harvest were shared by everyone. After the bones of the salmon were burned or, in some cases, buried or returned to the stream with proper invocations, the Indians believed that the bones found their way back to the home of the salmon people. There the bones became whole salmon, ensuring the fertility that would again bring the spawning salmon to the nets of the Indian fishermen in the annual cycle of renewal.

These Native American ceremonies exemplify the universal belief that prayers and offerings help ensure the abundance of nature. For example, the bear festival among tribes in Finland required that the bones of a slain bear be placed in a tomb with useful objects such as a knife and skis. The bear was honored, treated as a friend, and asked to tell the other bears about the honors paid to it by man. This ensured that the bear spirits would want to return in the form of the fully fleshed bear.

This festival is similar to the worship of the bear by the Ainu of Japan. If the Ainu captured a bear cub in the mountains, the cub would be brought to the village and treated like a visiting god. Nursed at a woman's breast until the cub became too large, even its caging would be gentle until the time came to send the bear to its spirit home. After the killing of the bear by arrow and ritualized strangulation, the bear's head and pelt would be arranged at the feast in its honor. This worshipful respect encouraged the bear spirits to return and share their renewed flesh with the Ainu in unending cycles of fertility.

HOW AGRICULTURAL SOCIETIES SOUGHT GOOD HARVESTS

Nor was it only hunting-and-gathering societies around the world which shared these beliefs. The development and evolution of agriculture, beginning nearly ten thousand years ago, was accompanied by immense changes in human behavior. The farmer became attached to the land. At the same time, the abundance of food encouraged the specialization of labor, the growth of cities, and the armies that built empires. Yet the priests, who had become a larger and more organized group, offered prayers and sacrifices so the spirits and gods would make the fields fertile. The failure of the crops threatened the farmers, and the rulers, priests, soldiers, and artisans, with the very real danger of starvation.

Fertility rituals are universal among agricultural societies. For example, the rain dance of the Hopi Indians is well known to tourists who have visited the parched mesas of Arizona in August. Their faces dark with soot and chins bright with white clay, one by one the priest-dancers of the Snake Society clamp live rattlesnakes between their teeth and circle the plaza of the pueblo. Other priests guide the dancers and soothe the snakes with feathered wands. All the while a chant reverberates that seems to come from within the Earth. Songs are sung about clouds gathering and rain falling. At the end of the dancing, the priests seize as many snakes as they can and carry them into the desert: to the east, the west, the north, and the south. The snakes are blessed and released to carry a message of renewal across the land and to crawl into the underworld depths, the womb of the world, and intercede with the spirits for life-nourishing rain.

This snake-dancing ceremony alternates each year with the flute ceremony, which also seeks to ensure the maturing of the crops and rainfall at the end of summer. These sixteen-day ceremonies are at the heart of a year-round procession of rituals. Beautiful and complex in their mythology and symbolism, many of the rituals seek to ensure that the nourishing rains will come and bring fertility to the land.

The annual round of ceremonies is not only about fertility but also about the relationship of humans to nature and the universe. This is shown in the marriage of the

Snake Maiden, a young virgin who is the living representation of two sacred statues of Snake Maidens, to the Antelope Youth, a young boy who has undergone purification. This marriage ritual, part of the sequence of ceremonies that culminate in the snake dance, uses corn, vegetables, seeds, and the milky fluid derived from the yucca root to symbolize the hoped-for fertility.

After the wedding, the young couple, married for this one night, sit together as sacred songs are sung and, at last, are taken home by their godparents. This ritual seeks fertility in its many unions: the joining of the Snake Society and Antelope Society in the ritual, the connection between the antelope whose horn rises to the sky and the snake which is capable of penetrating the earth, the joining of people with the natural world, and the merging of the masculine and feminine forces in nature.

To illustrate the universality of these rituals, we can compare the Hopi ceremonies to those practiced by the Greeks more than two thousand years ago. The Greek rituals were celebrated in cycles called the Lesser Mysteries (held in February) and the Greater Mysteries (held in September). These Mysteries were considered so sacred that death was the punishment for even speaking of them to the uninitiated.

What we know of the Mysteries suggests that the initiates, after a rigorous purification (which would include bathing and fasting), experienced a union with the Goddess Demeter. In the ecstasy of the rituals, the initiates felt themselves carried to Mount Olympus, the abode of the Gods, where they witnessed the sacred marriage of Demeter and Zeus, the highest of the gods. This divine union offered salvation. A voice thundered "A sacred child is born" and spoke of the "ear of corn in silence reaped." To these symbols of the ever-regenerating and life-giving Earth, the initiates shouted their thanksgiving *"Ye"* (for rain) and, kneeling, *"Kye"* (for giving birth).

The similarity between the rituals of these agricultural societies, separated by thousands of miles, and years, reveals the universality of the prayers and sacrifices adopted by agricultural peoples to placate and win the favor of the gods and spirits. To give a final example, in the nineteenth century each clan on the East Indian island of Buru concluded the rice harvest with a feast. All of the members of the clan had to contribute a small amount of their rice to this shared meal, and a portion of the rice was offered to the spirits. Called "eating the soul of the rice," this meal nurtured the clan with the vitality of nature. Our wedding ceremonies today contain a hint of such ritual practices; the throwing of the rice at the bride and groom is a vestige of ancient fertility rituals.

THE RAINMAKER IN BUSINESS

Today, in business, a rainmaker is someone who can put deals together and generate money for the other participants, who may not have the same access to powerful connections and financial resources. Such a rainmaker creates prosperity, not in the form of crops but as money. The rainmaker's exchanges are not with spirits or gods but with banks, investors, stockholders, clients and others who will benefit. These transactions are memorialized with agreements, such as promissory notes and limited partnerships, which connect the parties in the world of business.

What is missing, of course, is the beauty of the rituals which connect the tribal rainmakers to their gods and their own natures. What would it be like if every business transaction were celebrated like a wedding with the divine? If we could understand the origins of money and the marketplace, we might recapture at least a sense of the sacred rituals that once played so crucial a role in the creation of prosperity.

MONETA, MONEY, AND THE MARKETPLACE

What is the connection of these sacred exchanges between the human and the divine and the evolution of marketplaces and money? The Goddess Moneta offers us the key. Money is minted in her temples. She is also a representation of one of the many aspects of the Goddess Juno. This evolution of Moneta from Juno, who herself had evolved from earlier and more powerful Earth Goddesses, informs us that money evolves as an aspect of fertility. When the riches of the hunt and the fields were first offered back to the spirit world to ensure further renewal, there could be no doubt that this natural bounty was sacred. As cultures became more complex and specialized, this sacred bounty came to be traded outside of the sacrificial rituals binding human to god. It became a commodity, bartered at first and, later, either became money proper or was exchanged for money. So, inevitably, whatever the shape of money, it originated in the exchange between the human and spirit worlds.

But why did the sacred bounties of nature come to enter the marketplace as commodities? Why did money evolve out from religious ceremonies? Certainly money and market exchange had no place in the family, where food was shared because of love and familial responsibilities. This love feast served as the basis for sharing food in the larger community that developed from the family— that is, the clan or kinship group.

The saying of grace before a meal captures the feeling of the love feast. One form of grace, for example, is: "Bless us, O Lord, and these thy gifts which we are about to receive from thy bounty through Christ our Lord. Amen." This is a thanksgiving to God and a prayer that both family and food will be blessed.

The importance of circulating food is stressed in a passage from the *Rig-Veda:* "The man without foresight gets food in vain. . . . The man who eats alone brings troubles on himself alone." *The Bhagavad Gita* makes the distribution of food an essential element of the ritual of sacrifice: "The sacrifice contrary to the ordinances, without distributing food, devoid of words of power and without gifts, empty of faith, is said to be of darkness."

The sharing of food, its bestowal on others, is a way of circulating the divine essence in the human world. *The Bhagavad Gita* suggests the close relationship between the eater and the food, since it views both people and food as part of a cycle that requires sacrifice to connect with the divine. "From food creatures become; from rain is the production of food; rain proceedeth from sacrifice; sacrifice ariseth out of action."

On a practical level, sharing is also a way of trusting in one's family and community. If all will share, times of hardship will be far more bearable and scarcity will be less difficult to endure and survive. Eating alone makes one guilty, for it violates the trust, the love feast, that underlies the community.

In the Lord's Prayer there is a recognition of God as the source of our daily bread. "Bread," symbolizing nourishment for the body and the spirit, is also slang for money, as is the word "dough." But bread and dough are food, while money is neither food nor fertility. The origins of money are in fertility rituals, yet money is far more ambiguous than food in what it means to us.

MONEY, STRANGERS, AND THE LOVE FEAST

A story from *Aesop's Fables* suggests how money brings into the family circle strangers who lack the family's shared concerns. In "A Woman and Her Two Daughters," one daughter has died and the burial is arranged, including the hiring of mourners. The woman's surviving daughter is shocked to see strangers weeping and crying out with such grief over the death of her sister, while her own relatives show far less feeling. The daughter asks her mother how this can be. The mother answers that the kin are never the better for grieving, but the strangers gain money by it. So money can create the outward appearance of a feeling but not its inner reality.

A Jewish folktale also speaks of how money can distort our view of the world. Once a miser of great wealth came to the home of his rabbi and asked for his rabbi's blessing. The rabbi made the miser stand before a window and look at the people in the street. The rabbi asked the miser what he saw, and the miser answered, "People." Then the rabbi placed a mirror in front of the miser and asked again what he saw, and the miser answered, "Myself." The rabbi then explained that both the window and the mirror are made of glass, but the mirror also has a veneer of silver. Glass by itself allows us to see people, but glass covered by silver makes us stop seeing others and see only ourselves.

The danger of money, that we will be blinded by it and no longer see others, suggests how different a role money can play when compared to food. The love feast joins family and kinship group together in the sharing of food which is clearly seen as nature's gift. Money is needed to deal with strangers. In fact, money may encourage us to see others as strangers.

As societies became more complex, the likelihood of having to deal with strangers increased. Within the society itself, larger populations and specialized tasks meant that however large the family group, there would still have to be dealings with outsiders. Also, these complex societies developed the knowledge and the resources to send explorers, traders, and armies to new lands whose inhabitants were certainly strangers. At what point of blood relationship or geographic distance a person would be viewed as a stranger might vary greatly, but the love feast of the family at some point excludes the other, the stranger.

Unlike sacrifices and the intrafamily giving that connects the giver and ancestors to the renewing spirit world, exchanges with strangers promise no such renewal. Barter and trading are the way strangers deal with one another; when strangers meet, sacred circulation changes into the exchange of commodities in the marketplace. And, eventually, money in its many shapes came to be used to facilitate the circulation of these commodities.

Some scholars speculate that religious pilgrimages may have been one of the more important ways in which strangers came into contact with each other and served as an impetus to the creation of money. Far from home, the pilgrim would have to obtain food and other supplies, both to survive and make the required sacrifices. So traders would be encouraged to root themselves beside the temples, and pilgrims would bring various forms of wealth. Protected by the sacred association with the temples, fairs developed for the purpose of exchange. In fact, the German word for Mass—*Messe*—also means fair.

HOW THE TEMPLE AT DELPHI CAME TO MINT MONEY

One goal of pilgrims in the ancient world was to visit the famed oracle at Delphi in Greece. As early as 1400 B.C., a sanctuary of Gaia, goddess of the Earth and mother of the gods, existed on this mountainous site with its natural spring and panoramic views of Mount Kirfis and the Gorge of Pleistos running to the Gulf of Corinth. The myths tell of Apollo's killing of the female serpent that guarded the prophetic spring. Thus a male deity displaced Gaia, and from the eighth century onward Apollo, a culture-giving god of intellect, the arts, and prophecy, was worshipped there.

From all over the known world people came to consult the Delphic oracle for information from the gods. After paying a fee and sacrificing animals, the suppliant was brought into the inner shrine of the temple. Separated by a curtain from the priestess, who sat on a sacred tripod and breathed intoxicating fumes rising from the rocks, the suppliant could hear her incomprehensible words and shouts. Male priests interpreted these utterances in the form of brief verses.

It is surprising when visiting Delphi today to find the ruins of treasuries beside the ruins of temples. Corinth built the first treasury at the beginning of the sixth century B.C. The most powerful city-states followed suit until twenty treasuries lined the Sacred Way that ran through the sanctuary and past the Temple of Apollo. The word "treasury" comes from the same root as the word "thesaurus." It refers to a gathering of things, a repository. In addition to contributing to the support of the Temple of Apollo, the city-states also dedicated riches to their treasuries. These elegant marble buildings filled with gold, silver, and art, offerings that represented immense wealth. If necessary, especially in the event of war, the city-states could use these treasures as security for borrowing. In fact, the templelike architecture of many banks is a tribute to these ancient, and sacred, treasuries.

Delphi issued its first silver coins in the fifth century B.C., and temples which had the precious metal to mint coins facilitated trade by placing some of their silver in circulation as coinage. In this way, wealth offered as sacred treasure moved into the world of trade.

Many of the earliest Greek coins visibly show their origins in the temples. Gods, symbols for gods, mythological beasts and stories, and objects for sacrifice are the images most frequently selected for these coins. The busts of Olympian gods such as Zeus, Poseidon, Athena, and Apollo conferred trustworthiness on the new invention of money. We see the thunderbolt of Zeus, the trident of Poseidon, the owl of Athena, and the lyre of Apollo. Griffins, sphinxes, and the winged horse Pegasus show their fantastic forms and connect the spirit world to the realm of coins. Wheat, tuna, tripods (which first contained sacred offerings and later were themselves used as offerings), and double-headed axes are all sacrificial offerings that are portrayed on coins.

Of course, even the earliest coins are a recent, indeed a modern, development compared to the fertility rituals and offerings that originated with prehistoric peoples. Just as food and other offerings ultimately left the realm of the sacred to be traded with strangers, so coins left the temples to serve for trade. Scholars debate whether every early Greek coin came from religious sources, but most of these coins clearly do. These early coins are memorable not only for their religious types but also for the exquisite beauty of so many of the images. The busts of Arethusa (goddess of rivers and streams), Medusa (the snake-headed goddess), and Persephone (the daughter of Demeter and goddess of the underworld) are only a few of the aesthetic triumphs of the artists who created these coins.

One of the most important of these coins began to be minted in the temples of Athens in 525 B.C. Picturing a head of Athena on one side and her owl on the reverse, the preeminence of Athens made the Athenian tetradrachm widely and readily accepted. This facilitated trade across the Mediterranean world and beyond. On the tetradrachm, Athena's characteristic helmet symbolizes her role as protectress of the freedom of Athens. Many coins of the United States used images of Liberty or Standing Liberty that owe a debt to the images of Athena guarding the city of Athens. And, as Athena Medusa, Athena served as a goddess of fertility as well.

Today we feel a concern for the separation of Church and State which the ancient Greeks did not share. The divine and secular authorities in the city-states worked in unison. Despite the fact that coins in ancient Greece were minted in the temples, control of the mints either began with the rulers of the city-states or quickly passed into their hands. Nonetheless, several centuries passed before the face of a mortal as opposed to that of a god or goddess appeared on a coin. This first portrait, that of Alexander the Great, dates to approximately 300 B.C., about twenty-three years after Alexander's death. Alexander had declared himself a living god but was not officially deified until after his death. The use of his image reflected this deification and opened the way for living rulers to make godlike portrayals of themselves on coins.

WHY OUR MONEY SAYS "IN GOD WE TRUST"

Viewed against this background, many aspects of our coins and bills reflect the sacred origins of money. The Founding Fathers preferred simple busts of Liberty on the coinage of the Republic. Today the motto "In God We Trust" on all our coins and bills is accepted almost without question. We may not consider why such a motto appears on our money or realize that its first use was in 1864 during the agony of the Civil War.

On November 13, 1861, N. R. Watkinson, a minister from Ridleyville, Pennsylvania, wrote to Salmon P. Chase, Secretary of the Treasury, as follows:

> One fact touching our currency has hitherto been seriously overlooked. I mean the recognition of the Almighty God in some form in our coins.
>
> You are probably a Christian. What if our Republic were now shattered beyond reconstruction. Would not the antiquaries of succeeding centuries rightly reason from our

past that we were a heathen nation. What I propose is that instead of the goddess of liberty we shall have next inside the 13 stars a ring inscribed with the words "perpetual union"; within this ring the allseeing eye, crowned with a halo; beneath this eye the American flag, bearing in its field stars equal to the number of the States united; in the folds of the bars the words "God, liberty, law."

Secretary Chase advised the Director of the Mint: "No nation can be strong except in the strength of God, or safe except in His defense. The trust of our people in God should be declared on our national coins." A variety of mottos: "Our country, our God," "God, our Trust," "Our God and our country," led finally to the adoption of "In God We Trust," which first appeared in 1864 on the newly created two-cent piece.

Subsequent coinage acts allowed the use of "In God We Trust" on other coins. When, in 1907, President Roosevelt did not include this motto on the beautiful eagle ($10) and double eagle ($20) gold coins that he had commissioned Augustus Saint-Gaudens to design, a public outcry protested "Roosevelt's Godless Coins." In 1908, Congress passed a law requiring that "In God We Trust" appear on all coins of the United States.

An irony is that Roosevelt hardly had a godless motive in removing the motto; rather, he felt the very mention of God in the motto to be a sacrilege. It is interesting that the suggested motto of "God, liberty, law," which says nothing about trusting, became "In God We Trust." The Secretary of the Treasury added the concept of trust. It almost seems that we are being asked to trust in God when, in fact, the government really wants us to trust in the currency and the government which issues it. This might explain Roosevelt's feelings. Also the currency was not trustworthy when the phrase first appeared, since the Civil War was financed by debt and inflation rather than taxes. In any event, President Eisenhower signed legislation in 1955 extending use of the motto to paper currency, and since 1957 "In God We Trust" has appeared on bills as well as coins.

The all-seeing eye did not appear on coins of the United States, as N. R. Watkinson wished, but we are all familiar with its presence today on our currency. The Great Seal of the United States, adopted in 1782, has both its front and reverse portrayed on the back of the one-dollar bill. The reverse of the Great Seal shows an unfinished pyramid with the all-seeing eye contained in a triangle floating above it. This all-seeing eye is, of course, the eye of God contained in a triangle representing the Christian Trinity. Its presence on the Great Seal represents the desire of the Founding Fathers to have God oversee the continued building of the unfinished pyramid (nation) which they had begun. Not only was God's favor sought for the future, but His support for their efforts was unequivocally stated in the Latin phrase *"annuit coeptis,"* which translates "He [God] has approved our undertakings."

The color and motifs of United States paper money also arouse, at least unconsciously, associations with fertility cycles. The money is green on its reverse side and the decorative motifs are unfailingly of vegetation. This reminds me of an artist who told of his shock when he saw the Grim Reaper on the back of a Swiss thousand-franc bill. He had difficulty connecting money with the Grim Reaper, a death figure who scythes down humanity like a crop in the field. It jarred him, and yet he found it compelling. To give himself a feeling of financial security, he didn't spend that bill for a long while. Its value, about $500 at the time, could hardly explain why this image connecting money to cycles of life resonated with such strength for him.

More recently, when the Swiss government sponsored a competition for new designs for its currency, the winning entry portrayed photographs of famous Swiss artists in boldly colorful and contemporary designs. The idea of such new money outraged the public. Critics decried the designs as macabre, repulsive, like theater tickets, and suggestive of national decline. But how can pictures of artists be more macabre or repulsive than the Grim Reaper? Or does the Grim Reaper, by some paradox, speak to us of the ancient cycle of life and death, a cycle that promises fertility and prosperity in the very image of death? In any event, the outcry suggests that some sense of sacred propriety had been touched, and to this day the currency has not been modernized.

THE BIRTH OF THE DOLLAR

The very word "dollar" has a curious history that connects it with the name of a shepherd, Joachim, later St. Joachim. According to nonbiblical tradition, St. Joachim was father to Mary and grandfather to Jesus.

The expansion of trade in the sixteenth century increased the need for internationally accepted coinage. A valley, Joachimsthal (which means St. Joachim's valley) in what is now the Czech Republic, proved rich in silver. In 1518, the first coins minted from mines in Joachimsthal began to circulate. These coins quickly gained international popularity and took their name, Joachimsthalers, from their place of origin. Soon the name was abbreviated to the easier-to-say *taler* (or *thaler*). For more than three centuries, the taler and its many imitations, including England's crown, France's écu, Russia's ruble, and Spain's peso, became the standard for international trade.

In English-speaking countries, taler soon transformed to a more easily spoken word—dollar. Shakespeare made one of the earliest references to the dollar in *Macbeth*, in which a character speaks of a Norse king who had to pay "ten thousand dollars." In his 1782 proposal that the dollar be the currency unit for the United States, Thomas Jefferson wrote that the "dollar is a known coin and the most familiar of all to the mind of the people. It is already adopted from south to north." The dollar to which Jefferson referred was actually the Spanish peso (or piece of eight). Pesos remained legal tender in the United States until 1857, when more than 2,000,000 of them were redeemed.

THE SIGN OF THE DOLLAR

If the word for dollar traces back to St. Joachim, the sign for the dollar may have an equally surprising connection to religion. The origin of the dollar sign has been a subject of debate among numismatic experts. Since the dollar and its symbol existed before the United States, the popular belief that the dollar symbol evolved from the drawing together of the U and S in U.S. must be incorrect.

Another theory is that the dollar symbol evolved from the plural of the sign for pesos. This theory posits that P (for peso) and s (for the plural) gradually became superimposed in the late eighteenth century, but the graphic proof offered for this evolution is not fully persuasive.

The most intriguing explanation traces the roots of the taler itself. In the sixteenth century, Charles V not only ruled Germany but also Spain and its American possessions. On the reverse of his taler he placed two pillars to show his connection with Spain and entwined these pillars with scrolls. The ancient Phoenicians, famed for their explorations, built such pillars in Gibraltar when they erected a temple to Herakles near present-day Cadiz. These pillars derived from ancient coins from Tyre (in modern-day Lebanon) depicting the pillars of the temple of Solomon. Solomon's pillars had names: Jachin, which means "He shall establish," and Boaz, which means "In it is strength." So the dollar symbol is formed by the scrolls added by Charles V to the image of Solomon's pillars shown on the coins of Tyre. If this theory is correct, the upright of the dollar sign is a pillar with a meaning similar to that expressed on the reverse of the Great Seal and the dollar bill: "He [God] has approved our undertaking."

WHAT WE MIGHT LEARN FROM THE WORSHIP OF MONEY

We are taught to think of money in practical terms. Can we afford to buy a car or a dinner at a nice restaurant? Can we risk starting a small business or making an investment? Does our budget balance or must we cut our expenses or work harder to earn more? Are we threatened by bankruptcy or homelessness? Our hopes and fears constantly revolve around whether we will have enough or too little.

But Moneta does not speak only in terms of the everyday; she is not only a figure of our conscious lives, of the lives that we are aware we lead. She is also the wise woman in a dream that we struggle to remember. If her words remain with us when we wake, then we know that money speaks to us of cycles far larger than our own lifetimes. These cycles of birth, death, and rebirth are as true for the crops in the fields as for the farmers, the hunters, and even the urbanites.

Moneta's words imply that we might learn from the mysteries that make nature fertile. She reminds us of the love feast, the thankful sharing of the bounties of nature. In this we are made aware again of our desire for community and sharing. Ultimately, whether in a slogan like "In God We Trust" or simply by money's forgotten origins in religious ritual, Moneta arouses energies that once connected us to a higher realm, energies related to what is transcendent in the world and in ourselves.

Understanding the origins of money may let us be more forgiving of our desires to worship money. The adoration of money may have devastating consequences, as we shall see, but these consequences come from misdirected energy that, channeled differently, could have served us well. Gurdjieff spoke of harnessing the energy of a demon to do the work of an angel. If we can remember Moneta's words and bring her wisdom to our daily lives, perhaps we can regain and redirect these energies to more appropriate purposes.

But our quest has a fearsome aspect as well. The Grim Reaper is a reality: The abundance of nature flows always from death in endless cycles. This is another face of

Moneta, or any fertility goddess. To remember Moneta's dream words we may have to endure a journey through the underworld, the realm of the Grim Reaper. In this passage we may find in our own natures the richness and fertility that the shamans and priests sought by sacrifices to their gods.

CHAPTER THREE

MONEY AND SACRIFICE

When Money Feels More Important Than Life

THE CONNECTION OF MONEY to ancient rituals of fertility is lost to our conscious awareness today. However, an implication of this connection is everpresent: money issues can make us feel that our very lives are at stake. Almost all of us have struggled at one time or another with money shortfalls and found ourselves face to face with overwhelming fears. Our self-worth vanishes as we feel despair and see the future as futile. These feelings may not be a response to actual hunger or homelessness or an untended injury. Rather, they are a response to ideas about money, ideas that flow up from our unconscious and overwhelm our ability to reason and see reality.

The power of money to meet material needs, acquire status and power, and free us of many constraints does not explain why money can make us feel that our lives hang in the balance. As we shall see, the stories that begin this chapter, "The Rocking-Horse Winner," by D. H. Lawrence and the tale of King Midas, offer insights into how money arouses energies that once connected us to a higher realm. If these energies are misdirected, we risk losing our inner richness and our vital connection to family and community. We may gain wealth but at the cost of all that makes life worth living and, in some cases, at the cost of life itself.

To understand why this should be so, this chapter will explore an aspect of the ancient fertility rituals that is shocking today: human sacrifice. If we see that the exchange of our time and energy for money is a form of sacrifice that echoes ancient rites of human sacrifice, then we may be freed from a fearful attachment to money and be able to seek the deeper values which it symbolizes.

WHEN LIFE IS SACRIFICED FOR MONEY

In the short story titled "The Rocking-Horse Winner," D. H. Lawrence offers a penetrating look at the damage caused by the love of money. A boy named Paul knows that his mother does not love him or anyone, despite her appearance of being a loving mother. Although the family lives in a nice house and has servants, both father and mother have expensive tastes that they can't afford. Soon Paul and his sisters hear the house speaking to them, whispering "There must be more money! There must be more money!"

Paul's mother tells him that his father has no luck, and Paul confuses the word luck with lucre, "filthy lucre," as his Uncle Oscar once said. When his mother distinguishes luck from lucre, Paul tells her that he has luck. His mother doesn't believe him; Paul insists, saying, "God told me."

The family's gardener, Bassett, gambles on the horse

races. Paul is growing too old to ride his rocking horse but finds that when he rides the rocking horse with a frenzied, mad strength he somehow learns the names of the horses that will win the races. He and Bassett become partners in betting on the races, and Paul accumulates five thousand pounds. Hoping to silence the voices in the house that always whisper of money, Paul arranges through his Uncle Oscar to give to his mother one thousand pounds a year for five years as if it were a gift from an anonymous relative.

Paul is terribly hopeful that this money will quiet the voices in the house. Instead, his mother shows no pleasure in receiving the money. She goes to the lawyer who has served as intermediary and asks if the entire amount cannot be advanced to her. Hoping this will quiet her, Paul (through his uncle) agrees. But the voices grow louder and more insistent in demanding money, "More than ever!"

Paul knows that his mother does not love him. His primary reason for seeking the money is not to gain her love but rather to quiet the voices in the house, to quiet her insatiability. Such a child's effort to save a parent so the child's needs can be met is doomed to failure, especially if the parent is addicted and insatiable. Paul cannot change his mother's nature; his superhuman efforts only feed her yearning for more and more.

Lawrence suggests in several ways that Paul, in the grip of his obsession, is connecting to divine energies. Not only does Paul say that he knows he has luck because "God told me"; but Bassett, when telling Uncle Oscar of Paul's ability to name the winners, looks, "as if he were speaking of religious matters." Later Basset says to Uncle Oscar, "It's as if he had it from heaven," and Uncle Oscar replies, "I should say so!" This divine energy allows Paul to transcend what is normal. He becomes psychic, a word derived from Psyche, goddess of the Soul or Spirit; he is able to know what no ordinary human could know.

When we cross the boundaries between our material world and the higher realms, we expose ourselves to grave dangers. Shamans and priests perform rituals to give a form, a container, that allows for a transformative encounter with these higher energies and a safe return. The blind pursuit of money, even with the best motives, touches energies that can easily destroy us. Paul gives what is most precious and most powerful in himself, but he has no guide to help him on his journey. Even Basset and Uncle Oscar, good enough men themselves, become his fellow conspirators in using the uncanny information Paul has gleaned.

Finally, riding his rocking horse with superhuman force, Paul calls out the name of another winner. Then he collapses, unconscious, with a fever of the brain. He regains consciousness to learn that he has won over eighty thousand pounds for his mother. But he has sacrificed his very life for this money, and soon dies of the fever.

"The Rocking-Horse Winner" has many parallels with the well-known story of King Midas and the golden touch. While details vary from one version to another, Midas is always a lover of gold. In Nathaniel Hawthorne's retelling of the tale, Midas loves both gold and his daughter, Marygold. Unfortunately, Midas entwines these two loves and longs to bequeath to his daughter the largest pile of gold that has ever existed in the world. Midas loses his love of flowers (unless golden) and music (except for coins clinking together) and spends most of his time in the miserable underground vault—"little better than a dungeon"— where he plays with his gold and whispers to himself of his happiness.

One day a handsome stranger appears in the vault. Midas, certain that he turned the key in the lock, knows that this radiant young man must be a god. Soon the visitor, who is never named in the story, learns that Midas is not satisfied to have more gold than anyone else in the world. What, asks the beneficent stranger, would make Midas happy? Midas cannot imagine a large enough pile of gold, but at last conceives that his touch might turn everything to gold. The god asks if anything might ever make Midas regret having the golden touch. When Midas says that the golden touch will make him "perfectly happy," the god replies that the next morning Midas shall indeed possess this power. And the god, becoming brighter and brighter, at last vanishes like a sunbeam.

We are all familiar with how Midas's greedy joy soon disappears when he learns that he cannot eat or drink, for his food turns to gold in his mouth. Worse, he kisses his daughter, thinking that she is worth one thousand times more than the golden touch, only to have her turn to gold. Midas had liked to say his daughter was worth her weight in gold, but now this has literally become true. Stricken with misery, Midas suddenly discovers the god once again before him. When questioned by the god, Midas answers that a glass of water, a crust of bread, and certainly his daughter Marygold are all worth far more than the golden touch.

"You are wiser than you were, King Midas!" says the god, adding that Midas appears "to be still capable of understanding that the commonest things, such as lie within everybody's grasp, are more valuable than the riches which so many mortals sigh and struggle after."

The god tells Midas to wash himself in the river and pour water over all that he has turned to gold. If he is fortunate, everything, including Marygold, will return to what it was. And he is fortunate, for the story finishes many years later with Midas dandling his grandchildren on his knees and telling them how he came to hate the sight of gold, except for the golden hair of his daughter.

Paul's mother in "The Rocking-Horse Winner" has a great deal in common with King Midas. She is insatiable for money; he is insatiable for gold. She gains the golden touch in the form of her son's psychic powers; while Midas gains it directly as a gift from the god. She cannot save her son from death, and Midas cannot save his daughter from the death of becoming gold. Paul's mother is starving inwardly in a way that can never be satisfied; Midas's similar inner starving is reflected outwardly when his golden touch denies him the normal human joys of eating and touching.

But here the stories diverge. Paul's mother cannot love; she does not relate to her son and her family from an inner richness. Midas, while he is foolish and wrongheaded in asking for what will give him misery rather than happiness, does love his daughter. From this love, he is able to gain the wisdom that his love is far superior to acquiring gold. He is also able to see quite plainly his starvation and recognize that, for him, gold has become life-denying. He becomes richer within, richer in love and wisdom, because he learns from his experience and, according to Hawthorne's story, overcomes his obsession with gold.

THE GODS OF HUMAN SACRIFICE

Who is this golden god that visits Midas? Why does he come to that underground vault with such good will toward a mortal? And, having granted Midas one wish, why is he willing to intervene and save the foolish king from the folly of having wished for the golden touch?

King Midas, while probably a figure of myth rather than history, is said to have ruled the kingdom of Phrygia (in what is now western Turkey) at the beginning of the seventh century B.C. To show his piety, he is reputed to have sent his golden throne as an offering to the sanctuary at Delphi. He lived only a few generations before King Croesus, whose wealth we know to have been historical fact. The original story of Midas is Greek and, like so many Greek myths, was retold by a Roman poet, Ovid, in *The Metamorphoses*. As Ovid tells the story, Midas had no daughter at all, and Midas's gaining the golden touch is only one episode among many involving the golden god whom Hawthorne never named.

Ovid tells us that the god's name is Dionysus, lord of the vine and intoxication. Dionysus, or Bacchus as the Romans called him, had many drunken worshippers. One such worshipper was an old satyr named Silenus who weighed nearly half a ton from all his drinking. Trapped by peasants, Silenus is taken to their king—none other than Midas! Midas knows the drunken joys of Dionysus and has been inebriated with Silenus many times. So Midas treats his old friend to a drinking binge that lasts for ten days and nights. Then Midas takes Silenus home to Dionysus. The god, delighted by this, offers Midas a boon: any wish that Midas makes will come true. The balance of Ovid's tale about Midas is similar to Hawthorne's, so we will leave Midas to focus on the generous god Dionysus.

Son of Zeus and a mortal woman, Dionysus is plagued by madness. He wanders from kingdom to kingdom, from Egypt to Syria to Phrygia, and introduces in each place knowledge of how to cultivate the vine and make wine. In

Phrygia, Dionysus is initiated into the mysteries of the cult of the goddess Cybele. This goddess exemplified many of the terrifying aspects of fertility goddesses. As mother of the crops, the animals, and human offspring, the fertility goddess is endowed with immense powers. The cycles of life and death are the realm of Cybele or the very similar Mother Goddesses of neighboring lands.

As ruler over life and death the goddess herself must sacrifice. For Cybele, this sacrifice was Attis, the young shepherd whom she loved and, perhaps, had even mothered. Attis is slain by a wild boar or, in some versions of the myth, castrates himself and bleeds to death beneath the pine tree which is sacred to Cybele. After Attis dies, he is transformed into a pine tree and so finds new life.

The death of Attis led to the renewal of the land, the life of the new crops. This death was re-enacted each year in a great festival held around the spring equinox in March. On the third day, known as the Day of Blood, the high priest drew blood from his arms and offered this blood as a sacrifice. To the wild music of cymbals, drums, horns, and flutes, the worshippers danced to intoxication and gashed themselves so their blood flowed on the altar. In this frenzied state, some of the worshippers lifted their robes and castrated themselves, flinging their genitals on the statue of Cybele as an ultimate offering.

What purpose could be served by these terrible mutilations? Apparently the power of the male genitals was felt to be transformed by being sacrificed. No longer capable of impregnating mortal women, these genitals could be buried to impregnate the earth herself. So like the sacrifices of human blood, the severed genitals would serve to move life's great wheel from the season of death to that of birth.

From this description, it can be easily understood why Cybele was served by eunuch priests. Cybele had to sacrifice Attis, whom she most loved, to fulfill her role in making the land fertile. Likewise her worshippers at times sacrificed what was most precious to them—their manhood, their generative powers—to amplify her powers of fertility. In fact, the death of Attis strongly suggests that human sacrifice had been part of these fertility rituals. Not only the power of the genitals but the power of life itself would be offered in service to the goddess.

King Midas's benefactor, Dionysus, learned well from the frenzied rites of Cybele. As the cult of Dionysus spread, his worshippers would also aspire to a divine intoxication (often through the consumption of wine). In this frenzied state, they might see loved ones as beasts and tear them limb from limb. That his worshippers were often bands of women called maenads and their victims men (such as Penteus in *The Bacchae* by Euripides) suggests a re-enactment of the violent moments when the fertility goddess brings life from death by sacrifice.

The implication of human sacrifice in the death of Attis is made explicit in what we know of many fertility goddesses (and gods). The Old Testament is filled with references to the long struggle to end human sacrifice, often portrayed as part of the struggle between Yahweh and the pagan gods. We are told of King Ahaz who "did not do what was right in the eyes of the Lord [but] . . . even made molten images for the Ba'als; and . . . burned his sons as an offering, according to the abominable practices of the nations whom the Lord drove out before the people of Israel." Ba'al was a Phoenician god with power over the rain and thus over the fertility of the land. Often worshipped in the form of a calf or bull, the human sacrifices to Ba'al sought to make the land fertile. Human sacrifice was used to forge a connection to the divine by King Ahab, the warrior Jephthat, and perhaps even the prophet Elijah.

The worship of Ba'al and similar gods spread with the explorations of the ancient Phoenicians, who established colonies in many parts of the Mediterranean. In Carthage, founded by the Phoenicians, innumerable children were offered as sacrifices. As worshippers danced to timbrels and flutes that drowned the victims' screams, the children were placed in the hands of a bronze idol with a calf's head. From here they slid inexorably down into ovens filled with fire. Archeologists have found urns containing the remains of as many as twenty thousand infants who served as sacrificial victims.

Religious rites involving human sacrifice appear in many cultures around the world, cultures quite unrelated to each other. So the practice of human sacrifice was certainly not limited to the tribes and times of the Old Testament. When Julius Caesar conquered Gaul, he wrote of the fertility sacrifices of the Celts. At a great festival held every fifth year, condemned criminals would be sacrificed by the Druids (priests). The Celts believed that the more humans sacrificed, the greater the fertility of the land.

No culture made human sacrifice more central to its existence than that of the Aztecs. In the mythology of the Aztecs, the gods had sacrificed themselves to nourish the Fifth Sun. So the Aztecs believed their practices of human sacrifice came from the gods and that the continued existence of their universe depended on such sacrifice. Blood kept the sun in the heavens; and innumerable methods of bloodletting let the Aztecs put off the dread day when the sun would cease its movement through the sky.

The preferred sacrifice was of the human heart, for the

heart symbolized life to the Aztecs. They believed that the heart contained vital fluids that made it move and, through sacrifice, would make the sun continue to move and ascend the heavens each day. So priests would often pull the pulsating heart from the victim and hold it aloft to feed the sun. This tearing out of the heart also symbolized the husking of the corn; lifting the heart to the heavens aided the new corn to grow ever higher.

The Aztecs institutionalized a system of recurring warfare that allowed the taking of prisoners for the purpose of sacrifice. Although the sixteenth-century estimates of the sacrificial slaughter made by the Spanish conquerors are unreliable, such sacrifices were clearly widespread and systematic. Thus a mother who gave birth was said "to make a prisoner." One of the songs of Xipe, the Aztec god of the sun and the corn, speaks of his transformation into the war god Huitzilopochtli. So the blood of sacrificed prisoners feeds the growth of the corn.

Some sacrificial victims were actually made to act the role of a god or goddess. By doing so, these victims were given the sacred duty of representing the god or goddess. For example, each September there was a festival to celebrate the Maize Goddess Chicomecohuatl. After a strict fast lasting seven days, a beautiful slave girl, twelve or thirteen years old, would be dressed in the robes of the goddess with maize cobs about her neck and a green feather upright on her head. This feather symbolized the ripening maize which, at the time of the festival, would be almost ready to be harvested.

After a series of rituals, including perhaps a marriage of the girl to the war god Huitzilopochtli, each person had to come before the girl, squat (the equivalent of kneeling), and offer her a cup containing blood drawn from their ears as penance during the seven days of the fast. Later that day the priests would sacrifice the girl so that her blood soaked an altar piled with maize, vegetables, and seeds of every type. The body of the girl was flayed and her skin worn by a priest, who also dressed in the robes of the goddess. As the procession left the temple, this priest danced to the front to show the resurrection of the goddess.

If these examples of human sacrifice in fertility rituals seem far removed from contemporary life, we might consider how many people today are willing to kill for money. Listening to the news brings us endless varieties of this life sacrifice: cabbies killed for a few hundred dollars; shopkeepers shot down even after surrendering their money; and a tourist knifed to death for enough money to spend an evening at a disco. In his book *The Highest Altar*, journalist Patrick Tierney argues persuasively that human sacrifice actually takes place today in Peru. As remarkable as the fact of this sacrifice is its purpose: the murderers pray not for rain or good harvests, but for money.

When we first encountered Moneta, the Roman goddess of money, we spoke of the meanings hidden within her name. She is a goddess who warns, but what does she warn us against? Now we can understand Moneta far better, for we see her among her sister fertility goddesses. We know the sweetness of the Hopi ceremony which weds the Snake Maiden to the Antelope Youth in worshipping the Corn Mother. And we know the violence of the human sacrifices of the Aztecs in serving the very same goddess, the Maize Goddess Chicomecohuatl. Moneta promises us the new life that flows from the sacred marriage and warns us of the death that is inevitable in her endless cycles of fertility. In her most violent aspect, she demands human sacrifice to ensure her own rebirth, the annual renewal of the natural world, and the survival of humanity.

Moneta's message is difficult to hear, because our mortality is a painful and inscrutable truth. Yet neither the sacrifice of human victims nor the accumulation of vast amounts of wealth will allow us to escape from the cycles of life and death. When we contemplate money in this way, we may feel far greater sympathy for Paul's mother in "The Rocking-Horse Winner" or King Midas in "The Golden Touch." A son dead of brain fever or a daughter turned to lifeless gold are the sacrificial victims of parents who have no idea why they yearn for ever greater wealth. They know nothing of Moneta, much less Chicomeco-huatl. They have not plumbed the depths to learn the origins of their own passions and fears. Having failed to do this, they cannot see the paradox of wealth. For while money symbolizes the life force and abundance, it must be recognized as a symbol. To possess money without possessing the vitality and abundance that money symbolizes is to make money a dangerous illusion.

When people lived without money and hunted or farmed for their livelihood, abundance needed far less interpretation. But in recent centuries a worldwide migration of people to cities has separated us from the cycles of nature. Without trees we no longer witness leaves tumbling in autumn, the bare limbs of winter, and the green renewal of spring. Without crops we forget the plowing and planting of fields, the sprouting and ripening, and the harvest. Without wildlife or farm animals we divorce the meat filling the refrigerated bins of our supermarkets from the living animals that are the source of this nourishment.

In a way, cities are like the sacred grove at the ancient Greek center of healing in Epidaurus. Neither birth nor death was permitted within this sacred grove, making life the eternal constant. For someone who is ill, it must be profoundly healing to escape for a while the endless turning of the wheel of life and death. An important aspect of the cures at Epidaurus was a healing of the mind. After cleansing rituals and prayers, an ill person would sleep in a special chamber and hope to receive a dream from the gods. For the dream itself might heal or give an understanding of what course the cure should take.

Healing though it may be to enter the sacred grove where life neither begins nor ends, we cannot remain in such a timeless place. Both Paul's mother and Midas fail to understand the limitations of mortal women and men. They imagine that they can accumulate an infinite amount of the substance (money or gold) that symbolizes the life force.

Why can't Paul's mother or Midas evaluate money or gold and know when each has gained enough? They are grappling with the secret life of money. Unless they bring this secret life into the light of consciousness, they cannot possibly inhibit their compulsions and redirect their life energies. On one level, they are unaware that beneath money issues are fears and hopes about the fertility of nature, a fertility which is largely outside of their control. On another level, they are unaware of the sacrifices demanded in the cycles of fertility, sacrifices that would make all of us tremble if we allowed them to rise to consciousness. Yet that which we leave hidden from sight will always possess immense, destructive power. If we fail to face inner issues of fertility, sacrifice, and mortality, we risk losing what is most dear to us and receiving nothing in return.

The issue of sacrifice is embedded in money. This is true for all people and all cultures, because nature's cycles of life and death are universal. If we had been born as Aztecs and had to sacrifice our own blood to the Maize Goddess, we would recognize how we and our culture ritualized the attempt to offer our life energy in exchange for the divine energy that brings the richness of nature. Living in modern cultures that abhor such sacrifices of life, we have no easy way to see the connection between money and our aspiration to be blessed by the richness of the divine.

Such an aspiration, like so much touched by money, is paradoxical. On the one hand, we have the understandable hope that proper handling of money will bring well-being and prosperity for ourselves, those we love, and perhaps even the society of which we are a part. On the other hand, we hope that the accumulation of sufficient amounts of money will give us an excess of the life force. If we could gain such an excess, we could be like the gods, immortal, no longer subject to the rule of nature that decrees death as both the precursor and end of life.

Of course, we would ridicule anyone who expressed such a fantasy of living forever. In the conquest of the New World, the Conquistadors searched for two fabled sites: El Dorado (the city of gold) and the Fountain of Eternal Youth (which conferred immortality on those who drank its waters). Viewed through our lens of fertility goddesses who are the source of wealth (symbolized by money or gold) and also the source of life, we know that El Dorado and the Fountain of Youth are parts of the same mythical landscape. So Dionysus, the vegetative god of the vine, is capable of conferring infinite amounts of gold on Midas; indeed, capable of giving Midas the very power to create gold. What Midas risks losing in return is life itself, whether his daughter's life or his own.

THE COLLECTIVE UNCONSCIOUS AND THE BUSINESS CYCLE

Money, life, and sacrifice are not only connected in the unconscious of the individual but in the collective unconscious of the culture as well. This collective unconscious is the home of the archetypes, the larger patterns developed during human evolution and affecting each of us. During recessionary times we may read in the newspapers of some bureaucrat who declares that lowering the interest rate will pump new lifeblood into the economy. These are not the words of an Aztec priest who has pierced his genitals to let his blood nourish the earth and sustain the Fifth Sun in the heavens. These are the words of a secular official, perhaps a member of the Federal Reserve Board, who is unconsciously making the ancient connection between blood and abundance. In this case, however, the abundance is not of the fields alone but of a more complicated modern economy.

This economy depends, in large part, on the willingness of the people to consume. We have even developed measurements of Consumer Confidence. If Consumer Confidence rises, we can expect more consumer spending. This will have what the economists call a multiplier effect, since each dollar spent will be received by others who will be encouraged to spend more. Soon money will be flowing like life-giving blood through the system. But if the Consumer Confidence falls, people will be fearful about prosperity in the future and will spend less. The decreasing circulation of money-blood will ensure contraction of the economy with ensuing recession or depression.

Of course, the full complexities of the modern economy are beyond the focus of this book, but I would like to pose a simple question: Why are there recessions or depressions at all? Assuming for a moment that consumer spending is the key to boom and bust, what makes the consumer fearful or optimistic about the future? What animates this statistical consumer stitched together from the information contained in the index of Consumer Confidence? Where does he or she discover the facts that make prosperity seem more or less likely? What is the first cause, the prime mover, of this economic system?

Our consumer might ask someone else what is likely to happen. Based on the answer, our consumer might have soaring or plummeting confidence. But how did the second person have any information to give the first? Perhaps the second person has been laid off by a business. Then we would ask why did the business lay off the second person and cause panic about the future? If the answer is that the business is not selling as much as it used to because Consumer Confidence is low, then we have come full circle. How did the confidence of this business's consumers fall in the first place?

If someone answered that a drought has destroyed the crops in the fields and we need a prophet like Elijah to bring rain, then it would be easy to understand a low level of the index of Consumer Confidence. But in the world economy, such natural events rarely are the cause of economic contractions. In fact, the natural resources, the factories, and the skilled labor are all as available for use when the economy contracts as when it expands. What differs is our willingness to make use of these resources, which include ourselves, our life energy.

In an ideal world, perhaps a band of courageous people would agree to go against the trend. When the index of Consumer Confidence fell, they would begin a holy crusade of consumption by buying houses, lavish meals, clothing, and gifts until everyone around them would be employed as a natural result of their largesse. The multiplier effect would send waves of money through the economy, until the money inevitably returned to the very consumers who had originally banded together. Prosperity would ensue for all, even those who initially risked their assets (or perhaps went into debt) in order to consume.

We might call our hardy band the Consumers of the Round Table and reward the most prodigious among them with medals and feasts in their honor. In our Consumer Hall of Fame, we would enshrine golden statues of heroes and heroines—those who consumed not from self-love but in loving service to others. After several prosperous generations passed, with all the indexes of Consumer Confidence remaining at the highest possible levels, some misguided souls might begin to pray to these golden statues as gods and burn money on their altars to ensure that more money would be sent from the divine world back into our own.

What a grotesque fantasy! But let us use it for a moment to examine what the individual misses when facing the secular life of the modern economy. Basically, there is no way for the individual to make a meaningful sacrifice. We are not going to squat in front of some wooden idol and give it blood drawn from our ears. Yet if we fail to have some ritual by which the economy is positioned in the natural world, as well as in the artificial worlds of our industrial and informational revolutions, we may sense that a crucial link with the life-and-death reality of humanity has been lost.

That lost link condemns us to a statistical world. In such a world we cannot use sacrifice to re-establish our connection to the richness of nature and to re-establish our confidence. Instead of being active participants in rituals that strengthen the will of the society to survive, we become the victims whose lack of productivity is reflected in the unemployment figures. No goddess is sacrificed, but six or ten or fourteen percent of the work force is unemployed. Our sacrifices are hidden behind our statistics. Even these statistics do not suggest the full extent of the sacrifice. For example, the unemployment statistics do not include people who have given up looking for employment, who are underemployed, who are temporary workers but wish they were permanently employed, or who have started their own businesses from desperation when they were unable to find work. Those who are statistics, and those who are not even counted in the statistics, cannot make the community perceive any value in their sacrifices. They are left with no way to commune with the gods or their own natures.

Inevitably the people call for the sacrifice of the leader believed to be responsible for the recession, usually the president. Fearing to be voted out of office, he (or, someday, she) soon selects a trusted aide, usually a key advisor on economic policy, and, to use a common expression, gives this aide the ax. This scapegoating, a phrase which also comes from the lexicon of human and animal sacrifice, allows the president to blame the aide for sins (the recession or depression) that probably were not the fault of anyone. It is a secular counterpart of the Aztec priest sacrificing the goddess to renew the natural world.

However, the Aztec priest had the advantage of making the people believe that they were giving of themselves to nourish their gods. They were active participants in restoring the divine order that let the sun rise in the sky and the corn grow to be husked and devoured. Without recognition of this cycle of nature, a cycle which includes death as well as life, we are living in a culture out of touch with psychic realities as true for us as for the first man and woman who lived eons ago. We are denying our unconscious knowledge that there must be death, there must be a time when activity lessens or ceases. If unending growth is truly a goal that we desire, we must bring to the light of awareness our secret belief that such growth is as impossible for us as immortality. Only then can we evaluate whether such growth would be possible and wise.

No wonder "In God We Trust" appears on all of our coins and bills. In times of recession or depression, this slogan offers a way to understand why money fails us. Money, although a secular tool, requires our trust in the richness of a divine power. If we feel a constriction in the flow of money-blood, we will yearn for more life energy. If we feel that our political leaders are sacrificing us, then we (living in a democracy and not a theocracy) will demand their sacrifice. If a credible leader tells us that he or she can create more money and save us from the incompetents in power, that leader will find followers whose fervor seems religious.

Let us return to the Civil War, when, as we discussed in the last chapter, "In God We Trust" first appeared on a coin. Until 1862, the dollar had been defined as being worth a certain amount of silver or gold. The government would buy gold or silver at fixed official rates (which also created an official ratio between the value of gold and silver) for conversion into coins. However, the difficulties of financing the Civil War forced the issuance of paper money. Called greenbacks, these paper bills were not backed by gold or silver and quickly inflated the money supply. An ounce of gold rose to be worth twice as many greenbacks as the government's official rate provided. The marketplace determined the shifting relationship between gold and greenbacks by a floating exchange rate.

The desire for a more sound currency prompted enactment of laws in 1873, 1874, and 1875 that caused the United States Mint to resume purchasing gold in 1879 at the official exchange rate that had prevailed before the Civil War. However, the Coinage Act of 1873 failed to include a requirement that the government purchase silver for conversion into dollars. This omission meant that the United States had abandoned the bimetallic standard that had existed from 1792 through 1862 in favor of a gold standard. While I am omitting to discuss the complexities of the effect of the relationship between the prices of gold and silver established in the marketplace (which caused only one metal to be sold to the government during any given period, since the other metal would best be sold in commerce), many people believed that the failure to commit the government to purchasing silver as well as gold caused a continuation of the serious deflation that began in 1869 and reached its lowest point in 1896. That is why the Coinage Act of 1873 came to be called the Crime of '73 by supporters of bimetallism.

By 1896, deflation made goods cost only sixty-one percent of what they had cost in 1869. The effect on farm prices had been even more severe. In 1896, farm products cost forty-four percent of what they had cost in 1869. This deflation hurt debtors who had to pay back their debts with dollars worth more than when they had been borrowed. Farmers and small businesses, especially in rural areas in the South and West, sought a rainmaker who would relieve them of the onerous burdens caused by deflation. As banks failed (496 failed in 1893) and the unemployment rate rose rapidly after the Panic of '93—to 18.4 percent in 1894 and the still unacceptably high 14.4 percent in 1896—the nation languished in a depression, the like of which had not been seen since the 1830s and would not be seen again until the 1930s.

The Democrats came to their 1896 nominating convention divided into two wings, one which favored the gold standard and the other which favored a return to a gold and silver standard. Repudiating President Grover Cleveland, who had presided over four years of depression and favored a gold standard, the convention turned to a thirty-six-year-old newspaperman and former congressman from Nebraska named William Jennings Bryan. When Bryan gave his famous "Cross of Gold" speech and ultimately won the nomination, he framed this money issue with striking religious metaphors:

"I come to speak to you in defense of a cause as holy as the cause of liberty," Bryan said early in his speech, "the cause of humanity." Pointing out that his cause was not a dispute over personalities but over principles, he touched on human mortality: "The individual is but an atom; he is born, he acts, he dies; but principles are eternal; and this has been a contest over a principle."

This is marvelous oratory, but what eternal principle does Bryan refer to here? On one level, he is speaking of bimetallism, but in a deeper sense he is speaking of the prosperity that he believes would result from increasing the quantity of money in circulation. This eternal principle of prosperity flows from the confluence of death and rebirth over which fertility goddesses such as Moneta rule.

"With a zeal approaching the zeal which inspired the crusaders who followed Peter the Hermit, our silver Democrats went forth from victory unto victory . . ." Bryan continued, placing himself on the side of the "plain people of this country" whom he extolled: "The farmer who . . . by the application of brain and muscle to the natural resources of the country creates wealth, is as much a business man as the man who goes upon the board of trade and bets upon the price of grain; the miners who go down a thousand feet into the earth . . . and bring forth from their hiding places the precious metals to be poured into the channels of trade are as much business men as the few financial magnates who, in a back room, corner the money of the world."

In distinguishing those who labor to bring forth the riches of nature from those who are manipulators of money, Bryan glorifies the "hardy pioneers who have braved all the dangers of the wilderness, who have made the desert to blossom as the rose. . . ." Condemning the effect of monometalism, he speaks of how "the gold standard has slain its tens of thousands."

In contrast to the idea that "if you will only legislate to make the well-to-do prosperous, their prosperity will leak through on those below," Bryan avows that "the democratic idea, however, has been that if you legislate to make the masses prosperous, their prosperity will find its way up through every class which rests upon them."

This leads him to an interesting observation about the farms and the cities, the city voters having been generally supportive of the gold standard.

"Burn down your cities and leave our farms," he says, "and your cities will spring up again as if by magic; but destroy our farms and the grass will grow in the streets of every city in the country." So, as if Moneta herself stood behind him, he refers again to the necessity of natural fruitfulness. Like a shaman who can bring rain in the form of an increased money supply, he claims a superior knowledge of the secrets of fertility. He knows as well, therefore, that fertility demands sacrifice. He has stated clearly that he will sacrifice the interests of the capitalists and protect the interests of the working masses. This leads to the famous finish of his speech, a thunderous ending worthy of any god of rain-bringing storms.

"Having behind us the producing masses of this nation and the world, supported by the commercial interests, the laboring interests, and the toilers everywhere, we will answer their demand for a gold standard by saying to them: You shall not press down upon the brow of labor this crown of thorns, you shall not crucify mankind upon a cross of gold."

Bryan's fervent crusade for "the plain people" did not win him the presidency, but his imagery suggests the strong connection between money issues, productivity, and sacrifice. We may not keep this connection in our awareness, but an orator like Bryan, speaking in a time of crisis, can bring to light the ancient roots from which our economies have grown. When he speaks of sacrifice, he lets us glimpse our nature as individuals and, collectively, as a society. He may or may not have been correct in his beliefs about bimetallism (that debate continues), but his metaphor exposes truths of how we feel and experience money.

In a larger sense, the Cross of Gold is the power of money to create illusion. King Midas nearly lost his life, and his daughter's, on the Cross of Gold; Paul was indeed crucified, the madness of money too great a fever for his brain. Illusion is ever-present when dealing with money; our struggle is to find a microscope or telescope that will allow us to pierce the veil of illusion. Understanding the fertility myths with their legacy of sacrifice is one step toward deepening our understanding.

Looking back a century, Bryan himself seems transfigured. Running for president at the age of thirty-six, he conjures up the image of Attis, the shepherd boy loved by the goddess, the vegetative god sacrificed for the renewal of nature and productivity. In the election of 1896, Bryan was abandoned by the conservative eastern Democrats. His support in the Rocky Mountain states and the Great Plains could not overcome Republican William McKinley's success in the East and Middle West. McKinley won 271 electoral votes to Bryan's 176, and also won a decisive plurality of 600,000 votes.

Prosperity quickly returned to the nation. Deflation halted. The supply of gold increased both from new sources in the Klondike, South Africa, and Australia, and from the discovery of an inexpensive cyanide process to extract gold from low-grade ore. Harvests improved at home, while crop failures in Europe helped to keep farm prices high. On March 14, 1900, the Republicans passed the Gold Standard Act of 1900 which made the gold dollar the standard unit of value and required that all paper currency be redeemable in gold. Resurrected like Attis, Bryan ran for president again in 1900 but lost by an even larger margin. President McKinley could point to four years of Republican prosperity. Moneta had blessed him, answering not only his prayers but those of the "plain people" as well.

Yet Bryan, when writing his memoirs in 1925, sought to have the final word. He had fought for silver not for its own sake, but as a method of achieving an increased quantity of money. So he posed his question as follows: "Suppose the citizens of a town were divided, nearly equally, on the question of water supply, one faction contending that the amount should be increased, and suggesting that the increase be piped from Silver Lake, the other faction insisting that no more water was needed; suppose that at the election the opponents of an increase won (no matter by what means); and suppose, soon after the election, a spring which may be described as Gold Spring, broke forth in the very center of the city, with a flow of half as much water as the city had before used; and suppose the new supply was turned into the city reservoir to the joy and benefit of all the people of the town. Which faction would, in such a case, have been vindicated?"

Water, which Midas sprinkled on his possessions and his daughter to return them to their true reality, offers an apt metaphor for the flow of money. The very word currency comes from the Latin *currens*, which means to run or flow. And this flowing water has a deep source in the Cross of Gold, at once the symbol of sacrifice and of the tree of life. For the ancients sacrificed to bring the rainfall, to bring the inseminating and life-nurturing water. They offered blood in exchange for water; sometimes, in fact, their own blood and the blood of their loved ones. In Christianity, in the baptismal rituals, the sprinkling of or immersion in water is believed to bring about the most profound reality: the entry of spirit into flesh.

These are not ancient images fit only for academic study, but living images for us today. If we speak of King Midas instead of the fallen financiers of Wall Street's scandals, it is because the story of Midas is so obviously universal—as true in Phrygia seven centuries before Christ as on Wall Street during the junk-bond-financed mergers and acquisitions of the 1980s.

The connection of money to water, blood, and spirit can be ignored only at our peril. Money offers us illusions because of its own origins in temples and sacrificial offerings. It speaks to us of the inseminating power of water, the sacrificial efficacy of blood, and the eternal life of spirit. This is all implicit in the paycheck we carry home each Friday, the profit of our small business, the dividend on our stock, and the interest on our loan.

If we understand this, then we understand that our task is to dispel the illusions of money, so that we can see beneath and beyond money to the deeper truths of our lives. Money itself can then be placed in service to those truths, rather than to illusions. If we succeed in this process, Moneta will have served us well indeed.

CHAPTER FOUR

HOARDING MONEY

Why the Life Energy of Misers Is Stolen

ONCE THERE WAS a miller who loved gold. This love so possessed him that he sold everything he owned to buy what he loved. Then he melted all this gold into one large piece which he buried in his field. Each daybreak he would hurry to his field and dig up his glorious treasure.

But a thief must have watched the miller's furtive visits, for one night someone unearthed the miller's hoard and carried it away.

The next morning the miller dug and dug but found nothing. He howled with such anguish that at last a neighbor came to find out what terrible thing had happened.

When he heard that the gold had been stolen, the neighbor spoke to the miller as follows: "Why are you so upset? You had no gold at all, so you haven't lost any. You merely imagined that you had it, and you may as well imagine that you have it still. Simply bury a stone where you buried your money. Imagine that stone to be your treasure, and you'll have your gold again. After all, you didn't use the gold when you had it; and you will never miss it as long as you are determined not to use it."

The miller had a wise neighbor, but this hardly makes the neighbor's advice any easier to hear. The miller, like Midas, had fallen in love with gold. Misers are notorious for refusing to allow their great wealth to benefit anyone. If the neighbor acted more conventionally and sympathized with the miller over the theft of the gold, then an important truth would be lost. The mere possessing of something does not confer wealth; rather the wealth is conferred in the using of what is possessed. So money must circulate if it is to have meaning as money. Like blood, water, and spirit, money's circulation is a key to finding the wealth it measures.

Burying money in the earth symbolizes the removal of life energy from the human community. In fact, money is the least of what the miser withholds from the world, for it is a mere symbol of what might have been shared—love, kindness, joy, and creativity. The neighbor speaks for the community which the miller has denied and retreated from by being so miserly. This neighbor has no sympathy to give, but offers the miller a chance to see the illusory nature of wealth that is not used.

In this chapter we will explore the ways in which money symbolizes life energy. If we imagine gaining money to be the goal of any endeavor (or of our lives), then for a moment we lose sight of the underlying relationships that money was created to serve. Certainly in the context of the family, the using of money can be like the sharing of food or of love; in business, the flow of money can facilitate productivity and the creation of well-being for the whole community. If we hoard our energy and the fruits of our productivity, we gain little, and we steal from ourselves the connection to others and to community that makes life meaningful.

In each of the four stories in this chapter, there is an intervention from the spirit world. A boy becomes an eagle; a miser is visited by ghosts and spirits; the god of luck helps a peasant; and a king's wife proves to be a goddess in disguise. We might think of such interventions as thoughts or powers of imagination that live within each of us. At moments of crisis, we may suddenly encounter a new way of seeing an issue, a new way of thinking about money and possessions. If we are fortunate enough to have this spiritual intervention, what we experience is truly the power of self-healing.

THE PUNISHMENT OF THE STINGY

Our first story, from thc Chinook tribe of the Northwest, is titled "The Punishment of the Stingy." It illustrates how damaging it can be to refuse to circulate wealth—in this case, the wealth of food. By looking at the failure to circulate food, we see a concrete example of the social damage that results from refusing to circulate what is life-sustaining. In our culture, in which food can so easily be purchased, the equivalent would be the hoarding of money.

In the story, a harsh winter has brought hunger to the many people who live in their village built above a wave-swept beach. The chief has died and his only son is growing up to be a man. No food washes up from the sea, and the people eke out a meager sustenance from mussels and roots.

One day a hunter says the men should go to sea. Even if

they can't find anything to eat, at least they can gather more mussels. So all the men pile into two canoes and paddle until the village disappears from sight. When they reach a small island, they sight sea lions, spear one, and drag it ashore.

Now Bluejay, one of the hunters, says they should eat all of the sea lion and take nothing home to share with the women and children. None of the hunters argues with Bluejay, so the sea lion is boiled and eaten on the island. When another hunter, Raven, tries to hide a piece of meat in his mat to take home for the people who are hungry, Bluejay finds the meat and burns it in the fire. Then the hunters gather mussels to give to the women in the village.

The next day the chief's son wants to join the hunters, but Bluejay says the waves will carry the boy away and forces him to stay in the village. Again the hunters spear a sea lion. Again Bluejay says they should bring nothing back to the village, because it will make the chief's son want to come with them. The other hunters do not question this decision or the reason given for it, but Raven ties a piece of meat in his hair to bring back for the people. Bluejay discovers the meat and throws it into the fire. Before leaving the island, the hunters look for mussels, which they bring back to the women in the village.

On the third morning, the chief's son wants to go again, but Bluejay refuses to take him. Once again, Raven tries to conceal meat for the village but is discovered. The hunters feast on sea lion and bring back mussels for the villagers. The fourth morning these same events are repeated, and on the fifth morning, too.

On the fifth morning, the chief's son holds the side of the canoe until Bluejay hits his hands and makes him let go. Then the boy takes his bow and arrows and walks on the beach. When he sees a black eagle, he shoots and skins it and tries to put the skin on his body. However, it is too small to fit him, as is the skin of the second eagle that he shoots and skins. Then he shoots a bald-headed eagle and squeezes himself into its skin.

Soon the chief's son is flying and smells the smoke of fat cooking. He follows this scent to the island where the hunters are feasting on the meat of a sea lion. First the boy lands on a branch, but then he wants Bluejay to see him and circles the fire five times. Bluejay throws a piece of meat to the eagle, surprised that the bird has feet like a human (because the skin was too small to fit over the boy's feet).

The next morning, the sixth day, the hunters haul their canoes into the water, but the chief's son makes no effort to go with them. Once the hunters are gone, the boy calls together all the women and children in the village. He shows them the meat which Bluejay gave him and uses the meat to grease the heads of everyone left in the village. Then he pulls down all the houses but the one belonging to Raven. Sharpening the planks from the houses, he fastens a plank to the back of each woman.

Swim to the island and circle it five times, the chief's son tells the women, and you will become killer whales and always be able to kill sea lions for yourselves. But give nothing to stingy people.

As for the children, the chief's son says they will become seabirds. Lastly he splits sinews and ties the mussels to the rocks so that Bluejay and the others will always have the painful task of prying the mussels free.

Then the women swim to the island where their husband-hunters feast. The women-whales leap from the water as they circle five times around the island before heading out to the sea. Soon seabirds with blood-red beaks fly five times around the island until they, too, disappear from sight. Only Raven recognizes these birds as the children of the village.

Bluejay fears that he and the hunters have seen evil spirits. Now they not only gather mussels, but load their meat into the canoes as well. They rush home to the village, but the houses (except for Raven's) are all tumbled down and the women and children have vanished.

Bluejay laments until one of the hunters tells him to be silent. If you had not been bad, the hunter says, our chief would not have done this to us.

The women and children do not return. Instead the hunters live without shelter and scavenge for food on the beach. They eat roots and have to break the mussels from the stones. Bluejay is the most unfortunate of all, for he seldom finds food, and often hailstones cascade on him from the skies above. Only Raven, who had been kind-hearted, finds a seal or a sturgeon on the beach and has a shelter in which to live. But those who did not bring food to their families lose everything. This is how their chief punished them for their stinginess.

HOW THE REFUSAL TO SHARE AFFECTS THE COMMUNITY

We are often caught in the struggle over whether to follow a Bluejay or a chief's son. They are like our inner voices, one stingy and one generous. Sometimes, like the hunters, we nod assent and follow the wrong leader. Perhaps a voice like Raven's offers an opportunity to change our course, but such a voice can be difficult to hear.

Clearly the death of the chief has left its mark. Without good leadership, the hunters are unable to perform right actions. Bluejay benefits himself, for he and the men feast heartily. But he fails to circulate the wealth of food that should be shared with the villagers. This failure is immensely disturbing to the social order. When we looked at the roots of money, we saw its distant origins in sacrifices offered to ensure the abundance of nature. The story implies that there may be retribution from the world of nature, which is the source of richness, when wealth is not shared properly. Thus Bluejay's succulent feasts become the cause of life-long deprivation for the hunters.

The chief's son yearns to take part in several aspects of communal life. By seeking to join the hunters, he readies himself to be initiated as one of the men of the village. By his willingness to share the wealth of the hunt with the entire village, he shows his awareness of his duties to the community.

Bluejay's repeated rebuffs drive the boy to seek a higher justice. He slays three eagles and at last attires himself in the bald eagle's skin and gains its power of flight. The eagle symbolizes spiritual aspirations, the connection of the human to the realm of the spirit world. The eagle has the strength to rise above and destroy all the other birds (including the bluejay), so the eagle possesses the power to destroy what is base and evil. Kings, emperors, and nations have taken the eagle as their symbol, both to show their divine blessing and to manifest their power. When the boy draws on the skin of the eagle, he seeks the role and power of the father and the chief.

Drawing his strength from the supernatural world, the

chief's son sits in judgment of his fellow men. Since the men will not care for the women and children, the natural order of the tribe no longer functions. If the weak cannot rely on the strong, the chief's son will free them from their dependence. He transforms them into killer whales and seabirds that are capable of capturing prey. The men did not give the loyalty and love that would have been symbolized by sharing their wealth, so the women and children are freed from the social contract which made the village thrive.

A key aspect of the story is timing. The gifts of nature must be used when given; we must live in the moment. As each day passes, it becomes more and more difficult for the hunters to make amends. Five is a magical number, repeated numerous times in the story, and on the sixth day the village—and all that it represents, including the value of human connection—is destroyed. At last Bluejay and the others pile the meat into their canoes, but giving from fear or compulsion is not true generosity. By the time they are willing to give, their stinginess has been ruinous. Once the women and children have been transformed, it is too late to bring the wealth to the village.

Those who do not circulate lose what would have been circulated to them in return. The very word "circulation" implies this outcome, for it shares its root with circularity and circle. Circularity suggests that the energy given will return in some form to the giver, while a circle is a symbol of the connection of all things in the whole. Bluejay and the hunters deny this principle of circulation. They deny their connection to the whole. Only Raven, who was kind, is spared in some measure from the cataclysm that follows.

Repetition is like habitual thought. Bluejay and the

hunters do not fail once; they fail five times. Bluejay is not only stingy in refusing to share the food, but he also refuses to give the chief's son a proper role as a hunter and a man in the village. As the story repeats itself, so the habitual thinking of the miser is repeated. The miser must withhold; the miser fears what will happen if life's energies flow freely. But the miser cannot control the powers of richness that reside in nature. So the chief's son becomes a powerful man and, at the very end of the story, is acknowledged as the chief because of the wealth and rightness of his nature.

A CHRISTMAS CAROL

If these hunters lived in a more modern society, Bluejay would have convinced them not to share their paychecks with their families. Whether the substance not shared is food or money, the human issues remain the same.

The most famous tale of stinginess may well be *A Christmas Carol* by Charles Dickens. Set in the middle of the nineteenth century in London, this story's portrait of the miser Scrooge is even harsher than the portrait of Bluejay.

The hunter Bluejay and the money-lending miser Scrooge have one point in common: their refusal to circulate wealth to the less fortunate. Even at Christmas, Scrooge cannot overcome his miserly nature and join in the celebratory spirit of the season. Scrooge's nephew comes to wish a merry Christmas to his uncle, only to be rebuffed as always by Scrooge's famous "Humbug." The nephew tries to move Scrooge, speaking of how Christmas is "a good time: a kind, forgiving, charitable, pleasant time: the only time I know of, in the long calendar of the year, when men and women seem by one consent to open their shut-up hearts freely, and to think of people below them as if they really were fellow-passengers to the grave, and not another race of creatures bound on other journeys."

This speech moves Scrooge's clerk, who suffers from the cold in the office and dreadfully low wages and the fact that Scrooge begrudges him the day off for the Christmas holiday. But it does not affect Scrooge at all. Instead, Scrooge berates his nephew for marrying for love, refuses the invitation to come to Christmas dinner, and shows his nephew the door.

Next Scrooge is visited by two businessmen, who have formed a committee to make "provision for the poor and destitute, who suffer greatly at the present time."

In words that will later haunt him, Scrooge demands, "Are there no prisons? . . . And the Union workhouses? . . . Are they still in operation?" So Scrooge expresses his belief that he has no obligation to the poor, who can either go to prison or the workhouse.

One of the gentlemen speaks of how, especially at Christmas, "Want is keenly felt, and Abundance rejoices," and asks Scrooge what he will contribute, but Scrooge replies, "Nothing!"

When told that many would rather die than go to prison or the workhouse, Scrooge answers, "If they would rather die, they had better do it, and decrease the surplus population." So, with this pitiless reference to Malthus's *Essay on the Principle of Population*, Scrooge shows the gentlemen out.

Unable to give to others or care for them, Scrooge is

also unable to give to himself. He makes his clerk freeze by a tiny fire, but he does not allow himself very much more. At home, in fact, he must sit close to the fire and brood over it before he can feel the least sense of warmth. He does not feast for his dinner, but eats in "a melancholy tavern." His lodgings are a gloomy suite of rooms. He saves money by using only a candle for light and makes money by renting the other rooms in the house as offices (so he is alone at night). The miserly face that he shows to the world is the face that he shows to himself. If he yearns for warmth, a loving family, a Christmas feast, a brightly lit home, he can have none of it. He can no more give to himself than he can give to the poor.

In fact, the miser Scrooge suffers a living death; he has died to the joys that make human life worthwhile. To be saved, he must connect again to the source of richness. For Scrooge, this possibility of salvation comes in the form of a ghost and three spirits.

Scrooge once had a partner named Jacob Marley, who died seven years earlier. Scrooge has never removed his partner's name from the office sign, which read Scrooge and Marley. When Marley died, Scrooge was his "sole residuary legatee, his sole friend and sole mourner," for Marley had been as much a miser and just as unpopular as Scrooge. Now, on Christmas Eve in the dark, cold, and cavernous house that Scrooge inherited from Marley, Scrooge is rudely interrupted by the appearance of the ghost of Marley. His partner looks as he did in life, except that his body is transparent, and clasped about his middle is a chain "of cash-boxes, keys, padlocks, ledgers, deeds, and heavy purses wrought in steel."

This ghost terrifies Scrooge and warns that if a "spirit goes not forth in life, it is condemned to do so after death . . . and witness what it cannot share, but might have shared on earth, and turned to happiness!" Marley's ghost then says that Scrooge's own chain equalled Marley's in length, and that was seven years ago.

Scrooge is terrified and implores the ghost for some comfort. " 'I have none to give,' the Ghost replied. 'It comes from other regions, Ebenezer Scrooge, and is conveyed by other ministers, to other kinds of men.' " The ghost regrets that, when alive, his "spirit never walked beyond our counting-house" and says that "no space of regret can make amends for one life's opportunity misused."

Scrooge's only hope of a better fate, the ghost tells him, will come from the haunting intervention of three spirits. So Scrooge must face these forces from other regions in order to deal with issues of wealth and its circulation.

The Ghost of Christmas Past

The first spirit, arriving at one o'clock in the darkness of night, is the Ghost of Christmas Past—more especially, the ghost of Scrooge's own past Christmases. The Ghost transports him to visions of the characters in the books that he joyously read as a boy. He sees himself as a youth when his beloved sister, Fan, comes to bring him home from exile at school to live again with his family. The ghost reminds him that Fan died, but had a child— Scrooge's nephew.

Next Scrooge sees himself as a young man working for Old Fezziwig, a jovial and benevolent man who hosts a joyous celebration of Christmas. The young Scrooge and another apprentice speak of how they admire Fezziwig, but the ghost points out how little this party cost. Scrooge, forgetting the miser he has become, retorts, "The happiness he gives, is quite as great as if it cost a fortune." In saying this, Scrooge suddenly wishes that he could speak to his own clerk, Bob Cratchit, who is raising a large and happy family on a meager wage.

Lastly the Ghost of Christmas Past takes Scrooge to see the scene at which he parted from Belle, the woman whom he might have married. "Another idol has displaced me," Belle says to the young Scrooge, ". . . a golden one. . . . I have seen your nobler aspirations fall off one by one, until the master-passion, Gain, engrosses you." Saying that the man he has become would not choose a dowerless girl, she releases him from his promise to marry her.

Scrooge begs the ghost to show him no more, but nonetheless he sees Belle and her husband with their children. It is the Christmas that Marley died, seven years earlier, and the husband says how he passed Scrooge's office and saw Scrooge "quite alone in the world . . ."

Scrooge cries out to be removed from these scenes and tries vainly to extinguish the ghost's haunting light. At last he falls into an exhausted sleep. While he sleeps, we begin to see Scrooge in a new light. His encounter with the Ghost of Christmas Past has revealed that Scrooge was not always a miser. Once he had been a lonely schoolboy who loved his sister and yearned to go home to his family; once he had admired the joyful vitality and benevolence of his employer; once he had loved and been loved. Whatever hardened and limited him had come gradually, and had appeared to be a reasonable effort to lift himself from poverty. Scrooge, by his pain in what he sees in his past, reveals that he possesses the potential to change. He is not beyond salvation, but he has lost his way. Will these haunting ghosts, conjured from the redemptive depths of his own imagination, succeed in returning him to the loving exchanges that give life value?

The Ghost of Christmas Present

Scrooge sleeps twenty-four hours and wakes just in time to meet the next spirit, the Ghost of Christmas Present. This ghost transforms Scrooge's room, filling it with the light of a roaring fire and decorating it with so many leaves of holly, mistletoe, and ivy that the room seems "a perfect grove." A throne is formed by an abundant mound of different foods fit for holiday feasting, and on this throne sits "a jolly Giant."

This giant is the ghost, a striking figure with none of the spectral qualities that we would ordinarily ascribe to ghosts. He is dressed in a green robe, his chest bare as if he disdains artifice or concealment. The torch that he holds aloft is shaped like "Plenty's horn." He is joyous and unconstrained, and a green wreath of myrtle sits atop his flowing curls of hair. Around his middle is an antique sheath for a sword, but the sheath is rusted and empty.

This remarkable ghost is clearly a vegetation or fertility god. With his green robe, the wreath in his hair, his cornucopic flame, and his spontaneous vitality, he might be a brother to Attis or Dionysus. So the miser Scrooge is confronted by an image of the renewing richness of nature, the feast which calls out to be shared with others. The ghost takes Scrooge across the city and the countryside and far out on the ocean. Everywhere Scrooge witnesses people joyous and celebratory in the spirit of the season. The ghost brings him to see his clerk, Bob Cratchit, celebrating a dinner of goose with his large family. Cratchit's tight finances and fears for his ill son, Tiny Tim, don't lessen the family's joy in this feast.

Scrooge feels concern for Tiny Tim and asks the ghost if the boy will live. Unless the future is altered, the ghost answers, Tiny Tim will die. When Scrooge begs the ghost to say that Tiny Tim will be spared, the ghost quotes Scrooge's own words back to him, "If he be like to die, he had better do it, and decrease the surplus population."

Scrooge is overcome with grief and a feeling of penitence to hear his own words. The ghost tells him not to use such words until "you have discovered What the surplus is, and Where it is."

The ghost brings Scrooge to the home of his nephew, Fred, who is celebrating with his wife and in-laws. Fred laughs as he recounts his meeting with Scrooge and says, ". . . his offenses carry their own punishment . . . His wealth is of no use to him. He doesn't do any good with it. He doesn't make himself comfortable with it. . . . Who suffers by his ill whims? Himself, always."

Fred's wife plays the harp and Scrooge softens to hear music that he loved as a boy. He wishes that he could have heard this music years earlier and "cultivated the kindnesses of life for his own happiness. . . ." He finds himself enjoying the blind-man's buff and other games the party-goers play. When the ghost wants to leave, Scrooge begs like a boy to be allowed to watch until the guests go home.

The ghost allows him one more game, then carries him again across the world. Everywhere the ghost brings the rich joy of the season, but the ghost grows visibly older and his hair becomes gray as midnight approaches. When Scrooge inquires about this, the ghost replies, "My life upon this globe is very brief. . . . It ends to-night."

Now Scrooge sees something beneath the ghost's robe and asks what it is. In reply, the ghost pulls open its robe to reveal two children—"wretched, abject, frightful, hideous, miserable" as well as "yellow, meagre, ragged, scowling, wolfish; but prostrate, too, in their humility."

Scrooge asks if these children are the ghost's, but the ghost replies, "They are Man's. . . . This boy is Ignorance. This girl is Want."

"Have they no refuge or resource?" cries Scrooge.

Again Scrooge's earlier words are used against him, as the ghost replies, "Are there no prisons? . . . Are there no workhouses?"

These are the ghost's last words, for midnight comes and the Ghost of Christmas Present is gone—only to be replaced by the third and last of the spirits, the Ghost of Christmas Yet to Come.

The Ghost of Christmas Yet to Come

This phantom is "shrouded in a deep black garment" which conceals everything except a single outstretched hand. Scrooge trembles before this "dusky shroud," but tells the silent phantom that "I know your purpose is to do me good. . . . Lead on, Spirit!"

In several scenes it becomes apparent to the reader, but not to Scrooge, that Scrooge has died before the next Christmas. First a group of businessmen speak of a wealthy man who has died, but whose funeral will be cheap because no one is likely to go to it. Then, in a part of the city reeking with crime, several people come to sell booty that they looted from the dead man. Next Scrooge is in a room where the corpse lies on a bed beneath a ragged sheet. The ghost motions for Scrooge to draw back the sheet, but he cannot.

Scrooge begs the phantom to show him anyone in the city "who feels emotion caused by this man's death."

Two scenes follow. In one, a young couple is thankful because the man's death will allow them time to find the money needed to repay a debt that they owed him. But even if they cannot gather that money, the husband believes that they "will not find so merciless a creditor in his successor."

The second scene brings Scrooge again to the home of his employee, Bob Cratchit. The little boy, Tiny Tim, has died and the family is in mourning.

Scrooge demands to know who the dead man had been. At last the ghost brings him to a graveyard where Scrooge sees a neglected grave. On the stone is Scrooge's own name.

Pleading with the ghost, Scrooge says that he will live an altered life and begs for assurance that the future he has seen can alter too. "I will honour Christmas in my heart, and try to keep it all the year," Scrooge promises, only to see the dread phantom dissolve and dwindle into a bedpost.

Joyous to be alive, Scrooge leaps from his bed and celebrates with splendid laughter. He flings open his windows and learns from a boy that it is Christmas Day, so the three spirits actually visited him during a single night. He has the boy take a plump turkey to the Cratchits, then dresses himself in his best clothes. Meeting one of the gentlemen who asked him for funds to help the poor, he promises a munificent amount. He goes to church, talks to beggars, and pats children on their heads. He finds "wonderful happiness" at his nephew's Christmas dinner. The next morning he gives Cratchit a raise and promises to help the clerk's family.

Tiny Tim lives and Scrooge, we are told, "became as good a friend, as good a master, and as good a man, as the good old city knew. . . ." and ". . . had no further inter-course with Spirits. . . ."

TO RECOGNIZE MONEY'S ILLUSORY ASPECTS

The spirits bring the possibility of profound change to Scrooge. He is placed in the age-old drama between the human and spirit worlds, a drama of sacrifice and ex-change. The renewing richness of nature is symbolized by the Ghost of Christmas Present. But as we well know, such a fertility god is caught up in endless cycles of life followed by death. The empty scabbard that the Ghost of Christmas Present wears about his waist suggests the bond between fertility and death. This bond quickens our awareness that there is only the present in which to live; only the present moment, only the present lifetime. For Scrooge, Death comes robed as the dark phantom whom Scrooge welcomes as a messenger of good will, the Ghost of Christmas Yet to Come.

In seeing this struggle of elemental forces, this struggle which he experiences in his own life, Scrooge realizes how money has become illusory for him. He has pursued money for its own sake but has forgotten the richness of which money is but a symbol. When he dies, money will be of no value at all; it will bring no mourners to his grave-side. On Christmas Day, a day of birth (for both the sun and the light of the Christ), Scrooge himself is born into a new life. His only alternative is death, whether the literal death shown by his name on a grave marker or the meta-phoric death of a man who cannot offer his own vitality to the world.

It is a paradox, of course, that Scrooge must die to his old self in order to avoid the death that he has been living and the grave that awaits him. Once he is able to free the money that he has accumulated, his energy flows into the world and connects him to other people. And once he can give to others, he is far more generous with himself.

Scrooge is brought by spiritual trials to a realization of his proper role in relation to the world and himself. However, each person must experience their own spiritual journey in relation to the handling of money or material possessions. Thoreau, for example, would argue that he wanted nothing of ownership, since property can easily own people by the cares and worries that it imposes. Scrooge couldn't share this attitude, because his early poverty had raised the value of wealth above everything else. In fact, many community leaders in the nineteenth century believed that poverty served as a school where people learned the reward of hard work. Even if this were true, Scrooge failed to learn how to use what he possessed, both for himself and for others.

Scrooge at least was quite open about being a miser. Other stories illustrate how sharing wealth, or even renouncing the acquisition of wealth, may conceal inner feelings that are quite the opposite of generosity and loving connection to community. A folktale from China illustrates how stinginess may disguise itself as generosity.

MONEY MAKES CARES

Titled "Money Makes Cares," the story tells of two neighbors, one rich and one poor. The rich man, Ch'en Po-shih,

spends all of his time busy with his money: making invest-
ments, giving loans, paying taxes. He hardly has time to
eat, because dealing with the money fills his days and
nights. His wife begs him not to slave himself to death, but
he knows of no way to lessen his tasks.

The poor neighbor, Li the Fourth, works as a laborer.
Despite being a hard worker, he earns very little and has
no savings. When he comes home in the evening he gives
his wages to his wife. Combined with what she earns, they
have barely enough to survive. Nonetheless, Li and his
wife are happy, and after dinner Li often plays the mandolin and sings.

The rich neighbor never hears this music and singing,
because he is buried in calculating rent and interest. However, his wife does hear, and the happy music makes her
sad. She says to her husband that their wealth gives them
no happiness, while their poor neighbors are joyous.

Ch'en says that Li is only happy because he is poor and,
according to a proverb, the poor have plenty of time. The
way to make him stop singing, according to Ch'en, is to
give Li some money. Ch'en's wife argues that having
money will only make Li and his wife happier, but Ch'en is
certain that he is right.

The next day Ch'en invites Li to visit. When Li arrives,
Ch'en says that as old neighbors they share a common
bond. Ch'en observes that Li will never earn very much
being a laborer and offers to give him five hundred pieces
of silver. He suggests that Li use it to start a good business, but in any event it will not have to be repaid.

Li thanks him and rushes home to tell his wife of their
newfound wealth. He stops his work as a laborer and
thinks only of how to profit the most from the money. Unable to find solutions that satisfy him, he becomes like his

rich neighbor. He arrives home late for dinner and loses his desire to play music or sing. Instead he spends his nights worrying about what to do with this wealth.

Ch'en and his wife are delighted that the music and singing have ceased. Unfortunately for them, the deity of luck takes pity on Li.

After two sleepless nights, Li can barely get out of bed. Suddenly the deity of luck appears and warns him of the cares that money makes. Remember this, the deity tells him, and free yourself from these cares.

Li feels his energy return. He hurries to his neighbor and returns all five hundred pieces of silver. Thanking Ch'en for his kindness, Li feels relieved of an immense burden and sleeps soundly at last. The next evening the sounds of Li's mandolin and songs can be heard once again in the home of his rich neighbor.

According to this folktale, Ch'en soon lost all his wealth and lived in poverty, but the music and song coming from Li's home only increased in richness.

HOW HOARDING STIFLES THE POWERS OF IMAGINATION AND HEALING

Stinginess disguised as generosity may escape the notice of our friends and neighbors. It does not, however, escape the notice of the spirits that govern abundance. Not only does the deity of luck tell Li not to obsess about money, but the deity also tumbles Ch'en from wealth to poverty— for surely Ch'en lost the luck that gave him wealth.

Ch'en is much like Scrooge at the beginning of *A Christmas Carol*. He is possessed by his wealth; he, and his wife, have lost the ordinary joys that life offers. He, like Scrooge and the ghost of Marley, is certainly wearing a chain "of cash-boxes, keys, padlocks, ledgers, deeds, and heavy purses wrought in steel."

Among the ordinary joys denied to Ch'en are the ability to take pleasure in the happiness of others and the ability to enjoy music and song, which might be read in a larger sense as enjoyment of the world of the arts and the realm of the imagination. Ch'en is so absorbed with money that he does not even hear the music, while his wife in hearing it only wants to silence the joy that it expresses.

Observing the outer behavior of Scrooge and Ch'en, it might appear that each man has undergone a similar change of heart. Scrooge becomes able to give to the poor and befriend his own family, while Ch'en does give to the poor and seems to befriend his neighbors. Obviously, however, Scrooge and Ch'en have not changed in a similar way at all, for their motives are utterly different.

Scrooge, as we said before, contemplates his life and realizes that he must change. Otherwise he faces certain death, for he is already not living. On the other hand, Ch'en gives the silver because he cannot tolerate the joy of others. His giving is exactly the opposite of what it appears to be. It comes not from love of life and others but from hatred. He cannot free his life energy, stored in the form of loans and land and money, and let it flow richly into the community.

Ch'en meets no messengers from the spirit world. Nothing happens within Ch'en to bring about a personal transformation, so he is condemned to a life of poverty. The actual poverty inflicted on Ch'en at the story's end is merely the outer equivalent of the poverty that exists within him.

Ch'en makes a sharp contrast with Li the Fourth, who has such a peculiar name. We naturally imagine him to be the fourth generation of Li, or perhaps the fourth child. In a larger sense, however, the number four connotes completion. This view comes from numerology, the symbolism of numbers. One is unity, two is duality, three is change (because three is formed of one plus two, which is the potential for change when unity meets duality), and four is completion (because four is formed of three plus one, which symbolizes change becoming unity).

Li the Fourth is complete in himself; he is complete in his love of his wife, his humble work, and his joy in music and song. Since Li comes into the story as a complete man, he does not need the change of life offered to him by the five hundred pieces of silver. So the deity of luck intervenes when Li has lost his direction and been swayed by the lures of the world. This deity returns Li to his own path, to the richness of a loving family and the joys of music and imagination.

Scrooge and Li are brought by their struggles over money to a greater sense of who they truly are; they learn the secrets of their innermost selves. They do not offer us rules by which to determine our own conduct. If they did, we might conclude from Scrooge's example that we ought to seek wealth and circulate it, and from Li's example that we ought to give up wealth altogether. What we learn from them is that our dealings with wealth can be part of the process by which we discover ourselves and contact our deeper natures.

To deny one's own nature is perhaps the greatest form of stinginess. This denies what is rich within us; it refuses the possibility of change and growth. If a man like Scrooge comes to recognize his capacity for love and sharing, then he will be all the richer for having discovered himself. If a man like Li discovers that wealth is destructive for him and gives it up, then he, too, is the richer for the self-knowledge that he has gained. The point is not to renounce wealth but to embrace the journey through which we learn what to value.

THE KING WHO RENOUNCED HIS WEALTH

A king once ruled a vast empire in India. Despite his wealth, King Shikhidhvaja yearns to live a deeply religious life and find the highest truths. He sees many saints and wise men and practices many spiritual disciplines. At last he becomes convinced that the only way he can find truth and the peace that surpasses understanding is through renunciation.

He gives careful consideration to what he should renounce and to the timing of his renunciation. He possesses vast wealth in the form of land and precious possessions, controls armies and large numbers of servants, and lives an opulent and luxurious life. More than this, he deeply loves his wife, Queen Chudala.

Finally he decides that he will renounce his throne. He tells his wife of the anguish that he feels in his soul and his yearning for peace. He implores her to take care of the kingdom so that he can seek contentment.

The queen, a very wise woman, feels that her husband will not find the peace that he seeks by this process of renunciation. However, knowing that reasoning will not change his mind, she takes charge of the kingdom and proves an excellent ruler.

The king goes to the high peaks of the Himalayas, the mountains symbolizing the spiritual heights that he seeks to reach. He builds himself a crude hut and wears clothes of bark, sleeps on a deer skin, and bathes in freezing water. No matter how much he prays, meditates, chants, and practices asceticism, he cannot find peace. In fact, the harder he disciplines himself to follow these spiritual devotions, the more anguish he feels.

Because the king truly believes that peace follows from renunciation, he reasons that his continued unhappiness comes from not having renounced enough. He decides that he will renounce even more in pursuit of his goal. From the rich diet that he had enjoyed as king, he now eats only roots and fruits. But he feels even this to be too much, so he begins to eat only fruits. First he eats fruit every other day, then every third day, and finally every fifth day.

Still he suffers agitation and feels ever more troubled by his life. To overcome this suffering, he thinks constantly about what else he can give up. His body begins to wither. When the queen comes to visit and sees him in such a condition, she feels great sorrow.

Fortunately for the king, his wife is not only a queen but also a goddess. Unwilling to allow her husband to continue on this path to destruction, she takes the shape of a great sage named Kumbha and comes to the hut where the king is living.

The king honors this wise man and, in response to Kumbha's questions, tells the entire story of how he has given up his kingdom and come to live at such high and barren altitudes.

After the sage hears the entire story, he simply says to the king, "Peace follows renunciation."

With that, Kumbha vanishes and leaves the king in perplexity. After all, the king has already renounced so much. Yet he renounces even more: his straw hut, his clothes of bark, the deer skin on which he slept, and his water pot. Now he truly has nothing, yet he feels more miserable than ever.

The queen, in the guise of Kumbha, reappears and asks the king if he has found peace and happiness.

When the king answers that he feels anguish and desperation, Kumbha says once again, "Peace follows renunciation. You have not renounced enough." Once again Kumbha vanishes.

The king, meditating on the words of Kumbha, decides that all he has left to renounce is his life. He gathers wood and builds a huge fire. If the flames consume his body, he believes that he will have peace at last. Three times he walks about the fire, saying a farewell to his body. He tells his body that he gave it marvelous pleasures, but he has nonetheless failed to find peace.

As he stands poised to leap into the flames, the sage Kumbha appears and restrains him from this madness. Now the sage speaks directly to the king, saying that once the king has given up his body, who will find peace and who will enjoy it? Kumbha says that a man is formed from the fluids of his mother and father, and these parents are formed from the foods that nourished them, and this food came from the earth. The body created of the earth cannot belong to the king, nor can the divine awareness which enters into the body belong to the king. So in throwing his body into the flames, he is renouncing a life and an awareness which have been given to him but are not his. What the king must renounce, the sage concludes, is the illusion of "mine."

The king realizes that he has erred. It may be right for someone else to find peace through renunciation, but it is not the correct path for him. He must renounce his illusion that he can find peace through renunciation. He can only find peace through following his own nature, which calls to him to live a spiritual life in the material world. For the king, it is miserly to refuse involvement with the world; it is a withholding of his energy from the mixed life in both the material and spiritual realms that is most properly his.

What Kumbha has done in saying "Peace follows renunciation" is to bring the king face-to-face with the realization that he has interpreted this statement as if it were a rule, rather than searching for his own unique path that will lead to his self-realization.

We might interject at this point that the queen, in taking the shape of Kumbha, is pushing her husband to the limits of what he himself set out to do. Her love does not express itself by an attempt to dissuade him and lessen his pain; rather she seeks to bring him to a greater understanding of his nature. She understands that if he does not reach a point where he sees that renunciation is the wrong path for him, he will never escape his self-inflicted suffering.

What do we think of a spouse who will push a loved one to the brink of destruction for the purpose of self-knowledge? Of course, the queen is a goddess who can do safely what mere mortals would not risk. Her stance is as uncompromising as that of the spirits who visit Scrooge and sway him from his miserly descent to death.

The determination of the queen/goddess to see her husband find the path which is correct for him reminds me of the experiences of a friend, a mother, whose only son suffered from drug addiction. Gradually, with great heartache, she had to wean him away from her. She had to demand that he leave her home. Despite her natural generosity and her love for him, she had to ignore his pleas for money and give him nothing. Sometimes he would knock on her door and beg her to let him in; other times he would call and plead for money to eat. In the beginning, she might lose her resolve and give him money, only to find that he spent it on drugs. At last she overcame her motherly instincts and refused him a place to stay and food and money. She gave him the names of people who could help him enter twelve-step and rehabilitative programs. Like the queen/goddess, she had to let him go to the greatest extremity of danger in the hope that he would see his own error and find the life within him waiting to be lived.

I mention this because stories of millers, tribal hunters, Victorian misers, a Chinese peasant, and a king and queen of ancient India may seem remote from the concerns of contemporary people. Do these tales offer a mirror for our time, for our own psyches? We need only look and see that human nature has not evolved at the same speed as technology. Our hopes and fears with respect to material well-being remain with us. These hopes and fears have shaped attitudes toward wealth and money that have lasted not merely centuries but millennia.

WHY OUR LIFE ENERGY SHOULD NOT BE BURIED

The discussion of human sacrifice in the last chapter may have seemed unusual in a book about money, but, of course, this book is titled *The Secret Life of Money*. Outside of our daily awareness, the Goddess Moneta works her miracles of fertility. Her name speaks of memory, but we have largely forgotten her. We have forgotten how once we had rituals to reveal and quiet our fears about nature's abundance. Because Moneta rules in an archetypal world to which we seldom have access today, we are like bystanders taking part in a great event of which we know almost nothing.

Our lack of self-knowledge may encourage us to project our fears about prosperity onto money. Without even thinking of the human sacrifices offered Moneta and her sister goddesses, our unworded fears about prosperity cause us to begin the sacrifice of our life energies. The miller buries the gold that symbolizes the treasure, the energy, of his life. Riches that we do not use are truly stolen from us; such riches are our life energies, which we offer thoughtlessly to false gods. Like Bluejay, we may burn the excess meat rather than share with our tribe. Or like Scrooge we may refuse to give even to ourselves—much less to others. To give falsely like Ch'en or run from our true path in life like King Shikhidhvaja are simply other forms of stinginess, other ways to sacrifice our energies.

The spirits and deities in these stories of wealth and money are aspects of Moneta and of ourselves. We possess the power to understand the cycles of death and new life that make us wish to be misers and hoard our life force. If we can keep enough of that precious force, perhaps we imagine that we need never fear homelessness, hunger, or death. Of course, we don't articulate such thoughts to ourselves; we don't have a conscious awareness of what makes us stingy or withholding of money and life energy. We don't see money in its symbolic role as the offspring of Moneta.

When the spirits help Scrooge or Li or King Shikhidh-vaja, what we see is the power we possess to heal ourselves. If we are fortunate enough to have this kind of spiritual intervention, or open enough to receive it when offered by a friend, mentor, or group such as Debtors Anonymous, then our lives may change as our understanding changes.

Even an addiction is, according to psychologist C. G. Jung, a form of spiritual craving. Jung expressed this viewpoint in his correspondence with Bill Wilson, the founder of Alcoholics Anonymous. This understanding aided the development of the twelve-step approach with its central tenet of trust in a higher power. Terrible as the suffering of the addict may be—risking life itself in the case of my friend's son and many others—this suffering can also be part of the experience that leads a person to give up drugs, alcohol, or other compulsive behaviors and begin the journey in quest of his or her true self.

The central illusion of the miser is that life energies are finite, that such energies can be controlled and conserved by refusing to give. We mentioned earlier that one of the roots of Moneta's name relates to measurement. Money is such a useful tool for measuring and comparing the values of unlike objects and services. However, money in its psychic role as a sacred substance derived from exchanges with the spirit world is not subject to the same laws of measurement as money in its worldly role as a helpful servant to the marketplace.

Charles Dickens portrayed the Spirit of Christmas Present as a green god holding aloft a torch in the shape of a horn of plenty. We cannot measure such a cornucopia. It is larger than the national debt, larger than the value of all the precious possessions humankind has created in that brief time since we stood erect and imagined ourselves as a mirror for the image of the divine. But what cannot be measured can, nonetheless, be circulated. Inevitably this circulation will include money and the wealth we use so much of our lifetimes to create and possess. If this circulation is to be wise, we must look more and more deeply at the richness with which Moneta blesses us.

CHAPTER FIVE

THE SOURCE OF RICHES

Gaining a New Understanding of Supply

IN LAST CHAPTER'S STORY of the miller who buries his gold, only to have it stolen, the neighbor suggests that the miller replace his lost gold with a stone. This ordinary stone certainly appears to be valueless, but often valueless things come to have value if seen in a new light. Part of this process may involve seeing ourselves in a new light and unearthing inner riches of which we were previously unaware.

If we approach the miller's story from another vantage point, we might ask what the neighbor means by telling the miller to plant a stone in the earth. How can this stone take the place of gold? This chapter will follow the symbol of money to the source of richness within ourselves, and we will see how that inner richness can be freed in ways that encourage its increase and benefit our loved ones and our communities.

THE BOY AND THE STONE
Symbolic Imagination

Famed psychologist C. G. Jung tells of a game that he played as a boy of eight or nine. In the family garden, the ground sloped and a large stone jutted out. As a boy, Jung felt this stone belonged to him. In his game he would think: "I am sitting on top of this stone and it is underneath." But the stone could also have an "I," so the stone could say, "I am lying here on this slope and he is sitting on top of me." Jung would then struggle with the question of whether he was sitting on the stone or whether he was the stone on which he was sitting. The question fascinated him, and the answer was ambiguous, a pleasing mystery that led the boy to sit for hours speculating on his stone.

The image of a stone is that of an eternal substance. The stone will last after the flesh has vanished, so the stone will long outlast the boy. If the boy, on the other hand, is the stone, some life of the boy will survive the frailty of his own flesh. In other words, as Jung later recognized, his meditations on the stone were meditations on his soul, a soul as yet unnamed by the boy but existing nonetheless and awaiting the journey of discovery that became the central drama of Jung's life.

Most of us experience trials of the soul as inner struggles. Often these struggles lead to a deeper understanding of ourselves and the life to which each of us is best suited. This process might be called the discovery of the soul or, for those who prefer a more neutral term, the discovery of the potentials which each of us possesses. But when that potential is buried, the miller, or anyone like him, experiences the painful loss of not being all that one might be.

THE MINER AND HIS GOLD
Literal Thought

An extraordinary trial in the 1960s placed the existence of the soul at the center of its drama and revealed the inner wonderings and doubts of a man named James Kidd. Born in 1879, he worked as a pumpman at an Arizona copper mine from 1920 to 1948 and vanished, and presumably died, in 1949. His job had been low-paying, and his lifestyle had always been sparse. He lived in a small, bare room with blankets nailed over the windows. He frequented a local restaurant where he always hunted for a discarded newspaper, ordered the least expensive items on the menu, and never left a tip. He would nurse a five-cent cigar so it lasted all day, and he kept a small box to hold chewing gum to be used again. He never married and, in fact, seldom if ever invited anyone to visit his lodgings. Yet Kidd had friends who spoke of his yearning for quick wealth and his speculations about the source of life, the nature of death, and the soul.

After James Kidd disappeared in 1949, there seemed to be no will and very little to his estate. But as the years passed, stocks and bank accounts kept turning up. For Kidd had been a prospector for gold and had also played the stock market. Whether he pulled nuggets from the earth or won profits from the stock market, he died with a net worth of almost $200,000, easily a wealthy man by the standards of his day. Then long after his death came the surprise—Kidd had left a will, a very unusual will.

The will stated that he had no heirs and ordered that all his assets be sold. After his funeral expenses had been paid and $100 given "to some preacher of the gospel to say fare well [*sic*] at my grave," he directed to "have this balance money to go in a research or some scientific proof of a soul of the human body which leaves at death I think in time their [*sic*] can be a Photography of soul leaving the human at death, James Kidd."

One hundred and thirty-four claimants fought over what should be done with this money. Scientific organizations, psychic research groups, and reputed heirs all came forward to stake a position. In an initial ruling, the court determined that the will had created a charitable trust. However, the difficult issue remained of which claimant could best carry out the scientific proof required by the will. Extensive testimony about death and the soul led the court to award the estate to the Barrow Neurological Institute of Phoenix to help finance its research on the nervous system and the relationship between the brain and the mind.

What is striking about James Kidd, of course, is that he never spent his money on what would have given him pleasure during his lifetime. He never, for example, donated to an organization that might be doing the type of research that he wanted. He seemed content to hoard his money and speculate about whether the soul might exist. In his will, the one certain way he had to determine actions beyond his death, he, in essence, seeks to exchange his money for the proof that eluded him.

If we contrast James Kidd to C. G. Jung, we might see one man as a prospector and the other as an alchemist. James Kidd sought gold buried underground, but he seemed to have no idea of how to use this literal search or his growing net worth to deepen his sense of his own inner richness, and thereby prove, at least to his own satisfaction, the existence of his soul. Instead of beginning a journey into himself, he surrendered the responsibility for his search to outer authorities—to the courts of Arizona, and to the beneficiary they would choose to receive the money.

On the other hand, Jung created a philosopher's stone from that stone in his parents' garden. The medieval alchemists searched for such a philosopher's stone, a process by which base matter might be transformed to gold and, even more importantly, a way in which matter might be infused with spirit. Jung's dialogue with the stone began a lifelong exchange between the Carl Jung whose persona faced the outer world and the stone/Jung which represented the inner richness of the Self. Jung used the word "individuation" for this process of discovering the riches of the Self and integrating these riches into the ego.

MONEY IS THE SYMBOL, NOT THE SOURCE

The relationship between money, which is outer richness, and soul, which is inner richness, can easily confuse us. When we imagine, like the miller, that gold is all-important, we lose connection to our inner riches. The Bible frequently delves into this paradox which has always been so much a part of all of our lives.

As Jesus Christ starts for Jerusalem he is approached by a wealthy man who asks, "What must I do to inherit eternal life?" Jesus tells him to observe the Commandments, but the man says he has observed them from his youth. Then Jesus says, "Sell what you have and give to the poor, and you will have treasure in heaven; and come, follow me." But the man has great wealth and departs in sorrow. Of all those whom Jesus specifically invited to follow him, only this wealthy man refused.

Jesus then observes that "It is easier for a camel to go through the eye of a needle than for a rich man to enter the kingdom of God." So the largest beast in Judea can more easily pass through the smallest opening than a rich man discover the wealth of his inner life. Why should this be so?

The problem is easy to state but not so easy to understand or resolve in our daily lives. Because money has its origins in exchanges with the divine, it lends itself to the belief that it is the source of well-being and abundance. In this way, money appears to be the divine source. Thinking this way makes us worship money rather than the richness within ourselves.

Jesus frequently uses an increase in money to symbolize an increase in divine spirit. The parable of the pounds speaks of a master who must travel to a far country to receive kingly power. He leaves one pound each with ten servants. On his return, he praises the servants who have increased his money. The servant who increased the money tenfold is given ten cities to rule and the servant who increased the money fivefold is given five cities to rule. However, the servant who feared his severe master and merely has the one pound to return is castigated. The master asks, "Why then did you not put my money into the bank, and at my coming I should have collected it with interest?" The servant's one pound is given to the servant with ten pounds. When the people complain, the master says, "I tell you, that to every one who has will more be given; but for him who has not, even what he has will be taken away." The message is that those who possess inner wealth and work to increase it will receive more; those who lack awareness of inner wealth and refuse to work for its increase will lose what they have.

So money presents a paradox. On one hand, the very nature of money lends itself to use as a symbol for spirit. On the other hand, money is merely a symbol and cannot truly be a substitute for inner resources. Despite the many stories in which the increase of money symbolizes the increase of inner riches, Jesus declares, "No servant can serve two masters; for either he will hate the one and love the other, or he will be devoted to the one and despise the other. You cannot serve God and mammon."

The danger facing those with wealth is that they may worship it as a false god. This worship of money places the divine realm outside of the seeker, who loses the ability to search for and develop inner resources. Money, gold, and property will always be external to us and subject to the vagaries of good and bad fortune. In another parable, Jesus tells of a man whose situation appears to be somewhat like that of the miller: "The kingdom of heaven is like treasure hidden in a field, which a man found and covered up; then in his joy he goes and sells all that he has and buys that field."

Why is this man's fate different from the miller's? Quite simply, the treasure that he has discovered is his own spiritual life. The miller sold all of his worldly goods to hoard them in the form of gold. The man who sells all to buy the hidden treasure is transforming worldly wealth into spiritual wealth. He has begun the lifelong task of solving the riddle of his relationship to the stone, to what is eternal within him.

Jesus did not condemn the wealthy for their wealth but rather for their worship of that wealth. For example, in Jericho he stays with a man named Zacchaeus, a chief tax

collector who has made himself rich by collecting reve-
nues for the hated Roman rulers. People criticize Jesus for
being the guest of a sinner, but Zacchaeus promises to
give half his goods to the poor and restore fourfold to anyone he has defrauded. Jesus responds, "Today salvation
has come to this house . . ."

However, Zacchaeus is an exception among the
wealthy, because so many of the wealthy fall victim to the
illusion that money is godlike and worthy of worship. But
how can this illusion, of money and property as the source
of richness, be penetrated?

Jesus offers us the insight necessary to see the true
source of what supplies us:

> Therefore I tell you, do not be anxious about your life,
> what you shall eat or what you shall drink, nor about your
> body, what you shall put on. . . . But seek first his kingdom
> and his righteousness, and all these things shall be yours
> as well.

This is an insight into human nature that transcends a
particular religion or moment in time. Jesus also says,
"The kingdom of God is within you." If we trust that we
have within us the capacity to live a spiritual life, that we
possess an inner stone which Jung called the Self, then in
the natural process of living that inner life we will also
take care of our outer needs. The inner search is not a
denial of our outer needs, but rather in part a way of learning the right attitude and actions with which to deal with
the outer world—including money and ownership.

No perfect model is offered here. We cannot find rules
that will absolve us of the effort to undertake our own
inner quest. On the one hand, Jesus tells of a man who

stores enough food and drink to last for years and intends to take it easy. But God calls the man a fool because his very life is to be taken from him that night. This Parable of the Rich Fool concludes "So is he who lays up treasure for himself, and is not rich toward God." On the other hand, Zacchaeus retains half of his ill-gotten fortune and Jesus declares that salvation has entered his house. Whether outer riches should be kept or given, and to what degree, will vary from person to person. What does not vary is the need to embark on the journey of self-discovery.

THE STAR TALERS

A German folk tale tells of a little girl who has lost her parents and become homeless. She is so poor that she has only the clothes that she wears and a piece of bread given to her by a kind person. This is the condition that we all fear: to be without family, homeless, and, ultimately, without even clothes or food. When we have little or fear that we are facing financial catastrophe, how can we trust in our inner richness to supply us? How can we stop hoping to get money, with all the terrible anxieties which that hope brings, and focus on Jesus' insight that if we seek riches within then "all these [material] things shall be yours as well"?

The little girl in the story "put her trust in God" and went into the fields. There a poor hungry man approaches her and pleads for something to eat. She gives him the entire piece of bread. Next come three children, each cold and each asking for a different garment: a bonnet, a bodice, and a blouse. The girl gives to each. Night comes and she enters a forest where yet another child asks for a shift. If the girl gives away the shift, she will be naked, but she thinks that the night is so dark that no one will see her if she gives away her shift. As soon as she gives this last garment and stands naked in the forest, the stars start falling from the night sky. Each star is a taler (taler being the monetary unit from which the word dollar eventually derived). The girl finds herself dressed in a beautiful new shift of the finest linen. Gathering the talers in her new shift, she has riches for the rest of her life.

This may seem a simple tale; indeed, it's been criticized by feminists as perpetuating the idea that women should indiscriminately place their property and energies in service to others. That criticism reflects the difficulty that all of us have today in believing this story. Who wants to accept the motto on our coins—"In God We Trust"—as a step to giving away our money or property to those in need?

Yet the story has its own force; it tells us that the person who gives will, miraculously, receive. They will be beautifully clothed; they will have riches for life. For them, the stars of heaven will tumble to earth and become—of all things!—money. If this is true, counterfeiters would be well advised to try giving rather than printing, since no one is imprisoned for the possession of dollars that fall from the heavens.

The skeptic in us has to wonder whether wealth in spirit doesn't also imply poverty in the outer world. We know that a child can give away all she has to eat and wear, but when was the last time we saw stars fall to earth as dollars? What law of supply could cause this to happen?

THE CONCEPT OF SUPPLY

Let us visualize again the Ghost of Christmas Present in *A Christmas Carol* by Charles Dickens. This fertility god with his wreath on his head, green robe, and torch shaped like a horn of plenty is an image of the richness that we all carry within ourselves. The Ghost of Christmas Present is part of the inner life, the inner richness, of Scrooge. If one is aware of such a fertile and infinite life within, there is no need to fear whether clothes or food or money will be supplied without. The energy of this ghost will see that we are supplied with what we need. That is, we will inevitably take care of our material needs if we remain aware of the richness that lives within us. That richness is the source of our supply, not money, houses, clothing, and all the other manifestations of our energies working in the world.

In *The Infinite Way* by Joel Goldsmith, this concept of supply is expressed as follows: "Money is not supply, but is the result or effect of supply. There is no such thing as a supply of money, clothes, homes, automobiles, or food. All these constitute the effect of supply, and if this infinite supply were not present within you, there never would be 'the added things' in your experience."

This concept of supply is difficult to understand in an age so devoted to mass production, mass consumption, the advertising which seeks to link consumption and production, and laws of supply and demand seen in the marketplace. In contrast to all this, Goldsmith views the law of supply as our own consciousness, which he describes as "spiritual, infinite, and ever-present." If we are aware of this inner richness, this inner source which is continuously fruitful, we can come to accept money as "the natural and inevitable result of the law active within."

If this infinite supply is indeed within us, we find ourselves in an unfamiliar territory. We are used to dealing with limitation; we are comfortable with the familiarity of limitation. We have only so much money; we have only so much food, so much clothing, so much space in which to live. If we find a source of infinite richness within, however, we are no longer dealing with limitation. Suddenly the very nature of wealth changes.

The wealth of the outer world is increased by receiving: by wages, by profits, by income, by possession. The wealth of the inner world begins by being boundless. It cannot be increased by receiving. To enjoy the wealth that is inner richness, we must seek a way to circulate what we have. Goldsmith states this very well in *The Art of Spiritual Healing*. He says: "In spiritual truth, supply is not income; it is outgo. . . . There is no supply outside of your being. If you want to enjoy the abundance of supply, you must open a way for that supply to escape."

In cultivating an attitude of giving, whether what is given is small or great, we learn how giving increases our awareness of our own richness. Goldsmith suggests that giving may begin with giving up certain feelings that limit us—"the giving up of resentment, jealousy, and hate; the giving up of the desire to get recognition, reward, remuneration, gratitude, and co-operation." All of these feelings turn us toward the outer world. We wonder: Will we be as well off as others? Will others approve of what we do? So such feelings turn us away from the invisible inner richness that we seek to bring to our awareness.

While Goldsmith does not suggest that money be given away carelessly or without the use of common sense, he does stress the importance of making money circulate for "some impersonal purpose, not to family, not for one's own benefit, but to something completely impersonal." In

giving, we may feel gratitude for what we have already received, but to hope or expect either material or spiritual
rewards will diminish the realization of our inner richness. Of course, we might speak of giving love, understanding, support, shelter, or food as well as speak of
giving money. Giving money does not replace the flow of
other kinds of giving, but it may teach us about the nature
of giving itself. Also, money has the unique power to represent everything that is marketable, whether goods or
services, and so can purchase what is necessary to meet
innumerable needs.

Charitable giving springs from human compassion, the
natural concern that we feel in response to the suffering
of others. The Jewish religion views the giving of charity
as one of the finest expressions of piety. *Tzedakah*, the
Hebrew word for charity, suggests not merely giving but
also just and righteous giving. Two stories from Jewish
tradition illustrate how giving can be either heartfelt or
heartless.

ONLY THE DEAD ARE WITHOUT HOPE

In an ancient Jewish tale, "Only the Dead Are Without
Hope," a wealthy man fears that his riches will be of no
value to him when he dies. Taking the advice of friends, he
decides to make charitable gifts so that his kindness will
protect him in evil times. However, he imposes a limit on
his willingness to give. He will only give to someone who
has abandoned all hope in life.

One day he sees a man in rags sitting on a heap of trash.
Convinced that this man has abandoned all hope, the rich

man gives him one hundred pieces of gold. Amazed to receive this unasked-for and immense sum, the poor man inquires why he has been chosen from all the poor in the city to receive this benevolence.

The wealthy man tells how he swore that he would only give to one who had abandoned all hope in life. At this, the poor man flings the hundred pieces of gold back at him. Saying that he has faith in God's mercy, he berates the rich man for not seeing that God can as easily make him rich as poor.

Shocked, the wealthy man complains that this poor man feels no gratitude for the gift and is, in fact, abusive.

The poor man replies that the gift was the opposite of kindness. Only the dead have no hope in life, so the gift was like death.

Of course, the wealthy man entertained the notion of charity only from fear, not generosity. His fear caused him to impose a limit on his giving. He set himself in judgment over others, while at the same time failing to see that he himself was the one who had abandoned hope in life. He had misplaced the hope that flows from the richness of the inner life and trusted in his wealth instead.

THE FATHER OF THE POOR

An episode in the story titled "The Father of the Poor" offers a sharp contrast to the attitude of the wealthy man. "The Father of the Poor" is about Reb Nachum Grodner (1811–1879) whose tireless work to help the needy gave him a legendary status among the poor Jewish people who lived in the ghettos in Lithuania. Because of his popularity, the people called him by the more familiar and endearing Reb Nochemke.

Himself poor, Reb Nochemke would go to great lengths not to embarrass those needy people whom he helped. Once he was asked to be a godfather at the celebration of a circumcision, but he knew the father of the child had no money to pay for such a celebration.

Reb Nochemke asks the father if he is planning to go to another city called Kovno. The father is surprised and says he has no such plans. Reb Nochemke then says that he needs to have twenty-five rubles delivered to someone in Kovno and wants the father to deliver this money whenever the father should happen to go there. The father protests that he has no idea when he will go, but Reb Nochemke says there is no hurry. In fact, Reb Nochemke says that if the man should have use for twenty-five rubles before he goes, he may use the money and replace it later.

Of course the father spends the twenty-five rubles on the circumcision celebration. When he asks Reb Nochemke for the name and address of the person in Kovno, Reb Nochemke first says that he will have to find them at home and, after some time passes, says that he must have mislaid them. One day the father, never suspecting that he has been the beneficiary of charity, repays the twenty-five rubles to Rem Nochemke.

THE GOLDEN LADDER OF CHARITY

To be righteous and just in the giving of charity has been of concern since antiquity. In the eleventh century, Maimonides, the Jewish theologian, formulated many existing ideas about charity into the Golden Ladder of Charity. This Ladder has eight steps, each one higher than the last.

The first step on the ladder is the lowest form of charity. Here one gives, but with reluctance or regret. On the second step one gives happily but without regard for the degree of need of the person receiving the charity. Moving up to the third step, the giving is joyous and takes account of the degree of need, but the giver waits to be asked before giving. On the fourth step, the giver gives without being asked but puts the gift into the hands of the recipient. This causes the needy person to suffer with feelings of shame.

The fifth step conceals the identity of the recipient from the one who gives. Now the needy person does not have to feel shame for having been seen as needy by the one who gave. On the other hand, the sixth step conceals the identity of the giver from the one who receives. For example, the giver might anonymously leave a gift at the home of the recipient. On the seventh step of the ladder, the virtues of the prior two steps are combined so that neither giver nor receiver knows the identity of the other. In its time, the Temple in Jerusalem contained a room called the Chamber of Silence or Inostentation. Here those who desired to give could anonymously leave their gifts to be taken with equal anonymity by those in need.

The eighth and highest step is to prevent poverty and thus avoid the need for charity. This might be done by teaching a trade to someone, starting a person in business, or making a gift or a loan if that will enable the person to earn his or her own livelihood. By allowing the person to cultivate his or her own talents and provide for his or her own wants, the giver avoids the risk that the recipient will feel dependent, powerless, or shamed.

The Golden Ladder of Charity recognizes the importance of giving with the right attitude. Keeping this in mind, we can see why the wealthy man in "Only the Dead Are Without Hope" failed in his giving. Not only did he give from joyless self-interest in the hope that his own future would be without hardship but the very basis of his giving was his false belief in the poor man's hopelessness. In contrast, Reb Nochemke so artfully gave his charity that, in fact, it soon proved not to be charity at all.

HOW PURE GIFTS CONNECT THE MATERIAL AND SPIRITUAL WORLDS

Charity moves a gift from the material world, where individual ownership is the rule, to the spiritual world where the love feast offers each person a share of nature's bounty. In this, charity is like the fertility rituals which transform what is sacrificed by circulating it back to the spiritual realm. This circulation brings renewal. Jesus Christ, at the Last Supper, used this principle of circulation when he moved bread and wine across the boundary that divides the material and spiritual worlds. So he said of the bread, "Take, eat; this is my body." And of the wine that it "is my blood of the covenant, which is poured out for many for the forgiveness of sins." In asking the apostles to share bread and wine in this way, Jesus offered them a ritual by which the food of this world might give spiritual nourishment.

The issue is much the same with money. What are the ways in which money can be transformed like the bread and wine which, in the ceremonies of the Roman Catholic and Episcopal churches among others, are believed to become the body and blood of Jesus? What are methods by which money can be taken from our modern market economies and circulated across the boundary dividing the material and the spiritual? How can money be made to serve the increase of inner resources and inner riches?

One fascinating, contemporary phenomenon is the expert use of radio and television by preachers who promise salvation and plead for the contribution of dollars. A constant refrain from these media evangelists is that nothing heals the body and soul like giving, and they are not bashful about naming the organizations and addresses to which this money should be sent. While some of these ministers may be sincere, others are now convicted felons serving long sentences for fraud, conversion of money to personal use, and evasion of income taxes. Will a gift to such a minister, or his church or foundation, aid us in freeing our inner richness to flow into the world?

We observed earlier that the development of money and market economies may well have been aided by the needs of religious pilgrims. Far from home, these pilgrims needed to pay not only for their food and shelter but also for appropriate sacrifices and contributions in the course of the ceremonies. Today religious people the world over continue to journey to sacred sites in cities such as Jerusalem, Mecca, and Benares. To focus on the example of Benares, each year hundreds of thousands of Hindu pilgrims travel to this city on the banks of the Ganges. The pilgrims come for many reasons—to perform rites for the dead, gain a boon, expiate a sin, or simply for the merit of the pilgrimage.

Part of the pilgrimage involves the giving of *dana* or pure gifts to the priests, who help to perform the various ceremonies. Dana is made voluntarily and without any expectation of reciprocation or of material or spiritual reward. The ideal recipient of dana is a Brahman priest; many rituals are considered valueless unless dana is given to such a priest. The dana itself is not payment to the priest, but a gift in addition to the payment (which is called *daksina*).

This seems straightforward, except that the receipt of dana creates moral peril for the priest. The pure gift carries with it the sins of the donor. Whether the gift is money, which is preferred by the priests, or goods, the priest accepting the gift also accepts the sins of the giver. These sin-carrying gifts can only be cleansed if the priest rigorously performs certain rituals and gives away more than the value of the dana to others.

Since, generally speaking, the priests need to use what they receive in order to live and may very well neither know the complex cleansing rituals nor have the time to perform them, the receipt of dana condemns the priest-recipient to an unending accumulation of sin. We are told that these indigestible sins cause the priest to die an early and horrible death. In fact, the priest's body will not burn easily on the funeral pyre because it is so laden with sin.

Nor is the giver free from moral danger. The giver must find a priest whose character is perfected. This is because the giver is responsible for what the priest will do with the money. So if the priest is greedy and uses the gift instead of purifying it and giving it away, the giver will suffer and sink into hell with the priest.

The ideal of dana would place money in circulation at a high velocity. It would go from giver to priest and, no sooner had the priest performed the cleaning rituals, it would be increased and travel as gifts to others. The amount of money circulating in this spiritual realm would be constantly increasing; certainly it would never be hoarded or become venture capital used for profit. Since this ideal is seldom attained, the money used for dana is viewed as barren. If hoarded, it will be devoured by ants. If used for a business, the business will fail.

There are a number of gifts which are not dana, and therefore do not carry its moral peril. A gift in which reciprocation is expected, such as a gift to a friend, is not dana. Nor is a gift to a beggar (or an ascetic) or for the upkeep of a monastery considered to be dana, even though no reciprocation will take place.

If we think about dana, we see that it grows from a worthwhile insight. What value is giving to the poor if the ways in which we have obtained money to give—or more generally, the ways in which we live our lives—are reprehensible? If we are not trying to give away our sins, then perhaps we can make the "impersonal" and pure gift that dana must be. But if we make our gift to a religious organization or person that misuses it, we have not truly fulfilled the purpose of charitable giving. So the concept of dana suggests a higher level of responsibility that can inform the process of giving.

THE BEGHARDS

Our word "beggar" comes from the Beghards of Flanders, a brotherhood founded in the thirteenth century whose friars lived by begging. The best known of the medieval mendicant orders were the Franciscans, Dominicans, Carmelites, and Augustinians, but the roots of mendicancy (which comes from the Latin verb *mendicare*, "to beg") reach far into antiquity. Early in the Vedic period (which began around 1500 B.C. in India), Brahman priests followed strict rules in their solicitation of alms. The ancient Greeks and the Romans also had priests who solicited alms. While the practice of begging for alms faded away in the Western world with the end of the Middle Ages, in some parts of the world it continues to the present day. Among the Hindus, for example, renunciants are without a home or property, wander constantly (except for the four months of the rainy season), are celibate, and beg for their food and other necessities of life. The best home for such a renunciant is at the base of a tree.

What is the benefit to the mendicant who relies on the giving of others? In essence, this person is revealing faith that there will be divine supply and is literally following the words of Jesus: "But seek first his kingdom and his righteousness, and all these things shall be yours as well." What is the benefit to the society of which the mendicant is a part? The mendicant offers the opportunity for others to give, thus letting them free their inner richness. In this way, the pious life and the very survival of the mendicant are a reflection of the society's well-being.

The role of the mendicant did not survive the Reformation, which scrutinized both the concept of banking merit (which had been acquired by giving alms in the hope of future spiritual rewards) and the moral character of the recipient of the alms. So men like Benjamin Franklin, Andrew Carnegie, and John D. Rockefeller preferred to use their wealth and energy to create institutions, such as foundations, universities, hospitals, and libraries, that would better the lives of all men and women. Today our urbanized, post-industrial society has little place for people who would be poor by choice; so many are poor simply by the operation of the marketplace.

However, the mendicants who offered themselves as vessels to receive alms and the great industrialists who gave their wealth to develop institutions that would better the human condition both participated in the wise circulation of money. Both subscribed to the principle that the circulation of wealth increases the well-being of all. Both saw a way in which money could be taken from the marketplace and moved to a spiritual realm, where its circulation would serve purposes consistent with its sacred origins.

THE MARKER

Money is a marker in the experience of giving. Where we make our money flow—whether to those in need or to endow charitable, religious, and educational organizations—we realize that our love, understanding, compassion, and selfless volunteer work can flow as well. These sacrifices move us away from the worship of money (which is only a tool) and reveal to us the reality of human interdependence and inner richness.

At the source of our inner wealth, we are rich in so many ways. Giving money to help people and better society are ways to cross the boundary and find the treasure buried in the field. Giving of our feelings and time is another way. But there are even more inward routes to this richness: prayer, meditation, the joy of artistic creation, and the exploration of the imagination.

One important gift is the one we give to those aspects of ourselves which are poor. Just as Jung learned from the stone of his own eternal nature, so we can seek to heal ourselves by what we learn from the experience of our own inner richness. Scrooge possessed the vitality and fecundity of the Spirit of Christmas Present. When he crossed the boundary into the world of his own spirit, he found and brought back the cornucopic riches of the Self that could heal him. This crossing of boundaries is of value to us all. Even in the richest society in the world, many of us experience poverty within: The feeling that we are not worthy, that we are not loved or capable of loving, that we are not all that we might be, that we are not whole.

Both this chapter and the last chapter began with the story of the miller who sold all he owned to buy gold. Being a miser, he then buried this precious substance and refused to circulate it in the world. Since he could not move his energy into the world, he could not receive back the replenishment that we find in exchanges with others (whether of money, food, or emotions). He had buried his soul and lost the potential to grow inwardly.

In the realm of the soul, there is no resting place. If we do not grow—growth being the realization of our natural richness, the coming to know and the acceptance of what we most truly and deeply are—then we lose our precious treasure. One night, or night after night, a thief comes and steals what might have been ours. But if we are fortunate enough to take the advice of a wise neighbor, we may bury a stone in the empty hole that the thief has pillaged. One day, we may hear the stone speak a few words and, if we dare to respond, who knows what riches may be unearthed.

CHAPTER SIX

INHERITANCE

The Actual and Symbolic Wealth of Our Parents

ONCE UPON A TIME a man worked very hard for twenty years to build a business. Although his hard work took him from poverty to wealth, he finds that his twenty-year-old son will not work. When the father speaks of the pleasure of working hard and succeeding, the son replies that he will never choose a career because his father provides everything for him. Since the father loves his son and wants him to know the joy of work and success, the father sells everything that he owns and gives all his money to charities and to poor people. Then he tells his wife and his son that he has lost everything in bad business deals and the family is poor.

Yet the father is disappointed in his hope that his son will now work. Instead, the son solves the problem of poverty by planning to marry a wealthy girlfriend, who gives him $200,000 as an engagement gift. After throwing his son out of the house, the father discovers that he no longer has the drive which earned him his first fortune. Guilt-stricken to have deprived his wife and son of the comforts of his wealth, he decides to take his life by leaping from a bridge.

These episodes, part of an amusing film titled *For Richer, For Poorer*, are told in flashbacks. The film starts with the formerly wealthy man trying to leap from the bridge. A woman, a homeless beggar, approaches him and asks for his cash and his watch, saying that he won't need them anymore. Even at the moment of death, this man cannot escape dealing with what little remains of his property. When he realizes that he can't jump, he and the beggar befriend each other and he tells her his story.

The family dynamics of *For Richer, For Poorer* suggest certain truths about the inheritance of money. The generation which earns the money has the gratification of being very productive and successful. The next generation inherits the money, but often lacks ambition. It is difficult to find a reason to strive in the world. The wealth will take care of material needs, and the achievements of the parent can seldom be matched. William K. Vanderbilt, a descendent of Cornelius Vanderbilt who amassed an enormous fortune in the nineteenth century, observed that "inherited wealth is a big handicap to happiness. It is as certain death to ambition as cocaine is to morality." The challenge to the heir, if he or she wishes to overcome these obstacles, is to transform the relationship to money and to the parent who earned it.

A LARGER VIEW OF INHERITANCE

Throughout this chapter we will view inheritance in a larger sense as what is received from parents or family, whether in life or at death, and whether in the form of money, emotional patterns, moral values, or education that one generation can transmit to the next. For the heirs may inherit issues that the parent was unable to face or resolve. And even small amounts of money and property can carry the weight of emotions. The love that the child sought in life from the parent may be sought in a parent's will at death. The will is the final statement of the parent, the final division, often among siblings, of what the parent can offer the children.

The power to earn money is certainly not the power to control its effect on people. In the film, the father's desire that his son follow in his footsteps ignores the family relationship to money. The father valued the fact that everyone depended on his earning power. No wonder his son and wife show no interest in earning money. The son and wife enjoy the leisure that the father has never cherished. In a sense, the father is one-sided; he is all productivity, he shows no capacity for the pleasures of idleness. The son and wife must be idle for him; they live an aspect of the father's life that he has been unable to live for himself.

Perhaps the father's yearning for the son to be ambitious is not really about the son at all. Perhaps it is about a growing desire in the father to be indolent, to take time off, to discover another way in which he can live his life. One of the ways in which the father oversees his employees is by appearing in disguises that allow him to test their efficiency without their knowledge. These elaborate disguises suggest fantasies of other, as yet unrealized, possibilities in his life.

We might imagine that the beggar on the bridge approaches the father like a reflection of himself. The image of the beggar suggests that an aspect of the father is poverty-stricken. His pleasure in money comes only from earning it, but he recognizes that even that joy has faded for him. He needs to move into the world of the beggar, where money and work are the exceptions. In the film he does exactly that; he vanishes for two years and wanders across the country. During this odyssey he takes whatever work he can find and spends a lot of time not working at all. He sends small amounts of money to his wife but writes no letters to go with the money. The value of the money is no longer its purchasing power but its power to communicate.

When he returns home, he finds that both his wife and his son are working. His wife finds joy in no longer being dependent on a father or husband for support. His son lives on a divorce settlement of $5 million, but the son has realized that work is a form of community. Lacking his father's talents, the son works as a waiter for idealistic reasons. At last the father accepts that he need not be the only one who works; he can relax and discover the part of himself that is a beggar, a part that fails the measure of ambition but offers inner rewards that are not easily measured. Only by discovering this new aspect of himself can he accept that his wife and son have developed their own potentials in relation to work.

This gentle comedy is insightful about the universal issues presented by wealth. Symbolically, the wealthy man died on that bridge. He did not leap, but he began a process of change so radical that he became a new man. In a similar way, his son and his wife also found new lives. They have become neophytes, people who have discovered a new fate.

THE DEATH POWER OF MONEY

What may be unusual in *For Richer, For Poorer* is that the family has some resolution about issues of wealth, roles, and feelings while everyone is alive. So often money, whether in large or small amounts, is only transferred at death or as a part of an estate plan that constantly focuses on the approach of death. Both of the words "will" and "testament," which are instruments by which the person who dies instructs the living as to what should be done with property, are rooted in sexuality. In its origins, the word "will" suggests giving physical pleasure or being voluptuous, while "testament" shares the generative power of the testes, the testicles.

In this we see again the perplexing connection between sexuality, or the power to be fertile and productive, and death. This is much the same connection that we explored in the fertility rituals with their endless cycles of death inseminating life. So Hades, the Greek god of the underworld and the dead, is also the god of wealth. Wearing a helmet that makes him invisible, he rules Hades, as the underworld is called, without pity as he decrees death for all who live. Yet his epithets include "the wealthy one" and "the wealth giver." Why should money, in its role as wealth, be a substance of the underworld? And what does this mean?

A person who dies cannot transfer fertility by way of money. So we do not receive fertility by a will, only property. Looked at in this way, property is the residue of fertility. The property or the money is not the source of supply. Imagining that the inherited wealth is fertility, instead of seeking one's own inner richness, will lead to passivity and infertility. The will of the dead parent may overwhelm the life force of the child. How often does someone of nineteen or twenty have sufficient ambition to overcome the fact that a parent has provided enough money to last a lifetime? Such families must teach ambition unrelated to money, such as ambition to serve others, if the death power of the money is to be escaped.

To comprehend the death power of money, and how to transform this power, it may help us to travel to the underworld ruled by Hades. To understand what we inherit, and to learn who we are and how we differ from our parents, we sometimes have to descend into the underworld. If we can succeed in this journey, we return to our daily lives far wiser for our courage.

The god called Hades by the Greeks was called Pluto by the Romans. In our solar system, Pluto is the planet farthest from the sun and most recently discovered (in 1930). Smaller than Mercury and the moon, its orbit takes it as far as 4.6 billion miles from the sun's warmth and light. In 1978, astronomers discovered that Pluto has a moon, which they named Charon. In Greek mythology, Charon is the boatman who ferries the souls of the dead across the river Styx to the underworld. Then, in 1988, astronomers found that Pluto has a thin atmosphere of methane, and that this atmosphere will freeze to the surface of the planet for two centuries starting in the 2020s. Pluto remains the only planet not yet visited by spacecraft, although plans are under consideration for flights that would take seven or eight years and arrive early in the twenty-first century.

Pluto is hardly a place that we would like to visit. In fact, the planet Pluto is probably a very good image for the underworld ruled by the terrifying god Hades. It is a dark and frozen realm, far away from what we think of in our sunlit, day-to-day lives. We will only face the risk of travel to such a place under the greatest duress.

THE UNDERWORLD JOURNEY OF PERSEPHONE

Yet the affirming aspect of the journey to the underworld, the unconscious and unexplored realms within ourselves, is that we may find our own creativity and sources of renewal. With this in mind, we can turn to a myth which shows the very forces that shaped the underworld and, so, shaped our unconscious. This is the myth of Hades' abduction of Persephone, the daughter of Zeus and the fertility goddess Demeter.

Remember as this myth unfolds that we are speaking of inheritance in the larger sense. What we inherit is not merely money and only received at death, but it is everything, both good and bad, that we receive from our parents throughout our lifetime. When we examine such an inheritance, some of what we receive will be truly ours and worthwhile to keep. The rest we must learn to surrender if we are to get on with our own lives.

In the myth, Zeus, the ruler of the gods, gives permission to his brother Hades to marry Persephone. Zeus does not consult Demeter or Persephone about this, but, in essence, authorizes the incestuous and violent rape of Persephone by Hades, who is her uncle. So one day, as Persephone reaches to pluck a narcissus in a field, the earth opens in a great chasm. Hades, riding his golden chariot pulled by immortal steeds, appears from the darkness and carries Persephone away.

Persephone weeps and screams. Demeter hears her daughter. For nine days she searches for Persephone on the earth until at last she learns of the abduction and of Zeus's permission for Hades to marry Persephone. Although Hades rules a third of all creation and is a king, Demeter is inconsolable. Her rage against Zeus is so great that she leaves Olympus, the home of the gods, and wanders through the human world. She neglects herself and, finally, looking like an old and poverty-stricken woman, she sits by the Well of the Virgin in the town of Eleusis. The daughters of King Keleos come to draw water from the well. Feeling compassion for the old woman, they ask for and receive permission from their mother to invite Demeter to stay in the palace.

King Keleos has a new son, Demophoon, and his wife Metaneira entrusts the child to Demeter's care. The parents marvel at how Demophoon grows godlike under the care of Demeter. But, unknown to the boy's parents, each night Demeter dangles the boy over the leaping flames of a fire to make him immortal. One night Metaneira sees this and laments that she will lose her son and be grief-stricken.

Demeter is enraged and lays the infant on the floor beside the fire. Revealing herself as a goddess, she tells Metaneira that the boy could have been immortal but now must die like all men. Saying that she is a beneficent goddess who brings joy to both people and gods, she directs that a great temple and altar be built for her at Eleusis. In return, she will teach her sacred rites to the people.

King Keleos brings together the people to build the temple. But when they have finished, Demeter merely sits within the temple walls and mourns for her daughter Persephone. She will not let seeds sprout; nothing grows and people suffer a year of terrible misery. Zeus, fearful that there will be no people to offer sacrifices to the gods, sends one god after another to ask Demeter to return to Olympus. The gods implore her and offer her gifts, but she refuses them all.

At last Zeus decides to send a messenger to the underworld to meet with Hades. He chooses the god called Hermes by the Greeks and Mercury by the Romans. This handsome god carries a golden staff and often is portrayed wearing a winged helmet or winged sandals to show that he can move through all the worlds, from heaven to earth to the underworld. He is called the messenger of the gods, and is often sent from Olympus on missions of aid.

Hermes is the god of boundaries. On the earth he is the god who protects travelers. Because the early travelers were largely merchants and traders, he is also the god of commerce and of the boundaries set by commercial relationships. In the underworld he is the guide of souls, the god who brings us across the boundary from the world that we know to the world that is unknown. For those who journey within themselves, Hermes is the guide who helps us across the boundaries that previously we never saw and certainly never thought of crossing.

When Hermes comes he can use his golden staff to either mesmerize or awaken us. There is the danger that we will wander forever: grieving like Demeter, entrapped in the underworld like Persephone, or riding for years on the nation's highways like the father in *For Richer, For Poorer*. But, if we dare the suffering of the journey, we may be awakened by what is new and rich within us. For Hermes has the power to transform evil into good. He is a "giver of grace, guide, and giver of good things!" To express this another way, we have in ourselves immense healing powers if we see the ways in which we may need healing.

Hermes bounds from Olympus to the underworld depths. There he finds Hades and grieving Persephone, who yearns for her mother. When Hades hears that Zeus has ordered the release of Persephone, he smiles obediently and begs Persephone to see him as a worthy husband and come from time to time to visit him.

Persephone rises with joy, but Hades comes behind her and slips into her mouth the sweet seeds of a pomegranate. Then Hermes brings Persephone up from the dark realms and leaves her at the great temple in Eleusis.

Demeter embraces her with a happiness like intoxication, but the first question that she asks her daughter is whether Persephone ate anything in the palace of Hades.

When she learns that Persephone has eaten the seeds of the pomegranate, she knows that her daughter must return to the underworld.

Now Zeus sends his own mother, the goddess Rhea, to earth where all the fields lie barren. Rhea brings the promise of Zeus that Persephone may spend two-thirds of the year with Demeter, but must spend the other third with Hades. Rhea implores Demeter to let the corn grow again and nourish humanity.

Demeter agrees and once again the earth is lush with vegetation. As she promised, the goddess teaches her rites to her worshippers at Eleusis. These rites concern immortality and are so sacred that death is the penalty for revealing them outside of the ceremonies. Demeter also gives the knowledge of agriculture to humanity for its betterment. Only during a third of the year, when Persephone must live in the underworld, does Demeter withhold her nurturing abundance. That season, of course, is winter.

While humanity endures winter, Persephone sits on her underworld throne. She is the queen of the underworld, the wife of fearsome Hades. With him she rules the realm of the dead and of wealth. So she has entered adulthood, is no longer merely the daughter, and has found her own power and her role as a queen.

WHAT WE LEARN FROM THE UNDERWORLD JOURNEY

There is a beautiful epithet that applies to both Demeter and Persephone: *carpophorus* or fruit-bearing. Both mother and daughter are the bearers of fruits, of what grows and is nourishing. Looked at another way, the mother and daughter share the same essence; they are as one. They are both fertility goddesses. However, a crucial part of Demeter is missing. She can offer life, abundance, and vitality, but she appears to have no contact with death. Even she, a powerful goddess, is out of touch with a certain aspect of reality. She wants to keep Persephone with her always, so the daughter will have no experience of death or rebirth. She wants to make the infant Demophoon immortal, but she fails to see that humans by their nature must accept mortality.

Like the father in *For Richer, For Poorer*, Demeter has not dealt with death, the absence of productivity, the fallow period before the next time of growth. She has not dealt with idleness, with winter. As so often happens, the child must deal with what the parent refuses to confront. This is an aspect of Persephone's inheritance. Demeter's endless abundance forces Persephone to confront the meaning of death, emptiness, winter. Persephone must go to that dark and depressing realm where the atmosphere can freeze to the surface for two centuries.

The abduction of Persephone by her uncle Hades has been used as a model for incestuous sexual abuse, especially of a girl by her father or other male relatives. We may ask why Zeus, who is the ruler or ordering power among the gods, allows the painful penetration of Persephone by Hades. The myth never answers this question, but it seems that the oneness of the child with the parent must be violated. The child must separate. The rape is an image of how terrifying we may find the change forced on us by the unfolding of our own nature. Often this crisis comes in midlife as we undergo the stressful surrender of an old and outgrown identity. This identity may have pleased our parents. It may be part of our inheritance from them. Yet the stirring of our own power, our own sense of who we most deeply are, may force us to surrender what may in many ways be both secure and of value.

That the rapist is an uncle, a relative, suggests how closely related to us the force of the rape is. The energy of the rape is not the intrusion of a stranger, but rather the impact of a previously hidden energy within oneself. When this energy first appears, we feel darkness, depression, and disorientation. We do not like to change, even if the change comes from within.

Women and men alike experience this rising of unconscious materials into awareness like the penetration of a rape. Hades carries us away to the underworld; he penetrates us with his darkness. But when we return like Persephone to the light, we retain a knowledge of the darkness. We are more complete; we see more fully the truth of who and what we are. So Zeus, representing the highest principle of order within us, allows great psychic violence in the service of growth.

Hades feeds fruits to Persephone, who is the "fruit-bearing" goddess. His intrusion forces her to eat of her own nature. She is ingesting—becoming—herself. In this process she shows her mother Demeter, who acknowledges only abundance and immortality, that existence encompasses more than this. Through the descent of Persephone, Demeter, symbolizing the abundant part of ourselves, is brought into relationship with grief and mortality. This integration of unwanted aspects of life makes us more realistic and whole. Also, the pomegranate is not a fruit chosen at random. Many of the ancient Mediterranean peoples believed that the seeds of the pomegranate could be used as a contraceptive. So the number of seeds eaten by Persephone equals the number of infertile winter months. Yet the red juice and many seeds of the pomegranate were also considered a symbol of uterine richness and fertility. So Persephone eats of her own sexuality, discovering in her underworld journey the ways in which she is both barren and rich.

When we eat of our own natures, we become more and more ourselves. The alchemists (borrowing from the Gnostics) used an image of a snake that swallows its own tail: the *ouroboros*. Many snakes live in the darkness beneath the earth, so the snake symbolizes the ability to penetrate the underworld. By devouring itself, the alchemical snake forms a circle, its mouth grasping its tail, and the circle is an image of wholeness. When we eat of our own natures, we are both self-devouring and becoming whole in the image of being circular. It takes great courage to admit that we meet ourselves in the underworld. It may be easier to blame a parent and never eat the seeds of the pomegranate.

Several other aspects of the underworld journey are worth mentioning. We may need a guide, a Hermes, simply to find the entrance to the underworld or our unconscious. This guide may take many forms, such as a dream figure, a spiritual leader, or an analyst. Many cultures give the dead a coin or some wealth to take with them on their journey. So a price must always be paid to venture into the unconscious. We must also take with us offerings that appease terrible Persephone when we meet her enthroned beside her husband Hades.

For example, in *The Aeneid*, when Aeneas seeks the help of a prophetess to descend into the underworld and visit his father, Aeneas first must find a golden bough to bring with him as an offering to Persephone. This golden bough is such a holy offering that Charon, the ferryman, has no choice but to take Aeneas across the River Styx, while multitudes of other souls wait centuries for passage.

Aeneas must also offer something to the monster Kerberos that guards the gates of the underworld. Kerberos is a three-headed dog with the tail of a snake. The prophetess tosses a drugged scrap of honey and corn to Kerberos. The monster devours this and then sleeps while Aeneas passes. At last Aeneas honors the underworld goddess Persephone by setting the golden bough on her altar. When he sees his father, he tries three times to embrace him but clasps only the empty air. His father tells him that those who drink from the River Lethe in Hades will forget everything and be doomed to another life as a human.

Moneta's name, in its roots, suggests the importance of memory. Money, like the underworld journey, requires us to remember. If we drink from the River Lethe, we will forget what we have already experienced. In a larger sense, we will even forget the experience of our parents and of our ancestors. We will be unable to transform our inheritance, whatever it may be. Only if we remember can we bring the power of reason to bear on our own experiences and those of our family. Only this scrutiny protects us from falling into the illusion that these worn-out images are real. For if we are ruled by our past experiences, such as the patterns of childhood relationship to our parents, we will have no way to avoid repeating these patterns again and again—in essence, living the same life over and over without gaining spiritual insight.

Also, when we return from the underworld, we must not forget our experiences and insights there. Remembering is a putting together of parts, a reconstituting of ourselves. So memory allows us the understanding that leads to growth. When we review our experiences in the underworld, we understand that much of what we experienced as painful and frightening was, in fact, necessary and healing for us.

For example, Kerbéros is one of the great monsters of mythology. He is a three-headed hound of fearsome size. But we have to keep in mind that the dog is a friend of humankind. The first wild animal to be domesticated, the dog is part of humanity's extended family. So the dog in dreams and myths is likely to be on the side of human development. Kerberos as a dog is seeking to protect us from entering those parts of our unconscious that we are not yet ready to experience. He is fearsome, but he is serving us. In "The Wasteland" by T. S. Eliot, the narrator speaks of a corpse that has been buried, some aspect of life that people might prefer to avoid, yet the corpse itself may sprout and bloom. The narrator warns that the friendly dog should be kept away from such a corpse, because the dog may repeatedly dig up what we hide from ourselves.

Sometimes the dog, our friend and helper, seeks, like Kerberos, to protect us from knowledge of the underworld; other times such a dog insists on digging up and exposing to us unconscious material that we would prefer to bury. When we are ready to pass the gate that Kerberos guards, we are ready to face aspects of ourselves that have been hidden in our unconscious.

In *The Aeneid*, the drugged scrap of food that the prophetess feeds Kerberos is made of honey and corn meal. It is interesting that the prophetess, not Aeneas, drugs this terrifying guardian. In a way, the part of us that is prophetic, the part that can see into our own future, is the part that knows when the time is right to drug the guardian at the gates to the unconscious. Aeneas is like our conscious awareness. We do not consciously know the right moment to confront unconscious material, but like Aeneas we can be courageous in pursuing this unearthing once it has begun. Also, since Demeter is the grain goddess, the use of corn to drug Kerberos suggests that the very richness of our nature causes the guardian to sleep when the time is appropriate for entry.

The underworld or unconscious often expresses itself through paradox. So Kerberos is not only a dog but also a snake. And, as D. H. Lawrence says in his poem "Snake," the snake is "Like a king in exile, uncrowned in the underworld,/Now due to be crowned again." So the monster has two natures—that of the friendly dog and of the underworld god. The name Kerberos, by its similarity to the word *ouroboros*, suggests that the snake part of Kerberos's nature includes the circular image of the snake devouring its own tail. So, in the underworld journey, we find the image of the circle which represents integration and wholeness.

The golden bough symbolizes the mysterious connection between the world that we know and that which is unknown. Aeneas despairs of finding such a golden bough in the vastness of the forest. In fact, this golden bough is unnatural; it is not from the green world of vegetation but from the gold hidden in the underworld. That Aeneas can find such a bough in our world suggests that the moment is ripe for his entry into the unconscious. In the underworld he will meet his father and learn of his destiny, which is the inheritance belonging to him and his descendants.

The golden bough that Aeneas must offer to Persephone, in fact, came from the underworld. He is merely returning what already was hers. This gives us a fuller understanding of the nature of the underworld. It is the repository of wealth that awaits circulation. If the wealth does not circulate, then the underworld will truly be a frozen and terrible realm of deadness.

In everyday life, the golden bough might be a dream, a memory, or a feeling which we return to the underworld (the unconscious) by a process of contemplating its meaning and significance. Such golden boughs allow us to face the unconscious material that gathers within us from our daily lives, our family history, and the collective of the society in which we live. To refuse to deal with this material is to be frozen within.

If we dare the underworld journey, we may return with a greater insight. We may realize that abundance and barrenness are not opposites but reflections. So, too, are the harvest time and the time when the fields are fallow—productivity and idleness, and life and death—all reflections of one another. Money is like the golden bough, a residue or reflection of the richness of the natural world and our own natures. If we have enough insight, we may be able to use the inheritance from our parents as an offering on our journey of understanding. In doing this, we may transform our relationship to that inheritance, whether we viewed it as too much or too little, and to our parents themselves.

THE LAST WILL AND TESTAMENT
Dividing Property

We have been in the underworld long enough. Let us return to our own world, where money and property often perplex us. A difficult task faces the man or woman who must divide property by a will. Should his or her will convey some hidden, and perhaps unintended, message to those who receive inheritances and those who do not? Should the will seek to accomplish in death what could not be done in life, perhaps attempting to atone for not giving more of oneself? And do the beneficiaries understand their relationship to the person writing this last will and testament? Or should these beneficiaries, who may be adult children, search in the disposition of property for love and parental concern? The will is the last expression of the deceased. There is no opportunity for the beneficiaries to ask questions about intention and love, unless like Aeneas they seek their parents in the underworld.

In the Bible when a man in a crowd demands of Jesus to "bid my brother divide the inheritance with me," he speaks for so many of us who feel that we have not been given enough. Jesus refuses to be a divider of property, answering, "Man, who made me judge or divider over you?" Then Jesus warns the people in the crowd, "Take heed, and beware of all covetousness, for a man's life does not consist in the abundance of his possessions."

So a wise and industrious father in "A Father and Sons," one of *Aesop's Fables*, tells his sons on his death bed that he has hidden a treasure in the vineyard. After the father's death, the sons labor in the vineyard, turning over the soil in search of the treasure. While they find no treasure, their work makes the next harvest so rich that they profit from their labor. The moral given for this story is that good counsel is the best legacy, especially if the children also receive both the curiosity and inclination to follow the good counsel.

years old, and the boy thinks that many birds will have built their nests in its branches.

Suddenly he hears a voice crying, "Let me out, let me out." He clears away dead leaves and searches in the roots until he finds a glass bottle with a froglike creature in it that keeps calling, "Let me out."

The unsuspecting boy uncorks the bottle and a spirit flows out and grows larger and larger until it is half as big as the oak. This spirit asks the boy what he thinks his reward will be for letting it out. The boy says he has no idea. "I'm going to break your neck," the spirit tells him.

The fearless boy says that he's going to keep his head on his shoulders and not let the spirit touch his neck. And he says he would have left the spirit in the bottle if he'd known how it rewards people.

The spirit replies that its name is Mercurius, and that it is so mighty that the boy's wishes don't matter. The spirit's duty is to break the neck of the one who frees him.

The boy answers that he can't believe a spirit as large as Mercurius was in such a small bottle. If Mercurius will get back in the bottle and prove that it can fit, then the boy will allow the spirit to do what it wants with him.

Mercurius slips back into the bottle and the boy quickly corks it and tosses it among the roots of the oak. He starts back toward his father, but Mercurius cries pitifully to be set free. Mercurius promises the boy good fortune for the rest of his life.

At last the boy decides to take a chance. Mercurius may be telling the truth, and in any event the boy feels that the spirit can't hurt him. So he uncorks the bottle and again the freed spirit grows huge.

Mercurius honors the promise and hands the boy a piece of cloth as his reward. The piece of cloth looks like a bandage that might go on a wound. Mercurius tells the boy that if he touches the cloth to iron or steel, the metal will be transformed into silver. And if he touches the cloth to a wound, the wound will be healed.

The boy wants to try out this cloth. He takes his ax and strikes a blow that cuts through the bark of the ancient oak. Then he touches this wound with the cloth and immediately the bark is whole again.

The spirit thanks the boy for its freedom and the boy thanks the spirit for the gift. Then they part.

The boy returns to find his father annoyed that he has been gone so long. The boy says he'll catch up, but the father doesn't believe him. So the boy touches his ax with the cloth and strikes a tree. Instead of magically felling the tree, the ax has turned to silver and is bent and ruined by the blow. The boy says the ax was no good, but the father is enraged that he will have to pay the neighbor for the ax. The son says that he'll pay for the ax and the father calls the boy an idiot. The father says that the son has nothing but what he receives from the father, so how will the son get money to pay for the ax?

Soon after, the son says that he can't work anymore and suggests they both go home. The father refuses, saying he has work to do and won't sit idle. The son then says that he's never been in these woods and he won't be able to find his way home if the father doesn't show him.

The father gets over his anger and takes the boy home. He asks the boy to take the ruined ax to town and sell it. The father expects to have to earn the rest of the money to repay the neighbor.

The boy takes the ax to the goldsmith, who tests it and weighs it. The goldsmith says the ax is worth four hundred talers (dollars), but he can only pay the boy three hundred talers at the moment and will have to owe him the other hundred. The boy accepts and returns with this fortune to his father.

The neighbor wants one taler and six groschen for the ax, but they pay him double. Then the boy gives the father one hundred talers and says that the father will live an easy life from now on and want for nothing.

The astonished father asks how the son came by so much money. The boy explains what happened and how he was rewarded when he took the risk of trusting Mercurius.

The rest of the money is more than enough for the son to finish his courses at the university. Aided by the cloth that can heal all wounds, the boy becomes a doctor famed throughout the world for his healing skills.

WHAT WE FIND IN THE ROOTS OF THE FAMILY TREE

This marvelous tale offers a number of insights into inheritance. The father is a well-intentioned man. He has a difficult life, but he saves what he is able so that his son can achieve more than he did. We feel in this the father's belief that the family has a greater potential that it has shown so far. In the family genes are the possibilities of distinguished achievement that would be nourished by a university education.

However, the father is poor. He cannot, by his efforts alone, change the destiny of the family. What money he can save—that is, what life energy he can make available to his son—is not enough to let the son graduate from the university. Good though the father's efforts are, the son will have to live the woodcutter's life if he merely relies on what his father is able to offer him as an inheritance.

It is significant that the son is quite willing to strive as a woodcutter. He doesn't look down on this hard work, nor does he scorn his father. He isn't looking for someone to blame for the fact that he could not finish his university education. Parents so often receive this kind of blame. Whether the parent is alive or dead, the child may believe some flaw in the parent has crippled and limited the child's life. To become attached to this point of view is damaging, because the child fails to take responsibility for his or her own destiny. The child inherits the parent's life, instead of discovering his or her own life.

The woodcutter's son is quite willing to take responsibility for himself. He isn't filled with self-pity because he has been unable to complete the courses at the university. In fact, he shows how he respects his father and his father's work by wanting to join in the woodcutting. The father feels ambivalent about this, because he has an awareness that the son should rise higher in life. Yet the son's acceptance of the father's work shows that the son honors those from whom he will inherit. This attitude makes possible the son's inheriting far more than property or the cost of an education.

The father must borrow an ax if the son is to join him in the woodcutting. So the son receives something from the father which does not belong to the father. It will have to be returned or paid for, but in using the ax the son shows that he can expand the boundaries of what the father imagined to be possible. The ax itself offers an image of the dangers and possibilities offered by inheritance. The ax can be used both to build and destroy. So the son can use his inheritance to build or destroy his own potential.

The son wants to search for birds' nests in the forest while his more practical father prefers to rest at midday. Why should the son want to find birds' nests? Birds suggest the spirit, for birds can fly toward the heavens. So the boy is looking for a spiritual destiny of his own. The father has already found his place in life, but the son must venture deeper into the forest in search of what is his. By walking, the son uses his own power in his quest; by penetrating deeper into the forest, the son seeks his own nature beyond any boundaries set by the father.

What the son discovers is an ancient oak with a girth so great that five men could not put their arms around it. The boy imagines that this enormous tree will have many birds' nests in its branches, but what he actually discovers is a bottled genie in its roots. What we search for does not always present itself in the way that we imagine. The boy imagines his spiritual gift will come from looking to higher things, but in fact he must look down, toward the underworld, if he is to inherit any gift from the family tree. He must look at the roots of this angry oak to find the genie who, like the ax, can destroy or help build the boy's life.

This immense oak is described as angry. How can a tree be angry? A family tree can be filled with anger, carried from generation to generation. The father has an intuition that the family can achieve far more than it has. But this potential is unrealized. Perhaps many generations in this family have seen this glimmering of potential, but crushing poverty and social circumstances have made it so very difficult to rise to a new status. The father is frustrated at his own failure to earn and achieve more. He yearns to give more to his son but is frustrated in this as well. In his frustration is anger for the family fate, a fate that he cannot see how to alter.

The son searches among the roots of the family tree for

a voice that he hears calling. He does not know whose voice this is, but he knows that it cries out to be free. At last he finds a bottle with a froglike creature hopping inside it. If he does not examine what is in the bottle, he will live the same life that his father has lived. He will carry the family frustration and rage. But to examine this unseen aspect of the family history is dangerous; it lets the genie out of the bottle.

Alchemists used many different images of Mercurius, including one image of a boy with wings imprisoned in a bottle. This symbolized the concept of spirit imprisoned in matter. Being within the bottle is a way of containing and examining emotions and feelings without simply acting on them in the world. The boy's inner looking leads to understanding and growth.

Mercurius, as we said earlier, is Mercury or Hermes, the god who guides us on our underworld journey. He both makes boundaries and enables us to cross them. With his golden staff he can either awaken or mesmerize us. In this tale, he appears as a genie, a spirit encapsulated in a bottle. The word "genie" shares its roots with such words as genetic, genital, genitive, genuine, and genius. And the Latin verb *genere*, to beget, gives the derivative *gens*, which refers to male descendants of a free male ancestor—that is, a clan.

Apuleius, the second-century Roman author of *The Golden Ass*, wrote of how a man might honor his genius by sacrificing to it on his birthday. This use of the word genius, however, was quite different from its usage today. The genius to which a man sacrificed was the family spirit. These sacrifices, by honoring and revering the clan, made a man abundant in all ways. The genius would become a household god and protect the family. But if a man failed to honor this genius, it would become a restless and destructive influence on the family.

In our tale, Mercurius appears to be such a restless and destructive spirit. No honor has been given to Mercurius, no sacrifices have been offered on its altar. Faced by this violent aspect of the family history, the boy is fearless. His quest for a higher life has somehow prepared him for this meeting, but he is unaware of the form that the family spirit will take. At first, surprised, he thinks he will keep this spirit bottled up. Often that seems the safer way to deal with those aspects of our inheritances that are tormenting.

However, the boy is courageous. He has an intuitive sense that the spirit will not harm him and may keep its promise of giving good fortune. By opening the bottle a second time, the boy offers himself as a sacrifice to the spirit. If the spirit breaks his neck, the boy will live a broken life—a life in which his spirit and imagination (symbolized by the head) and his emotions and instincts (symbolized by the heart and body) are never brought together in a harmonious unity.

By risking his own life, the boy transforms Mercurius into a protecting spirit, a beneficent household god. The boy has honored not his personal genius, which would be mere narcissism, but the genius of the family. He has drawn from something larger than himself; he has realized the gift that Mercurius has waited centuries to give. Now that Mercurius has given the gift of healing to this generation of the family, the role of guide is no longer needed. So Mercurius is free to return to the realm of the gods and spirits.

At first the boy misunderstands his gift. He thinks that it will magically cut down trees so that he can be his father's equal as a woodcutter. Having transformed the ax to silver, his first blow destroys the ax. So the boy's fate is not to match his father's. That is not his life issue nor should it be his life goal. If he uses his gift in that way, he will render it of no value. The boy's complaint that the ax is no good is his momentary failure to see the true nature of his gift. He must use the gift in achieving the new and unique shape that his own life will take.

To do this, however, he must leave the father's world, symbolized here by the forest. The father is enraged that the boy has damaged the borrowed ax. This rage shows the poisonous effect of the anger in the family tree. The father feels that the family has no genius, that the son is, of course, an idiot. The only way to success is the hard work of woodcutting, so the father at first refuses to lead his son out of the forest. He feels that he must continue to labor as he always has.

But the father truly loves his son. That is why he tried as best he could to send his son to the university. His anger passes quickly enough. After all, it isn't really anger at the son but rather at the condition of the family. By showing the son the path out of the woods, the father accepts and even encourages the son to begin his new and gifted life.

The son sells the silver ax and gives his father the enormous sum of one hundred talers. A taler was obviously worth a lot more than a dollar is today, because this fortune will enable the father to live at ease for the rest of his life. Certainly this ease includes material well-being, but it also includes the spiritual joy that comes from at last seeing the healing realization of the family's gift. The son has touched his healing cloth to the wound in the family tree; he has healed it. The father is ready to hear how his son's destiny will be different from his own, so his son tells him the whole story of his meeting with Mercurius.

The son shows great wisdom in his use of the gift. He is no Midas. He does not use the cloth to convert more and more metal into silver. He merely uses the money received from the sale of that one ax to pay for his university education. With the help of the healing cloth, he realizes the potential of his ancestry by becoming a famed doctor and healer. The fact that he receives only three hundred talers and is owed another one hundred talers by the goldsmith suggests that what we inherit is so vast that it must come to us in installments received over time. We cannot be given (or understand) our inheritance in a moment of realization; rather, a gradual process is required by which our understanding deepens.

A MYSTERY SOLVED
The Thief Who Steals from Misers

We have discussed the tale of the miller who sold all that he owned to buy gold that he buried. One night a thief came and stole the hoard of gold. But who was this thief? It may come as no surprise that Hermes (Mercury) is not only the god of commerce, but the god of thieves as well. So if we suspect that Hermes stole the buried treasure, we are likely to be correct. But, unlike most thieves, Hermes will often offer something in return for what he steals.

The story of Hermes' birth reveals not only how Hermes became the god of thieves but also shows how Hermes felt unjustly treated in what he inherited from his father. Hermes' father was Zeus, ruler of the gods, while his mother was a nymph named Maia. Zeus had also fathered Apollo, the god of light, healing, music, poetry, and prophecy. However, Apollo's mother was Leto, so he and Hermes were half brothers.

On the day of his birth, Hermes performed two remarkable feats. First, he took the shell of a tortoise and invented the lyre, a stringed instrument on which he made beautiful music and sang joyously of his own birth. Next he went to where his brother Apollo kept a herd of sacred cattle. Hermes stole fifty cows from this herd and made them walk backwards so that their tracks could not be followed. After hiding the cows in the depths of a cave, he sacrificed two cows to the twelve immortal gods (including himself among these dozen deities).

In the ancient Mediterranean world, cattle were used to measure value, served as wealth, and were a valuable sacrificial offering. When Hermes steals the cows of Apollo, he is stealing the equivalent of gold or money. Apollo quickly realized that his younger brother had stolen the cattle, but he could not prove it. He accused Hermes of the theft, but Hermes changed shape and returned to his cradle as a baby. Hermes told his angry brother that he was newborn and knew nothing of any theft.

Since both Apollo and Hermes knew that Hermes had stolen the cattle, these gods were playing a game with each other. The game is much like the disputes of human siblings who feel their parents have favored one or the other. The game conceals the bitterness that the less favored sibling feels toward the parent. Even when Apollo and Hermes bring their grievance to Zeus, Hermes lies shamelessly. He says that Apollo accused him of theft without any witness and that Apollo threatened him, but he completely denies having stolen the cattle. Hermes says that Zeus should help him as the younger son.

Zeus, not touched by the anguish human parents often

feel in trying to give fairly of themselves to children, bursts into laughter. He tells the brothers to be reconciled and commands that Hermes lead his brother to where the cows are hidden. Hermes and Apollo go together to the cave, and Hermes brings the cattle out of the darkness. Then Hermes plays on the lyre. He plays so beautifully, singing of the gods, that he appeases his brother's anger.

This leads to a remarkable exchange and reconciliation between the brothers. Apollo admires Hermes' ingenuity in inventing the lyre. He wants the instrument and feels it to be worth fifty cows or even more. For his part, Hermes gives the lyre to Apollo.

In return, Apollo gives Hermes not only the fifty cows that had been stolen but also a golden three-leaved staff capable of bestowing wealth. While Apollo keeps for himself the gift of high prophecy, he gives to Hermes certain soothsaying powers as well as the lordship over animals which had formerly been Apollo's. He also gives Hermes the important offices as guide of human souls to the underworld and messenger of the gods.

So Hermes' theft of wealth ends with Apollo receiving a marvelous gift, the lyre, which makes the sounds of a new and beautiful music. It is this music that we seek when we examine our inheritance. Of course, we may rage against parents and siblings for a time. Either we have been given too little of what we wanted, too much of what we did not want, or not a fair portion compared to what someone else received. The most obvious symbol of this giving is money, but love, attention, encouragement, and so much more are also part of our inheritance.

If we explore in the roots of the family tree, we may develop an understanding of our families that will deepen the understanding that we possess of ourselves. Confronting parental shortcomings and the behavioral patterns that we have adopted to compensate for their anger, abuse, lack of love, or lack of understanding may allow us a greater freedom.

In "The Spirit in the Bottle," the woodcutter's son finds this freedom when he risks his neck to gain the genie's gift. He surrenders his attachment to the familiar life that he knows. If he remains under the spell of the anger that is so ominous in the immense presence of the family tree, he will share with his father a dumb sense of suffering and rage for the family's unrealized potential. He will never realize his own potential. Instead he goes through a process by which he comes to a more objective understanding of his family's potentials and shortcomings. Through this process he frees himself from the patterns of the past. By taking responsibility for his fate, he is able to receive from Mercurius an inheritance as marvelous as music—that of healing.

CHAPTER SEVEN

INDEBTEDNESS

How the Debtors' Tower Connects Earth to Heaven

ON A SATURDAY AND SUNDAY, February 20 and 21, 1822, in London, a weeping boy ran desperate errands through the streets in an effort to keep his father from going to debtors' prison. His father had been arrested and detained in a sponging house, a halfway house that would be followed by prison if the debt could not be paid. A baker, who sold bread and pastries to the family, had brought suit to recover forty pounds, a small part of the total debt owed by the boy's father to many creditors.

February had been a terrible month. The boy had turned ten years old, and his family had obtained employment for him in a blacking shop, where he applied a dark finish and labels to pots. His weekly wage of six shillings was decent pay for such a boy, the daily hours of 8 A.M. to 8 P.M. acceptable by the standards of the day. "No words can express the secret agony of my soul," he wrote years later in his autobiography, "as I . . . felt my early hopes of growing up to be a learned and distinguished man, crushed in my breast. . . ."

As the boy wept and ran from relatives to family friends seeking aid on that weekend, he must have felt the world that he had known—the world of childhood and of a whole and happy family—coming to an end. On Monday, February 22, the debt remained unpaid and the boy heard his beloved father say that "the sun was set upon him for ever." These words made the boy feel his own heart had broken. Later in the day, his father was taken to Marshalsea Prison and confined as an insolvent debtor.

That boy of ten was Charles Dickens.

DEBT AND IMPRISONMENT

The fate of John Dickens may seem severe, even inhuman, when judged by contemporary standards. The English legal system sought to prevent default on debt by the imposition of severe penalties. A seventeenth-century English judge, Sir Robert Hyde, didn't mince his words on this point: "If a man be taken in execution, and lie in prison for debt, neither the plaintiff, at whose suit he is arrested, nor the sheriff who took him, is bound to find him meat, drink, or clothes; but he must live on his own, or on the charity of others; and if no man will relieve him, let him die in the name of God, says the law; and so say I."

We would do well to consider how recent is the change in our thinking about whether personal freedom can be sacrificed as a penalty for nonpayment of debt. In this chapter we will explore how the powerful symbol of the debtors' prison has been lost to our awareness. Bankruptcy, which is used more and more frequently by overburdened consumers and businesses, does not require imprisonment and so does not warn of the way in which debt can deprive us of time, the very essence of life. Beyond this, however, we must face the debt that we owe for the miracle of life, a debt that may confuse us when we come to deal with everyday debts. And since debt is a statement about our ability to make payment in the future, it is also a statement about how we imagine that we will evolve and what productive role we will play in society. If we are wrong in our assessment and cannot repay our debts, we take the assets and life energy of others.

AN OATH OF POVERTY

Debtors' prisons were by no means limited to England. The colonies and, later, the states also imprisoned people for debt. Massachusetts, for example, dealt legislatively with debt collection laws more than seventy times in the seventeenth and eighteenth centuries. Seeking to ameliorate the harshness of imprisonment, Massachusetts experimented with a number of reforms: making the creditor pay for the cost of keeping the debtor in jail, allowing the debtor a limited freedom to leave the jail in search of work during the daytime, and letting debtors swear an oath of poverty and go free. However, swearing such an oath did not give relief from the debt itself.

In fact, in the 1820s, England also allowed the taking of an oath of poverty. In a larger view, it is curious that as the wandering monks, who took vows of poverty and lived by begging, no longer flourished in the western world, this new, secular oath of poverty emerged. John Dickens feared to take this oath, because he felt the disgrace would cause him to lose his job in the Navy Pay Office and the pension that would one day be his. Yet his creditors refused to enter into a new schedule for debt repayment, so the oath of poverty was his only option if he wished to leave prison. To qualify for such an oath, all of the clothing and personal property owned by him and his family could not have a value exceeding twenty pounds. As part of this process, Charles had to go before an official who, smelling strongly of beer and with his mouth full, examined the boy. Charles worried that the silver watch in his pocket, a gift from his grandfather, might be of too great value to keep and was relieved when the official merely glanced at his clothing and dismissed him.

In New England, Yankee merchants used the debtors' laws to their benefit by plying laborers with rum and whiskey. When the laborers could not pay for the liquor bills, the merchants would put them into indentured servitude to work off their debts in the Newfoundland fishing grounds. By the 1820s, when Dickens's father found himself within the walls of Marshalsea Prison, as many as ten thousand petty debtors were under close confinement in Massachusetts prisons. If we think of the debtors in jail in the other states, and the estimate that thirty to forty thousand people were arrested for debt in England in 1837, we can see that imprisonment for nonpayment of debt must have created fear for a great many people.

Reviewing a few examples from Massachusetts reveals that imprisonment of debtors, while perhaps serving as a deterrent to default on debt, often punished those who were already victims of hardship. In 1824, in Springfield, a girl of nineteen with a nursing baby was imprisoned for a debt of about seven dollars. That same year in Boston a blind man with a dependent family went to jail for a debt of six dollars. In Salem, a seventy-six-year-old veteran of the battle of Bunker Hill found himself imprisoned for a debt of a few dollars; while in Marblehead the local infantry raised $22.18 to release a sixty-eight-year-old veteran of the Revolutionary War from jail.

All of the states had laws governing debtors who could not pay, and in most of the states the pendulum of reform swung back and forth. If we imagine that the United States was founded by hardy pioneers who refused to borrow, we would be indulging in a fantasy. The capital and credit to support many merchants in the New World came from Europe, especially from England. Personal debt was also common, since food and other items often were purchased on account from a local merchant. While we may imagine that debt is a uniquely contemporary problem, debt has, in fact, a long history and almost certainly existed in prehistoric times.

TO SELL A WIFE, SON, OR DAUGHTER

Debt most frequently is measured in money and is an important aspect of the secret life of money. However, even before money existed, people borrowed such things as seeds, tools, and goods for trading. The earliest documented laws, the Code of Hammurabi set down in Babylonia about 1750 B.C., provide that "If a man be in debt and sell his wife, son, or daughter or bind them over to service for three years, they shall work in the house of their purchaser or master; in the fourth year they shall be given their freedom."

To imagine a man selling his wife, son, or daughter to

pay his debt shocks us, but the Bible frequently places before us the dangers of debt. In one parable, Jesus tells of a king whose servant owes him a debt too large to pay. The king orders the servant, his wife, his children, and all his belongings sold so that the debt can be paid. But the servant falls to his knees and begs for more time to make payment. Moved by this plea, the king releases the servant from the debt.

This would make a happy ending, except that the servant is also owed a debt by a fellow servant. This debt is much smaller, but the first servant no sooner leaves the king then he comes upon the second servant and seizes him by the throat and demands, "Pay what you owe!" The second servant pleads for more time, but the first servant is merciless and has him thrown into prison.

The king is filled with rage when he hears that the first servant did not offer the same mercy he had received to the second servant. So the king delivers the first servant to the tortures of prison until he makes full repayment of his debt.

While this parable used debt to show that people should forgive one another as God forgives them, it also illustrates how the debtor who failed to pay ran the risk of prison, indentured servitude, and even slavery. Under Roman law, a creditor who had obtained a judgment could force the seizure and sale of a debtor's assets for the benefit of all creditors. Such a proceeding would also cause the loss of the debtor's civil rights. To alleviate such a harsh result, the Roman law allowed the debtor to petition a magistrate for the voluntary surrender of the debtor's assets. By choosing this course, the debtor's civil rights were preserved.

The Middle Ages saw the bankruptcy laws change and

evolve. Debtors who sought to conceal or abscond with assets were targeted for especially severe penalties. As national laws developed, debtors who could not pay remained at risk to lose all assets and, in some cases, to suffer criminal penalties and the loss of civil rights. Some countries only allowed merchants to go bankrupt, while ordinary debtors could never find relief from their debts. In addition, the social view of bankrupts was extremely negative. The debtor who slipped into bankruptcy was often subjected to professional and social sanctions, including, in some cases, the requirement to wear clothing indicating this degraded status.

Social attitudes have changed, but we live in a world where debt is as ever-present as money. And as with money, the constant experience of debt dulls us to an exploration of its deeper nature. Of course, on a superficial level, we know that debt is usually created by our borrowing money or other valuables from someone else and promising to repay what we have received. The mortgage on a house, the installment loan on a car, the monthly balances owed on our credit cards, and the loan from a friend to tide us over until the next pay day are all forms of debt.

THE UNDERWORLD POWER OF DEBT

This mundane debt, so easily understood, conceals the historical power of debt to deprive us of our freedom. Even today, we need only read the newspapers to find examples of how debt is used as a tool of enslavement. In Brazil, for example, laborers on remote farms are paid wages in scrip that can only be used to purchase food and

supplies at the company store. Since the scrip is not sufficient to meet the needs of the laborers, they fall deeper
and deeper into debt and, in effect, become slaves. In
Europe, women from the East are promised work in
shops or restaurants in the West, only to find that they are
brought to brothels and forced into prostitution to repay
"debts" for agency fees, transportation costs, meals, and
rent. This illicit trade can also be found in the United
States. In one case, a young woman from China was co-
erced into prostitution to repay the $30,000 debt incurred
for her passage to New York City. In the conservative
town where she had grown up, she had never held hands
with a boy. Abhorrent as these stories are, they illustrate
the power of debt to be destructive of human liberty and
dignity.

The liberal bankruptcy laws that the United States
adopted in 1898 (and amended a number of times) actually serve to conceal the destructive power of debt and the
more ancient and punitive attitudes felt toward debtors.
Today, in the United States, individuals and business own-
ers are free to go bankrupt and find relief from debt without fear of prison or servitude. The startling rise in total
filings for bankruptcies, from less than 30,000 in 1910 to
360,000 in 1981 to nearly 1,000,000 in 1992, is in part a reflection of changed social attitudes toward the failure to
repay debt.

While debtors' prisons can hardly be defended, they did
serve a symbolic purpose, which has largely been lost
today. They advised us that debt must be repaid; if it cannot be repaid in money, it will be repaid by the deprivation
of freedom. To take our freedom is to take life itself. If
debt can take life, then debt is clearly an aspect of the underworld, the invisible world where wealth accumulates
and the dead reside.

While the reform of our laws relating to bankruptcy has certainly had benefits, it has not contended with the underworld aspect of debt. The impulse for social reform—the obvious wrongness of keeping someone in prison for debt, especially when being in prison defeats any possibility of paying the debt—does not deal with the place debt occupies in the human mind. If such an issue remains invisible, then changing its manifestation in our world (to one million bankrupts in a single year rather than a single soul in debtors' prison) simply allows new forms of suffering.

Anyone who has overspent and been pursued by bill collectors knows the terrible stress and anxiety of being unable to pay debts. Charles Dickens, in his autobiography, recalled the warnings given him by his father in debtors' prison: "My father was waiting for me . . . and [we] cried very much. And he told me, I remember, to take warning by the Marshalsea, and to observe that if a man had twenty pounds a year and spent nineteen pounds nineteen shillings and sixpence, he would be happy; but that a shilling spent the other way would make him wretched." This view of debt recognizes that freedom, beauty, and the vitality of life itself can be lost through dependence on debt.

Debt's ancient origin is reflected in biblical admonitions about debt, and the interest payments which often accompany debt. So Solomon warns, "The rich rules over the poor, and the borrower is the slave of the lender."

In Exodus, when God specifies the ordinances for the Jewish people, he includes the admonition that "If you lend money to any of my people with you who is poor, you shall not be to him as a creditor, and you shall not exact interest from him." This passage shows that debt should not be used to oppress poor people. If a poor person gives a garment to secure a loan, the garment should be returned before nightfall so the poor person does not suffer. Nor should a person's means of earning a living be taken as a pledge, because that would deprive the debtor of both livelihood and a way to earn enough to repay the loan.

Solomon is especially vehement about not becoming a surety or giving a pledge for someone else. This is an arrangement in which one person guarantees the payment of another person's debt, usually as an inducement to the creditor to make the loan in the first place. The words of warning are forceful and urgent: "My son, if you have become surety for your neighbor, have given your pledge for a stranger; If you are snared in the utterance of your lips, caught in the words of your mouth; then do this, my son, and save yourself, for you have come into your neighbor's power: go, hasten, and importune your neighbor. Give your eyes no sleep and your eyelids no slumber; save yourself like a gazelle from the hunter, like a bird from the hand of the fowler." The reason for this urgency will become clear later in the chapter, when we discuss the considerations that make debt either wise or foolhardy.

Debt existed before written history. As with language and money, we rarely wonder about the birth of debt and how debt came to be so much an aspect of our society. As individuals we suffer from debt, but we seldom study debt to understand its deepest implications. If we fail to take debt as a subject worthy of inquiry, then debt will remain invisible to us. Of course, we will know the principal and interest payments that we must make to maintain our standing as good debtors, but we will not understand our deeper impulses and reasons for entering into and remaining in debt.

HOW DEBT CAME TO ASHANTI

A folk tale may help us gain insight into the way in which debt first became part of the human community and what that debt means to us. "How Debt Came to Ashanti" is a tale about how debt came to the kingdom of Ashanti, now a region of Ghana in West Africa. This story features Anansi, the spider, who is the trickster hero of the Ashanti and Akan people. He is constantly seeking to outwit animals, men, and even the gods. Sometimes he is wise, but more often he is unscrupulous, greedy, and selfish. As a culture hero, he is like Prometheus who brought fire to humankind. By outwitting the hornets, the python, and the leopard, Anansi became the owner of all stories that are told. His escapades sometimes lead to the creation of customs, institutions, and practices—such as debt.

However, Anansi is not the first one to bring debt to the Ashanti. In "How Debt Came to Ashanti," a hunter named Soko flees from his own village because he owes a debt that he does not want to pay. When he arrives in the lands of the Ashanti, the people are worried because they have never known debt. They send their old men to Soko to tell him that he must rid himself of the debt if he wishes to live among them.

Soko cannot imagine how to do this, but Anansi has heard about Soko and his debt. Anansi comes to Soko and finds him making palm wine. Anansi wants the wine and tells Soko that getting rid of the debt is easy. All that Soko has to do is say, "Whoever drinks my palm wine will take the debt."

Soko says this and Anansi offers to drink the wine. By drinking the wine, Anansi drinks the debt as well. After

Anansi has drunk the wine, he plants his field and says that whoever eats the grain will take the debt.

A bird eats the grain and takes the debt. When the bird lays eggs, she says that whoever breaks her eggs will take the debt. A falling branch breaks the eggs and causes the tree to have the debt. The tree then says that whoever eats its blossoms will own the debt. A monkey eats the blossoms and takes the debt, and the monkey says that whoever eats him will in turn own the debt. When the monkey is devoured by a lion, the lion also says that whoever eats him will take the debt.

One day Soko is hunting and kills the lion. He returns to the village and shares the meat with all of the people. Because all the people eat, everyone owns the debt. This is the story of how the hunter, Soko, and the trickster hero, Anansi, brought debt to the kingdom of Ashanti.

THE DEBT WE OWE FOR LIFE

Soko is an interesting figure. He comes alone, an outsider, carrying a burden that appears to be uniquely his. The people that he comes to fear contamination from him. He must rid himself of the taint that he carries. But the story does not tell us what debt Soko owed or why he sought to evade it. Yet the debt is clearly not what we ordinarily think of as debt. If it were, Soko could simply change his mind and pay it. However, the unfolding of the tale reveals that this debt cannot be repaid.

In an apparent turn of good fortune, Soko is told by Anansi the way in which he can rid himself of debt. He need only say that whoever drinks his wine will inherit the debt. Anansi, being a spider, is a spinner, a weaver of human fate. While Anansi appears to offer a solution, what he really does is free this new force, this debt, to begin its circulation.

The debt quickly travels through all aspects of the world. Its first transfer is connected with palm wine, which may suggest that debt has its own intoxicating force. Having arrived with a hunter, the debt passes with grain and so is part of agriculture. It enters the realm of the animals when the bird eats the grain, and penetrates the nonagricultural realm of vegetation, the wild, when the bough breaks the egg. Soon it travels through the animal kingdom from monkey to lion and returns at last to humankind.

When the debt returns in the form of the lion's flesh that is devoured by all the villagers, we see that Soko could not permanently rid himself of the debt. The debt is far too powerful for that. The debt, in fact, is shared at a communal feast, which seems much like the love feasts that we discussed in chapter two. This communal feast would usually involve thanksgiving to the gods for the nourishment of the food. And the communal feast is part of the cycle of death and rebirth, whether the death of the animals whose bones are enfleshed again in the spirit world or the annual death of the vegetative world from which renewal comes with the new harvest.

If we understand the tale correctly, everything that is received from nature comes with debt. This debt is an aspect of the natural cycle of life and death. In the largest sense, the debt that we owe to nature is the debt for life itself. When we think, however fleetingly, of the miracle that we have life, we can experience a sense of gratitude for that very fact. But we are accustomed to this most profound debt and our daily lives leave little time for such contemplation, so for the most part we live unaware that such a debt exists.

If we owe a debt to nature for life, it can be repaid only by death, as we have seen in the many rituals in which sacrificial death is meant to fecundate new life. So we may wish to deny that we receive gifts from nature, and that we are indebted for these gifts. In fact, we might prefer to blame someone or something for this indebtedness. "How Debt Came to Ashanti" presents Soko as an outsider, a stranger, a defiler of the purity of the Ashanti. But Soko sounds like a scapegoat, a man singled out to carry the accumulated sins of a tribe into the wilderness. The tale claims that he came from another place, but what place?

If we have a powerful desire to avoid knowledge, nonetheless some inner force may make us seek for truth—even the truth that we might prefer to avoid. This seeking while desiring to avoid truth is an aspect of the collective mind as well. For the individual or the group, the truth that we feel most shameful about ourselves is the very one we often project on others. In Jungian psychology, this hidden truth, the truth that we do not know about ourselves, is called the shadow.

Soko appears to be the one chosen to carry the shadow of the village. He is called a stranger, but the power of debt resides in nature itself. Debt is not brought by Soko, but rather has been with the Ashanti from their first taking of nourishment and life from the world. Anansi, the trickster, is simply bringing to everyone's awareness what has always been true. Each time something is drunk or eaten or given, debt passes with it. Often this takes the life of the plant or animal consumed, but from this consumption life regenerates.

TIME AS MONEY (OR DEBT)

If we owe a debt for life, then we may be able to understand why the penalty for failure to pay debt was the deprivation of liberty. This imprisonment is a form of taking life, of taking the time of which a life is composed. We know the saying "Time is money," which means that time can be measured in terms of the amount of money that could be earned in a given period of time. Debt too can be measured in money. In fact, money is curiously like debt. Each of us offers something of ourselves for sale, our time and energy or some product that we create with that time and energy. It is almost as if we are indebted to those who have money, because money is a means of calling forth what we offer of value to the community. Through the measuring scale of money, time can equal debt.

Of course, the system of imprisonment for debt did not offer uniform justice. A person did not spend a month in jail for owing one dollar, two months in jail for owing two dollars, and so on. Many people made compacts with their creditors and never went to jail at all. Others fled or hid their assets. And of those who went to jail, some spent the rest of their lives imprisoned for a small debt, while others had friends or relatives who quickly paid their way to liberty.

No doubt the conscious rationale for debtors' prisons was the desire to punish harshly and thus prevent defaults. But if the unconscious rationale was that we are indebted for our very lives and, therefore, our time may be taken to repay debt, then we are really discussing two very different kinds of debt. One debt is existential—the debt we owe for our existence and the nourishment we are given by nature. This debt, if ever repaid, is repaid by our death. The other debts are the daily debts, usually measured by money.

We must distinguish between these debts. It is true that we can buy dinner with a credit card or, as John Dickens did in the 1820s, have an account with a local baker for the purchase of bread and pastries. However, the debt that we owe to the credit card company or the local merchant is obviously quite different from the debt that we owe to nature for our life and sustenance.

Looked at in this larger view, we see that the Bible in the book of Genesis suggests a debt very similar to that incurred by the Ashanti. On the sixth day God created humanity in the image of God, and gave to humanity dominion over the animals and the plants so that humanity might be nourished and multiply. God shaped "man of dust from the ground, and breathed into his nostrils the breath of life; and man became a living being." So we owe not only our life and the nourishment that we gain from plants and animals to God. We also owe God for our very image, that sense of selfhood that allows us to seek what is divine and attempt to live in harmony with it.

God placed humans in the Garden of Eden and sought to let them live unaware of their debt by forbidding them to eat of the tree of the knowledge of good and evil. But the serpent, a king of the underworld, the world of the unconscious, tempted the humans. The serpent said that eating of the tree of knowledge would make them like God. They would know good and evil as God did, but they would not die as God had said. So the serpent, like Anansi the trickster, brought to awareness an aspect of the human condition that had previously not been understood. Adam and Eve did not die physically after they ate the fruit, but they did die to what they had been before ingesting this knowledge. For the first time humans felt fear and anxiety over death. As God said to Adam, "You are dust, and to dust you shall return." Yet eating the forbidden fruit also allowed an awareness of the moral nature of humanity and the debt to the creator whose image we share.

RAPUNZEL

There is another story of eating forbidden fruit. Once upon a time a man and his wife yearned for many years to have a child. From their back window this couple could see over a high wall to a beautiful garden filled with flowers and vegetables. A fearsome witch owned this garden, but the wife conceived a desire for the beautiful rapunzel (a type of lettuce) that she could see growing there. As her craving grew, she began to pine away, for she knew that she could never eat what she desired.

When her husband asked what ailed her, his wife said that she would die unless she could eat the rapunzel. The husband thought to save his wife whatever the cost. So one night he stole into the garden and brought home some rapunzel. But as soon as his wife devoured this, her craving grew even greater.

Finally the husband returned to the garden for more of the rapunzel, but the witch loomed up before him and said she would punish him harshly for his theft. The man pleaded for mercy, explaining that he stole to satisfy his wife's craving.

This quieted the witch's anger. She offered the man as

much rapunzel as his wife desired, but on one condition: that the couple would give to the witch the child that would be born to them. The terrified man agreed.

Needless to say, his wife became pregnant. When she delivered their longed-for baby, the witch appeared to claim what was hers. Naming the girl Rapunzel, the witch carried her away. When Rapunzel was twelve and the most lovely girl alive, the witch locked her in a tower in the middle of a forest. The tower had no door and no stairs, but when the witch called from below Rapunzel would let her golden tresses of hair fall down from the window of her room atop the high tower. The witch would then climb up on this golden hair.

Several years passed. Rapunzel would often sing to ease her loneliness. One day a prince, passing near the tower, heard this beautiful singing and saw the witch climb up on the golden tresses to the tower. When the witch had gone, the prince called for Rapunzel to let down her hair, and he climbed to the tower. After overcoming her fright at her first view of a man, Rapunzel felt the prince would love her far better than the witch and agreed to marry him and travel away with him. She took his hand to seal their marriage, and soon became pregnant.

Unfortunately, before she could flee, Rapunzel naively asked the witch why she was heavier to pull up than the prince. The enraged witch cut off Rapunzel's hair and banished her to lonely misery in a far-off desert.

When the prince came to the tower, the witch let down Rapunzel's hair and pulled up the youth. Hearing the witch tell him that he would never see Rapunzel again, his grief overwhelmed him and he jumped from the tower. While the prince didn't die from his fall, his eyes were pierced by the thorns of brambles. Blinded and grieving for his lost wife, he lived in abject poverty and wandered in the forest.

One day, after several years of wandering, the prince heard a voice that he knew. He had come at last to where lonely Rapunzel lived with their infants, a boy and a girl. Recognizing and embracing him, Rapunzel wept, and her tears healed his eyes. When they reached the prince's kingdom, Rapunzel was received with joy, and they lived for many years with great happiness.

THE DEBTORS' PRISON AS A PLACE FOR GROWING AWARENESS

"Rapunzel," which comes from *Grimms' Fairy Tales*, reflects again how the child must often pay the price for the debts of the parent or the family tree. In the tale, the mother will die if she does not eat of the vegetative world which is symbolized by the rapunzel. By eating the rapunzel she seems to fill her stomach with a baby, whose origin in the vegetative world is confirmed when the witch names the baby Rapunzel. The mother owes a debt for the rapunzel, the lettuce which has not only saved her life but has also given her the life of a child. She must pay with Rapunzel; she must pay with her baby's life for the gift of fertility.

This would be bad enough. But this witch, who in her power to give and withhold vegetative wealth and life reminds us of Demeter, Cybele, and Chicomecohuatl, imprisons the girl in a tower that has no entry. This tower is the debtors' prison; here the daughter sacrifices her life for the debt of her mother. Yet the tower also suggests the ascent of the spirit, the upward rising of the material world toward that which is divine. In this tower, Rapunzel is imprisoned until, like Persephone, she comes in contact with the aspect of herself (symbolized by the prince) that is able to force a separation from the aspect of the mother (symbolized by the witch) that would never free the daughter to live her own life.

The tower's self-containment suggests that Rapunzel is undergoing a process of deepening her knowledge of her own feelings. Only her golden hair allows her contact with the outside world. Like the golden bough that Aeneas found in the green forest, this golden hair shows the wealth that is part of Rapunzel and awaits her discovery. While the journey to self-knowledge is painful, dry, and lonely, ultimately it is healing as well.

"Rapunzel" suggests that the debtors' prison may be a place for the painful evolution of self-knowledge. If we thought more often of this debt we owe for life, then we might have a better understanding of the daily issues of debt that we often face. We might examine whether being in debt on an existential level in any way predisposes us to enter into money debts as well. If we find ourselves locked in the debtors' tower, we might contemplate the value of this image of imprisonment. When we suffer from anxiety over money debts and the fear of bankruptcy, we lose the precious moments of our life as surely as if we are imprisoned. How can we use the upward thrust of this tower, its reaching toward spiritual heights, to understand which debts are truly ours? If we can confront ourselves, debt may be a challenge that offers us a deeper insight into our own nature.

A striking feature of "Rapunzel" is that the daughter pays for her mother's debt. This is reminiscent of our discussion of inheritance. It is almost as if the daughter has inherited a debt from the mother. In terms of inheritance laws, of course, if an estate has only debts and no assets, then the heirs receive nothing. They are not obligated to pay the debts; rather the creditors of the person who died lose whatever they were owed. As Shakespeare wrote in *The Tempest*, "He that dies pays all debts." However, Rapunzel paid dearly for the rapunzel that gave life to her and her mother.

HOW DEBT RESEMBLES INHERITANCE

There is an uncanny resemblance between debt and inheritance. For example, money received by borrowing feels much like money received by inheritance. We receive something for which we do not work; our present resources are increased and we are better off. Of course an inheritance does not have to be repaid, while debt does. But repayment is a future consideration; in the moment of receiving the money we are like heirs, richer than we were before.

William Thackeray, the contemporary of Charles Dickens, made the following observation about debt in *Vanity Fair:* "Everybody in Vanity Fair must have remarked how well those live who are comfortably and thoroughly in debt; how they deny themselves nothing; how jolly and easy they are in their minds." While Thackeray is satiric, he certainly captures the sense in which debtors may imagine themselves to be heirs—at least, until the time when the debt must be paid.

Even the story of John Dickens languishing in debtors'

prison shows the peculiar similarity between debt and inheritance. Dickens had been imprisoned in Marshalsea for a little over two months when his mother died at the age of seventy-nine. In her will she gave her son 450 pounds, more than enough to pay off all of Dickens's debts and let him and his family begin a new life. On May 28, John Dickens walked out of Marshalsea a free man, an heir and not a debtor. While John Dickens never returned to debtors' prison, his son Charles carried the burden of that experience for the rest of his life: "My whole nature was so penetrated with the grief and humiliation of such considerations, that even now, famous and caressed and happy, I often forget in my dreams that I have a dear wife and children; even that I am a man; and wander desolately back to that time of my life."

THE BRIDGE OF CH'ÜAN-CHOU

A folk tale from China, "The Bridge of Ch'üan-chou," may help us understand this curious connection between debt and inheritance. Many stories are told about this bridge, which was first built in the reign of Emperor Shen-tsung (998–1022). Before the building of the bridge, the cruel spirits that lived in the Loyang River tormented the people who crossed the river by boat. The building of the bridge required many miracles and the help of supernatural workers.

Our story is not about the building of the bridge, but about its rebuilding more than seven hundred years later. In the reign of Emperor Ch'ien-lung (1736–96), there lived a free-spending youth, Li Wu, who was the fifth son and whose name meant fifth. Although the young man spent freely, he did not work hard and so he was often in debt. All the shopkeepers feared to sell him anything, except for the butcher, who was always willing to take a note from Li Wu. This butcher actually told Li Wu to buy as much as he wanted and never pressured Li Wu to pay the many notes that he had given for his debts.

At last even Li Wu became curious about the butcher's behavior. After paying for a purchase of meat, he hid outside the shop and then followed the butcher to a hilltop shrine dedicated to the earth deity. Moving aside some grass, the butcher put Li Wu's note into a grave and brought out of the grave a piece of silver. When Li Wu looked in the grave, he saw many pots of silver, one of which was only half full but also contained all of the notes that the butcher had accepted from Li Wu.

Suddenly the earth spirit spoke, saying that all of this silver belonged to Li Wu. The spirit had guarded these riches, but now could surrender its post because the owner of the silver had come. So the butcher's generous offering of credit to Li Wu had been based on the butcher's knowledge of how to convert the notes into the silver of this secret treasure.

Li Wu was now a rich man, and soon he had a strange visitor named K'ang Chin-lung, who claimed the ability to find buried wealth. K'ang came to evaluate the character of Li Wu who, having himself changed to a better man, treated K'ang excellently. He even gave his guest golden bowls in which to bathe his face each day and, when K'ang threw these bowls into the lotus pond, Li Wu made no complaint. After several months, K'ang left without any farewell.

The next chapter of Li Wu's life was not so pleasant. He

had once insulted a man, who now falsely accused him of being a bandit. How else could Li Wu have obtained such wealth? All of his riches were confiscated and he was taken to the court of the emperor to be put on trial for his life. In chains, he crossed the bridge over the Loyang River. Seeing that the high tides caused the water to come over the bridge, he swore to raise the bridge three feet if his life were spared.

As the guards and Li Wu neared the emperor's court, Li Wu saw vast expanses of fields with his name as the owner. Inquiries brought word that K'ang had purchased these fields for Li Wu. At the court, K'ang made a golden shell within which he placed a living snail. Li Wu gave this miraculous gift to the empress, who persuaded the emperor to let Li Wu go free. Then Li Wu took the golden bowls that K'ang had thrown into the lotus pond, and managed the fields that K'ang had bought for him, and became so rich that he kept his vow to add three feet in height to the bridge over the Loyang River.

THE DEBTOR'S JOURNEY TO UNDERSTANDING

This tale directly connects the debtor to the heir. Li Wu thinks that he is a debtor, a view shared by everyone except the butcher. However, Li Wu is, in fact, an heir, not a debtor. A spirit guards his inheritance, the silver that comes to him from the grave. Like Mercurius, the spirit has waited a long while to give this treasure to its owner and, once its task is done, the spirit is at last free to abandon its post.

Whose spirit is this? Why does it guard an inheritance that belongs to Li Wu? This spirit may be an aspect of Li Wu that he has not yet discovered. In a sense, this spirit holds Li Wu's future. Curiosity, the same curiosity that took the woodcutter's son deeper into the forest, makes Li Wu follow the butcher up to the hilltop shrine. On this high and sacred place, Li Wu encounters what is truly his, his silver treasure.

This tale suggests how our existential debt and our daily debts meet one another. The silver from the grave is something that Li Wu owns but is unaware of. This treasure is guarded by the earth deity, which is the source of life itself. Not just the silver, but everything—life and nourishment—springs from the earth.

But every debt that we incur also gives us an asset. Our existential debt, not being measured by money, may leave us in doubt as to the extent and nature of the asset we have received. In the last chapter we discussed the underworld descent that the heir must make to learn the deeper meaning of his or her inheritance. Debt, too, requires a journey to learn the nature of the assets we have received, assets that may require a lifetime of self-exploration to discover their true worth.

For each of us this process of discovery is unique. Some may discover that money debt is not for them; perhaps their inner richness will not yield large sums of money to repay debt. Others will see that debt is appropriate for them, because the richness of their nature will bring the money that will repay borrowing. Li Wu had the earth spirit and, later, K'ang to protect the wealth of which Li Wu was unaware. In the case of Li Wu, the wealth of his nature was such that it yielded a wealth of money and valuables in the world.

It is easy to see the negative aspects of debt, the oppressive and strangling effect that debt can have on life, but debt is not one-sided. Like inheritance, debt yields us an asset. With existential debt, the asset is our very life. With daily debt, the asset is the increased energy that money allows us in the world. The tale of Li Wu may even be read to suggest that we will be able to pay our daily debts of money if we gain a sufficient understanding of our own nature. Or, if we have this understanding, we will not incur money debts that conflict with our actual capacities to earn money in the world.

Contrasting debt and inheritance may help us understand this process. The reason that we do not have to pay for an inheritance is because it comes from the past. It is given to us by the generation (or generations) that have come before us. Where, then, does money debt come from? Let us imagine that it comes not from a bank or lender but from the future. When we take a debt, we are making a statement about our capacity to earn money in the future. We are saying what we will become. In a way, we are speculating about the unfolding of our own nature. The debt of Li Wu reflected the potential that he would discover, a potential known to the earth spirit and the butcher long before Li Wu discovered his silver from the grave.

This is why no simple rule can govern whether we should enter into debt. If we understand our capacities to be productive, taking on a debt may be a way to increase what we are able to produce far beyond what would have been possible without the debt. Debt allows us to take the frozen wealth of the underworld and make it circulate in the green, sunlit world where we live our lives.

The danger is that we may fail to understand ourselves

and our situation. We may borrow against our future time and energy and find that, in fact, we did not increase our productivity and face bankruptcy. As an heir must be self-examining to make a wise use of inherited money, so we can use the possibility of indebtedness as part of the process by which we seek who we truly are. But when considering debt, we should keep before us the image of the tower without entry, the image of the debtors' prison. Debt places our very freedom at risk; Anansi brought it to humankind like Prometheus brought fire. It can be both beneficial and terribly destructive. It must be handled like fire, like the elemental force that it is.

We can return now to Solomon's warnings with a far better understanding of his concerns. Solomon warns against becoming a surety for a neighbor or giving a pledge for a stranger. Both situations make one person a guarantor for the debt of another person. The problem with this is exactly as Solomon describes it: ". . . you have come into your neighbor's power." The burden of debt is onerous enough if we carry it for ourselves, but at least we may incur such a debt because we believe that our inner nature will unfold in a way that brings money sufficient to pay this debt. But if we become the guarantor for the debt of another, we are speculating about their inner wealth and the future form of its unfoldment in the world. To risk our freedom for this hardly seems wise. If we wish to help someone else, it might be far better to give a gift that we know we can afford than to guarantee debt that we hope we will never have to pay.

The confluence of existential debt and money debt suggests why the amassing of vast fortunes reflects a hidden wish for immortality. We spoke earlier of The Fountain of Youth which, in the minds of the Conquistadors, poured forth its waters in the land of limitless gold (El Dorado). Yet human life is the encountering of limits. We do not possess limitless wealth, limitless strength, limitless life. Even the Pharaohs died, despite having the power to force slaves and followers to die with them in order to serve as company for the death journey. One of the richest of the Romans, Crassus, saw his son's severed head flourished on a spike by the Parthian cavalry and soon thereafter lost his life and his head as well. Every day in the obituaries we read of people whose vast wealth could not insulate them from the existential debt that we must pay with our lives.

Viewed from this perspective, we see another facet of inheritance. The heir views inheritance as the receiving of an asset, but the person who dies gives up all assets. Whether these assets are great or small, the surrender of them—with life—pays all debts in full. The ineffable yearning for immortality vanishes with the wealth that failed to make us superhuman. So death alone brings an egalitarian redistribution by taking all from rich and poor alike. But what if we could avoid this debt to life? What if we could live forever?

ALCESTIS

This is the subject of the play *Alcestis* by Euripides. The god Apollo had a dispute with his father, Zeus. Because he angered his father, Zeus ordered him to serve a mortal—King Admetus of Pherae in Thessaly. Surprisingly enough, Apollo found that he loved Admetus for being a just and immensely hospitable man. Wanting to give a boon to his host, he persuaded the Fates to allow Admetus in his hour of dying to send someone in his place to the underworld. If someone would volunteer to die in Admetus's place, then he could go on living. He would not have to pay a debt for his life but could actually live the fantastic dream of being immortal.

Unfortunately for Admetus, no one is eager to die in his place, not even his old father. The only one willing to die for him is his young wife, Alcestis, whom he loves deeply. While a modern feminist would hardly approve of Alcestis sacrificing herself for her husband, Alcestis acts from love and for the honor of wifehood. In any case, once Alcestis has pledged herself before the gods, no one, not even Admetus, can save her. Yet as time passes, Admetus finds that he loves her more and more; he cannot imagine living without her. The thought of her death brings daily grief to him, but he cannot change her fate.

This is all background to the play, which begins on the actual day that Alcestis is to die. The play opens with Apollo confronting Death (who appears as a character) and pleading for the life of Alcestis, but Death refuses to let her live. Soon we see Alcestis in her death scene telling her husband how she ". . . would not live on, torn away from thee." She says that she can never be fully paid back for giving up her life, "For naught there is more precious than life," but asks that Admetus not remarry so their children will be saved from the hatred of a stepmother. Grief-stricken, Admetus assures her that he will never remarry, ". . . dead, mine only wife/Shalt thou be called . . ." When Alcestis has died, the Chorus sings to Admetus, "From us, from all, this debt is due—to die."

In the midst of Admetus's grief, a traveler comes to his door. This traveler is none other than the hero Herakles (called Hercules by the Romans), who is renowned for his prodigious feats of strength and daring. Mothered by a mortal woman but fathered by Zeus, the king of the gods, Herakles is half-man and half-god. His own father, Zeus, has decreed that hospitality must always be shown to travelers. This hospitality is to the larger world what the love feast was to the tribe in its village. As people travel for trade and pilgrimage, they more and more frequently encounter strangers. How are these strangers to be treated? Zeus's edict to offer hospitality is a command to share both shelter and food. In this god-sanctified sharing resides the same love and thanksgiving for nature's bounty that animates the sharing of food in the love feast.

Admetus is abundantly hospitable. Despite his grief for Alcestis, Admetus lies and says the mourning is merely for a servant so that Herakles will stay in his home. A servant tells Herakles the truth about who has died. Herakles vows to "save the woman newly dead" and repay his host, who was so hospitable even in bereavement. While Herakles goes to save Alcestis, Admetus continues his inconsolable grieving. Then Herakles returns, leading a woman who is silent and wholly hidden in veils. When she is at last revealed, the woman is Alcestis. Herakles tells how he ambushed Death and tore Alcestis from Death's arms. So Admetus and Alcestis are reunited.

LIMITLESS, LIKE A GOD

Admetus is a fascinating man because he has little sense of limitation. He is both unreasonably demanding and unreasonably generous. The expectation that anyone should die in his place, including his father, is shocking. Why should his father give up his life so Admetus can live longer? Admetus is no god to whom the living are sacrificed. Whatever his relationship with Apollo (in some versions of the myth they are lovers), the gift from the god makes Admetus forget his own nature. He loses touch with his human life, with his understanding of the needs of others. And, as with so many magical wishes, the reality of immortality includes a striking disadvantage: to outlive all those we love.

On the positive side of the ledger, Admetus is the most generous of hosts. Here, too, he lacks a sense of limitation. It does not matter if he is mourning for his wife; he is willing to lie in order to make certain that Herakles will receive the hospitality decreed by Zeus. Certainly Admetus recognizes the debt implied in the love feast, that nature's bounty belongs to all of us and must be shared. This generosity gained him Apollo's boon in the first place and, at the play's end, moves Herakles to restore Alcestis to him.

In Admetus we see the warring impulses aroused by our existential debt. On the one hand, we want to deny the debt. We do not want to die. We long to be what physically we cannot be—immortal. From this perspective, immortality is a condition of debtlessness. This refusal to accept limits leads to selfishness, whether revealed in the belief that a father should die in place of a son or in the hoarding of wealth as if its energy might ward off death.

On the other hand, an awareness of our existential debt may lead us to be self-sacrificing, to be selfless. In the Bible, Paul shows his understanding of this when he writes, "Owe no one anything, except to love one another." If we feel the debt that we owe for life, we are im-

mediately brought closer to all humanity. We are all debtors—both those who give and those who receive. In an
economy based on money, we may wish to honor the
spirit of the love feast by making our money circulate in a
way that will alleviate suffering and work toward human
betterment.

If the world of Admetus seems remote, fictional, or ar-
chaic to us, we can easily find contemporary parallels. For
example, the enormous debt of the federal government is
shifting wealth between generations. Projections suggest
that future taxpayers will pay a far higher proportion of
their earnings in taxes than today's taxpayers, who benefit
from the increased debt because their taxes are lower. If
this is true, the generation that incurs the debt is taking
the life energy of subsequent generations, just as Admetus
was willing to take the life energy of his young wife. Another example would be the rationing of life-saving drugs
and operations that any reform of the health care system
is likely to require. Since the wealthy will be able to go
outside such a system and buy whatever medical services
they need, like Admetus they will gain greater life expec-
tancies compared to those who must accept the limitations of rationing. In fact, there is actually an illicit trade
in body organs, such as kidneys, which are sold by people
in poorer countries for transplant to people in richer
countries who seek longer life. On the other hand, there
are also altruistic people who donate body organs because they desire to help others. In this, they are certainly
like Alcestis. Such acts of altruism are closely scrutinized
by medical centers to be certain that coercion, however
subtle, has not influenced the decision to give the organ.

To see how Admetus lives in each of us, can we think of
a real person so hospitable that no guest would ever be

turned away from his or her door? Someone who would give even if impoverished by doing so? Or, in contrast, someone who yearns to have more and more life, even if it means taking from others? And what would the taking of "life" from others mean? How could this be done? If we found someone like Admetus, vastly willing both to be hospitable and to take the life energy of others, we might find a mirror that would allow us to see ourselves ever more clearly.

DEBT TORMENTS EVEN THE GREAT

When we think of those whose accomplishments are great, we seldom think of debt. Yet, while John Dickens languished in debtors' prison, a revered American found his old age blighted by worry over debt. The man who proposed adopting the dollar and decimal system for American currency—inventor, architect, farmer, author of the Declaration of Independence, and president of the United States—Thomas Jefferson's abilities and accomplishments enriched his country and left a legacy to humanity.

Despite this legacy, Jefferson suffered great anxieties because of his money debts. While he appeared to be wealthy from several inheritances of land and slaves, in fact these inheritances included much that was mortgaged. These debts only worsened as his public career took him to France and, later, to Washington. In 1787, at the age of forty-four, Jefferson wrote from Paris to confide in a friend that "the torment of mind I endure till the moment shall arrive when I shall owe not a shilling on earth is such really as to render life of little value." But that debt-free moment never arrived; in fact, Jefferson's old age was filled with worry over debt.

Notwithstanding his debts, Jefferson showed unusual generosity throughout his life. In the public sphere he gave unstintingly of his time and energy even while he felt the allure of a more private life. "The whole of my life has been a war with my natural taste, feelings and wishes; domestic life and literary pursuits were my first and my latest inclinations. . . . The circumstances of our country, at my entrance into life, were such that every honest man felt himself compelled to take part, and to act to the best of his abilities."

In his private life he honored the rituals of hospitality. Not only invited guests and friends, of which there were many, but strangers, too, could rely on being fed and sheltered at Monticello. When his daughter Martha complained that the constant company left Jefferson no time to be sociable with her, he replied, "The manner and usages of our country are laws we cannot repeal." So he lived by laws much like those decreed thousands of years earlier by Zeus.

Jefferson kept meticulous account of his day-to-day spending, yet seemed unwilling to keep closely in mind his overall position. After serving two terms as president, he discovered on leaving office in 1809 that he owed $10,000 more than he had thought. This is a significant sum today, but a huge amount at that time. In 1814, Jefferson told his grandson that "if he [Jefferson] lived long enough he would beggar his family, that the number of persons he was compelled to entertain would devour his estate." Yet he did not change his course, bound as he was by the laws of hospitality and his own pleasure in company. Even as Jefferson entertained, Monticello fell into disrepair. To take a small example, visitors sat on handsome chairs with leather bottoms, but the bottoms had worn through so that the hair stuffing the seats stuck out in all directions.

Jefferson's finances suffered from fluctuations in the agriculture markets and tight money which made his lands difficult to sell at a good price, but he also acted more from friendship than prudence. In 1818, he signed as a personal guarantor for a $20,000 loan that a close friend, William Cary Nicholas, was seeking. In doing this, Jefferson ignored Solomon's warning not to become the guarantor of the debt of another. Jefferson delivered himself into his "neighbor's power." Nicholas, who was thought to have a net worth of $300,000, declared bankruptcy in 1819.

Jefferson called this the "coup de grâce," for now he could never hope to be free of debt. As he approached and passed the age of eighty (in 1823), he worried that he and his daughter and grandchildren might be turned out of Monticello and have no means of support. "For myself," Jefferson wrote to his grandson, "I should not regard a prostration of fortune, but I am overwhelmed at the prospect of the situation in which I may leave my family." The possibility of the family's impoverishment held up to Jefferson "nothing but future gloom," and, except for his concern for them, he felt he would "not care were life to end with the line I am writing."

The depressed market closed off the avenue of land sales to pay debt. Instead, Jefferson conceived of the idea of a lottery to raise money. Such a lottery, in which the winner would receive land, required the approval of the state legislature. When the lottery bill passed in February, 1826, the news of Jefferson's plight traveled across the nation. In the North and the South, citizens rallied and raised funds to ensure that the patriot who had done so much for his country would not be impoverished at the end of his life. New York City collected $8,500; Baltimore $3,000; Philadelphia $5,000; and the citizenry of other cities contributed as well. So, like the sharing of food in the love feast, Jefferson's generosity was met by the generosity of the citizens whom he had served so many years.

Jefferson's health declined sharply in May of 1826, but he hoped to live until July Fourth, the fiftieth anniversary of the signing of the Declaration of Independence. As he drifted toward death, he believed that the subscriptions from the various cities had solved his struggle with debt and saved Monticello for his daughter and grandchildren. On July 2, he lapsed into a coma, but regained consciousness several times to ask if July Fourth had come. On the evening of July 3, he asked for the last time, "Is it the Fourth?" to which his doctor replied, "It soon will be." With this answer Jefferson slipped again into unconsciousness and died at approximately one o'clock the next day—July 4, 1826.

The very date of Jefferson's death emphasized the legacy of his life—the hospitality of his nature not only as a host at Monticello but as a man who gave so much of himself in service to the nation for which he had drafted the Declaration of Independence. Yet Jefferson also took what was not his. His deathbed belief that the subscriptions of money would pay his debts proved to be in error. In fact, his debts at his death amounted to more than $100,000, an enormous sum. His daughter and grandchildren had to give up Monticello, which remained empty several years before finally being sold for $7,500.

The $100,000 owed by Jefferson came from the life energy of others; it belonged to them. Like Admetus's desire for the life energy of his father, Jefferson added to his energies by the sacrifice forced on his creditors. His remarkable life, already benefited by inheritances, gained in vitality from the spending of the money represented by these unpaid debts. The debts dwarfed the value of Monticello and Jefferson's other assets.

There is another way in which Jefferson took life energy that was not his. The rituals of hospitality, a system that Jefferson accepted as law, rested on the foundation of slavery. Slaves in the fields produced the food to feed the guests; slaves in the household saw to the preparation of meals, the housekeeping, and the laundry. Without such unpaid labor, Jefferson would have found it far more expensive and perhaps impracticable to honor the law of hospitality.

Nor was Jefferson unaware of this taking of the lives of his slaves. He had penned the Declaration of Independence, including the famous opening sentence: "We hold these truths to be self-evident, that all men are created equal; that they are endowed by their Creator with certain inalienable rights; that among these, are life, liberty, and the pursuit of happiness." In fact, Jefferson abhorred slavery, yet owned slaves. In his *Notes on Virginia*, published in 1785, he indicted the slave system: "And can the liberties of a nation be thought secure when we have removed their only firm basis, a conviction in the minds of the people that these liberties are the gift of God? . . . Indeed I tremble for my country when I reflect that God is just."

So Jefferson took what he believed to be the gift of God, liberty, from the slaves who served him. To say this is to see how the best and most abundant of us can live with compromise and moral ambiguity. Slavery, which Jefferson believed to be unjust, and debt, which caused Jefferson immense personal anguish, both allowed him to sustain a life greater than he might otherwise have lived. Rather than condemn Jefferson for this, we might better seek to understand how each of us may (like Admetus) demand the life energy of others or (like Alcestis) surrender to others the life energy which is ours.

THE INCALCULABLE DEBT

The image of the debtors' prison forges a symbolic connection between debt and freedom. Today that symbol of the imprisoning power of debt has vanished, so the imprisonment of debt is more elusive and harder to understand. We must exercise our imaginations if we are to comprehend the image of the debtors' tower. We must cross the boundary from our day-to-day world and enter the life of the unconscious, where credit cards buy nothing and existential debt is the gift and burden of our birth. In this way, our relationship to debt, and to money, has the potential to become a creative relationship, an expression of our inner nature formed from the same inspiration that breathes life into poetry and art.

C. G. Jung wrote of the play of fantasy that precedes any creative work. "Without this playing with fantasy no creative work has ever yet come to birth. The debt we owe to the play of imagination is incalculable." This incalculable debt allows us to seek the depths of our own nature. In this play of the imagination is the opportunity to bring to awareness what is unrevealed and hidden in ourselves. Fantasy allows the conscious and unconscious worlds to meet. It allows the prisoner to realize that the imprisoning tower soars upward toward the life of the spirit. It allows each of us to measure our money debts as merely one aspect of the far greater debt that we owe for life. And the exploration of debt, whether owed for money or for life, may reveal assets as unimaginable to us as the silver guarded by the faithful earth spirit was unimaginable to the spendthrift youth named Li Wu.

CHAPTER EIGHT

CHANGING SYMBOLS

Money, Credit Cards, and Banks

ONCE UPON A TIME a merchant carved a wooden statue of Mercury and offered it for sale in the market. But no matter how he touted the beauty of the statue, no one wanted to purchase it. So he changed his tack and started crying out, "A god for sale! A god for sale! One who will bring you good fortune and keep you lucky!" Finally someone asked why, if Mercury brings such good fortune, the merchant does not keep the statue and the good fortune that will go with it. "I'll tell you why," answered the merchant. "It is true that he brings gain, but he takes his time about it; whereas I want money at once."

Titled "The Image-Seller," this story from *Aesop's Fables* implies that the merchant is a charlatan whose puffery about his statue far exceeds the truth. If the statue could really do what the merchant promises, why wouldn't he wait and enjoy good fortune over time? In fact, he imagines good fortune only in terms of money. He does not think of what money symbolizes, such as life energy and the sharing of productivity within the community. Perhaps the merchant would do far better to meditate before his carved statue. As time passed, he might gain a deeper understanding of the creative process by which he created the statue, the value of finding images like Mercury that may connect us to our inner richness, and the role of money as a symbol and tool rather than a goal.

Yet the merchant's attitude is, in many ways, quite contemporary. The desire to have "money at once" is reflected in many aspects of the world in which we live: the heavy burden of consumer debt, governments that run deficits year after year, and bankruptcies of individuals and businesses at levels that would have been unimaginable only a short while ago. We are all aware of the magnitude of the federal government's debt. But when we realize that individual debt (including consumer and mortgage debt) as a percentage of annual disposable income has increased in the United States from about thirty-five percent in 1950 to more than eighty percent today, we may wonder at the effect of such a burden on our day-to-day lives.

To understand why we have become so accustomed to debt, we have to appreciate the ways in which the symbols around us have changed. For example, although the nature of the images on our money have remained much the same throughout the twentieth century, our money has changed profoundly. Our currency is no longer backed by the precious metals of gold and silver but has become simply paper. Beyond this, the symbolism of money now faces a competing symbolism from credit cards, which are such a ubiquitous tool of our consumer-oriented economy. The advertising for credit cards, not to mention the way in which the debt may not have to be repaid immediately, encourage us to believe that the cards are magical and in essence create "money at once." Credit card debt is a significant contributing factor in the unprecedented number of bankruptcies. Finally, the banks themselves have changed both their relationship to the community and the symbolism of their architecture. In 1900, hardly any bank would lend to a consumer, while today bank profits from credit cards are a crucial component of the overall profitability and survival of the banks.

These changing symbols and new relationships are like pieces of a jigsaw puzzle. This chapter seeks to fit together these pieces so that we can have a better understanding of how each of us, and our society, are affected by the desire for "money at once." This is not to say that we face catastrophe, but it is at least an acknowledgement of new realities with respect to money. We cannot use money as a lens to search within ourselves if we do not understand its changing nature in the world outside us.

THE TRANSFORMATION OF MONEY

In an earlier chapter we discussed the extraordinary battle waged by William Jennings Bryan to make silver a monetary metal as well as gold. His Cross of Gold speech made explicit the profound symbolic power of gold. While he triumphed over President Grover Cleveland to win the nomination of the Democratic party, he was soundly beaten by Republican William McKinley in both the 1896 and 1900 presidential elections.

The Republicans inaugurated the new century by enacting the Gold Standard Act of 1900. Key among its provisions was the confirmation of gold as the primary monetary metal and its enshrinement as the standard of value. The Act provided, "That the dollar consisting of twenty-five and eight-tenths grains of gold nine-tenths fine . . . shall be the standard unit of value, and all forms of money issued or coined by the United States shall be maintained at a parity of value with this standard." Silver was not eliminated as a monetary metal, but its main use was for small bills (ten dollars and less) and coins. All paper money, including greenbacks, could be redeemed for gold at the Treasury. The Treasury could only issue gold or silver certificates up to the amount of gold and silver held as trust funds in its vaults.

Quite simply, paper money symbolized a certain amount of gold or silver held on deposit in the Treasury and available for exchange. So a twenty-dollar bill might state, "This certifies that there have been deposited in the Treasury of the United States of America twenty dollars in gold coin payable to the bearer on demand," while a five-dollar bill would refer to "five silver dollars payable to the bearer on demand." These bills were called "gold certificates" and "silver certificates."

However, if we look at our paper money today, we find no mention of silver or gold. Rather, we carry and spend Federal Reserve Notes. A financial panic in 1907, marked by a lack of adequate credit for businesses, strengthened the sense that a mechanism was needed to make the money supply more elastic. This mechanism was the Federal Reserve System, which created a network of Federal Reserve banks authorized to issue Federal Reserve Notes. Without delving into the technicalities of this system, it allowed liquid assets of the banks (such as commercial paper acquired from businesses) to be used as reserves against which the banks could issue Federal Reserve Notes. While the Federal Reserve Act of 1913 required that part of this reserve be in the form of gold, new banking laws introduced by President Roosevelt to counter the Depression eliminated any gold backing for the dollar and actually made it illegal for United States citizens to use or hold gold coins. It is extraordinary that thirty-three years after enactment of the Gold Standard Act of 1900, gold should not only have gone out of circulation, but United States citizens would also be forbidden by law from hoarding gold or using gold as money.

Gold continued to be used as a reserve in international monetary dealings, although gold did not flow from country to country as the classical economists of the nineteenth century believed necessary to keep international trade in balance. After World War Two, the United States dollar served as the international currency, the trusted standard of value. Yet as more and more dollars circulated throughout the world, aiding economies struggling to rebuild from the war, the gold reserves held by the United States became inadequate to pay for the dollars in circulation at the official exchange rate of thirty-five dollars per ounce of gold. On August 15, 1971, President Nixon suspended payments of gold for dollars held by foreign central banks. The price of gold was no longer defended at thirty-five dollars per ounce. By 1979, gold had risen to $450 per ounce and today fluctuates around $400 per ounce.

Not only had gold vanished first from our hands and eventually from international exchange, but silver also vanished from circulation. In the 1960s, as the silver content in our coins became worth more than the face value of the coins, people began to hoard these coins. In 1965, the right to exchange silver certificates for silver at the offices of the United States Treasury was suspended.

In addition, the silver content of coins was sharply reduced or eliminated. The quarter with the bust of George

Washington, for example, had been made of ninety percent silver and ten percent copper from 1932 through
1964. Starting in 1965, the composition of the quarter
changed to seventy-five percent copper and twenty-five
percent nickel. These new coins were neither as valuable
nor as beautiful as silver coins. Following Gresham's law,
the less valuable coins immediately drove the more valuable coins out of circulation. Why pay with a quarter that
might have a silver content worth more than twenty-five
cents, when payment could just as well be made with a
quarter made of metal worth far less than twenty-five
cents? So not only gold, but silver too, ceased to have a
role as money.

Certainly gold and silver are metals prized by people
since the earliest times. Their beauty and usefulness for
ornamentation gave them value long before market
economies used them for purposes of exchange. In aban-
doning both gold and silver as the metallic backing for our
currency, we have given up metals with deep symbolic
meaning. Of course, part of the trust placed in such metals
was based on their scarcity. The difficulty of locating and
mining the metals made sudden increases in supply un-
likely. However, the symbolic power of gold and silver
also made people trust in their value.

Gold symbolizes the light of the sun, the powerful radiance of divine intelligence. So gold represents what is
most superior and conveys this quality to objects in the
material world. The golden crown of kings suggests divine
power and illumination, while golden money implies a divine superiority. Silver, too, is superior, symbolizing the
radiance of the moon, brightness, purity, innocence, chas-
tity, and even eloquence.

There is a symbolic tension between these two metals,
gold being equated with the sun and the masculine while

silver is equated with the moon and the feminine. This may partly explain the ferocity of the battle between supporters of a gold standard and supporters of a bimetallic standard. For example, after silver supporters passed a bill in 1878 that required the United States Treasury to purchase a certain amount of silver each year for conversion into silver dollars, President Rutherford Hayes showed the depth of his belief in gold by vetoing the bill as a "violation of sacred obligations." Certainly, when William Jennings Bryan addressed the complex issue of whether currency should be backed by gold alone or also by silver, an unseen aspect of the debate was the profound and ancient symbolic content of these two metals. We cannot value this symbolic content in dollars, francs, or yen; but we must realize that our money today is backed by neither gold nor silver. Its value is based totally on the productive abilities and assets that we possess individually and as a society.

Not only has the symbolic nature of our money changed, but its size has also been altered. On July 10, 1929, the dimensions of our paper money were reduced from 7⅜ by 3⅛ inches to 6³⁄₁₆ by 2⅝ inches. The larger bills had been issued since 1861, but the government sought to economize on paper costs, and scholars of money refer to our present paper currency as small-size notes. It is curious that this shrinking of the paper money came so close in time to the Depression with its shrinking of the productivity of the economy. More immediately to the point, however, is that as we use money we almost never think that it has changed: that the bills are no longer gold and silver certificates but rather Federal Reserve Notes, that the size of the bills has been reduced, and that our coins are no longer made largely of silver.

WHY USING CREDIT CARDS IS NOT THE SAME AS SPENDING MONEY

Even though our money is no longer backed by precious and beautiful metals such as gold and silver, we continue to be affected by its symbolic power. Without even knowing why, most people are more reluctant to spend cash than to use credit cards. To pay with cash still symbolizes the sacrifice of life energy, while credit cards play off the possibility that the debt incurred may never have to be paid.

Today the credit card is ever-present. In the United States, there are more than one billion credit cards. More than seventy-five percent of American households have either Visa or MasterCard or both, not to mention cards from American Express, Diners Club, oil companies, and retail stores. Without a credit card, some of the activities that we take for granted, such as renting a car or reserving tickets, become extremely difficult or even impossible. The advertising for credit cards presents images of acceptance, pleasure, and success. American Express emphasized prestige value with the phrase "Membership Has Its Privileges." Visa sought exotic locales where American Express cards weren't accepted and claimed: "Visa. It's Everywhere You Want to Be." And MasterCard championed people who "Master the Moment," as if the credit card itself might be the key to living life to the fullest.

The credit card is a recent invention, first conceived of in the Utopian novel *Looking Backward 2000–1887* by Edward Bellamy. Published in 1888, this novel devotes itself to describing the ideal social system that exists in the year 2000. Julian West, the hero of the novel, falls asleep in 1887 and wakes in the year 2000 in a Boston which is strikingly different from the city in which he went to sleep. As he converses with his host, Dr. Leete, Julian hears of a city, and a world, in which money is no longer used.

Dr. Leete explains, "But as soon as the nation became the sole producer of all sorts of commodities, there was no need of exchanges between individuals that they might get what they required. Everything was procurable from one source, and nothing could be procured from anywhere else. A system of direct distribution from the national storehouses took the place of trade, and for this money was unnecessary."

Dr. Leete then shows Julian a credit card, which is a "piece of pasteboard," and tells Julian that the card "is issued for a certain number of dollars. We have kept the old word, but not the substance. The term, as we use it, answers to no real thing, but merely serves as an algebraic symbol for comparing the values of products with one another."

This piece of pasteboard is the first description of a device that did not exist in 1888 when Edward Bellamy wrote his novel. Some hotels began issuing credit cards to their most prestigious customers as early as 1900 and in 1914 department stores and chains of gasoline stations followed suit. Beginning in 1947, railroad and airline companies also offered credit cards. However, the key to the modern growth of credit cards was the "new" kind of credit card introduced by Diners Club in 1950.

Instead of using the credit card to sell more of its own goods (as had the department stores and other retailers), Diners Club acted as an intermediary. A cardholder might purchase a meal in a variety of restaurants that accepted the card; Diners Club would then pay the restaurant and collect the balance from the cardholder. The next year, in 1951, the first bank credit card was introduced by the Franklin National Bank. Such bank credit cards, now the most popular cards in use, can be used to purchase an endless variety of goods and services.

So credit card has come to have a different meaning than Bellamy imagined when he created the phrase. Today a credit card is a card that allows the user to pay for goods or services without having any money in an account (as Bellamy's card would have required). In effect, the credit card user borrows money. This is allowed because the company issuing the credit card is relying on the creditworthiness of the cardholder. When the bill comes, the cardholder can pay and extinguish the debt.

In fact, each transaction using a bank card involves five parties: the merchant, the customer, the merchant's bank, the credit card company (such as Visa or MasterCard), and the customer's bank. The merchant has the benefit of consumers who buy more than if they had to pay cash. The customer has the advantage of the card's convenience. The merchant's bank earns a fee which is several percentage points of the total purchase. Both the credit card company and the customer's bank share in the fee paid to the merchant's bank. In addition, the customer's bank, which issued the credit card, charges the cardholder an annual fee that may be in the range of twenty to thirty-five dollars and charges interest on amounts that the cardholder does not pay on time. Such interest income accounts for more than seventy-five percent of all credit card revenue earned by banks.

These charges have made credit cards a source of great profits for the banks. In 1989, net profits from bank credit card operations reached $4.11 billion, twenty-six percent of the total bank profits of $15.73 billion for that year. While credit card profits fell in the ensuing recession as consumers purchased less and paid down credit card balances, credit card operations remain a crucial foundation for bank profits. After the debacles of nonperforming loans to real estate developers at home and to underdeveloped nations abroad that closed the 1980s, the banks in the 1990s will continue to be relentless in their pursuit of credit card customers.

We can understand why banks want consumers to have credit cards, but why are consumers so willing to turn a profit for the banks? Beyond the convenience factor, and perhaps the need to borrow money in order to make purchases, is a more intangible sense of wealth that credit cards can give, a magical feeling of expansiveness and power. It brings the world under our control. As American Express repeatedly tells us, "Don't Leave Home Without It." By carrying a card, we make our homes portable; we ensure that strangers will treat us like family and shower us with gifts and favors. They will honor the laws of Zeus that command hospitality be given to strangers. No doubt the ancient warrior pictured on each American Express card is there to reassure us that we are safe, heroic, even noble as we use our cards.

Underneath that sense of magical power is, once again, the elusive promise of immortality, eternal youth, limitlessness. It is no accident that the American Express cards are green or gold. Green, of course, is the color of the vegetative world that is constantly in its cycles of death and rebirth. The greenness of the cards may even suggest that the money we spend by using the card will inevitably replenish itself like vegetation. Gold is the metal of underworld wealth, whether the literal gold which is mined from the earth or the symbol of our inner richness. That is why so many of the bank cards are also gold (or silver, which ranks second to gold as a symbol of richness).

By using this imagery, credit cards offer us the illusion of debt which need never be paid, an illusion reinforced by the fact that the bank cards require only the payment of a monthly minimum and not payment of the full balance. If we pay our minimums, we are in good standing, we are creditworthy. We have captured extra energy from that debt (in the form of what we have consumed); we possess more vitality. A recent advertisement from American Express shows that its cards are accepted by a chain of shops selling ecologically-sound products, and concludes by telling us that American Express is "welcomed at . . . places that are good for your soul." Clearly such a credit card is not a mere ticket to exotic locales and the possession of prestige consumables but is a succor to us in our imperishable depths.

The advertisements for credit cards may seem deceiving, but we should hardly blame the advertisements for the deception. Such advertisements would not succeed if we didn't have a desire to believe and a willingness to imagine ourselves as actors in the fantasies created in the advertisements. Basic to this self-deception is our reluctance to distinguish between what we have already earned and what we hope to earn someday, or to distinguish between what we are and what we hope to be. So one advertisement speaks of the credit line that goes with the credit cards and ends by saying, "You've earned it."

This is misleading, but pleasing to the ears. We seem to be hearing that those who are hard workers and good earners are the ones who are offered credit lines. A naive listener might even imagine that when "You've earned it," you must own it in the form of savings. Of course, nothing could be further from the truth.

Quick to leap on the bandwagon of condemnation for the profligate 1980s, the most innovative advertising for credit cards seeks to distinguish and even define the 1990s. No longer are we fun-loving hedonists eager to buy useless baubles and idle away our hours on island beaches. The 1990s have reformed us all (including the credit card companies that urged us to spend and enjoy in the 1980s), so that we are now frugal and intelligent consumers.

"Master the Moment" did not gain MasterCard its hoped-for market share, so MasterCard found a new advertising agency to invent anew the role of credit cards for the 1990s. As the television screen reveals exotic vacation vistas, a man's voice asks, "You know those credit card commercials where they tell you to jaunt off to some exotic paradise? This isn't one of them, O.K.? We're taking our MasterCard to the supermarket." The visual changes to the interior of a supermarket and the "friendly" voice asks, "How's that for exotic?" The wisdom of this choice is explained at the checkout counter when the Master-Card is used to buy the groceries. The knowing voice informs us that "it's smart to use your monthly statement to keep track of your monthly grocery spending."

The commercial closes with deft assurance: "Master-Card. It's not just a credit card. It's smart money." The problem with slogans like "You've earned it" or "It's smart money" is their implication that the banks are seeking informed and creditworthy consumers to use their cards. Such upstanding consumers would naturally pay their bills in a timely manner. However, consumers who pay on time are not the people that the banks really seek to have credit cards. In credit card parlance, such good payers are called "free riders." They are almost thieves, problematic people who dare to enjoy the convenience of the credit card without making their fair contribution to the interest charges that generate seventy-five percent of the banks' credit card profits.

Once the banks realized that good payers were not their ideal customer, they began to go after people who would be more likely to pay the monthly minimum and carry a revolving balance on which interest had to be paid. College students are an especially desirable target group for the credit card companies. More than half of the 5.6 million full-time college students enrolled in four-year programs have credit cards. An added bonus in reaching the young is brand loyalty. MasterCard believes that sixty-five percent of people will continue to use their first brand of credit card for fifteen years or more.

So a flier for Citibank MasterCard—titled "Special Student Offer—All Students Eligible"—states "Citibank knows that students like you become responsible, creditworthy cardmembers. That's why we're extending a special student offer to you." The flier advises the student, "You always have the option of paying your purchase balance in full within our interest-free grace period, or spreading your obligation over time. You decide what's best for you—Citibank gives you the choice." After referring to how this credit card "can help you build your credit history better," the flier promises, "We'll start you off with a credit line to meet your needs and reward responsible payment behavior with credit line increases as your financial needs grow."

This sales pitch has a surprising clincher: "No co-signer or minimum income is needed—so apply now!" This is truly magic, if a credit card with a credit line can be obtained by a youth who has no income. Not surprisingly, many college students are no more able to handle credit card debt than their parents. So we hear of a freshman at the University of Houston who had neither a job nor a credit history, but quickly obtained eight credit cards (including three Visa cards). She found that she couldn't control her impulse spending. By her junior year she had a debt of $6,800, no credit cards, and a bad credit history.

Such stories could be multiplied. They are the inevitable result of the banks' use of credit cards to gain interest income. To the banks, the college student who defaults is simply a negative statistic in an overall profitable enterprise.

Self-deception is hardly limited to college students. For example, during the 1980s many people simply denied that they paid interest on their credit cards, when in fact two-thirds of them did. By denying that any interest was paid, these cardholders avoided the necessity of asking what the rate of interest might be. Had they asked, they would have discovered that the rate of interest averaged nearly twenty percent throughout the 1980s. Consumers who believed they would pay off their revolving balances next month gave billions in profits to the banks.

The insensitivity of credit card customers to interest rates had been shown as early as the 1950s. The average interest charge for credit card balances came to be 19.8 percent, and this rate did not lower as interest rates fell through the 1980s. With the recession in the early 1990s, interest rates paid by banks to depositors fell to the two- to three-percent range by 1993. At the same time, the banks were charging nearly twenty percent to their credit card borrowers. This differential made the credit card business very profitable and may well have saved some banks from failing due to unprofitable real estate loans.

An extraordinary battle in Congress finally helped raise the awareness of credit cardholders. On November 12, 1991, President Bush gave a speech in which he urged banks to lower their credit card rates. He believed this would encourage consumers to spend and boost the economy. On November 13, Senator D'Amato, a New York Republican, offered a bill to cap credit card interest rates at fourteen percent, far less than the state usury ceilings which generally ranged from eighteen to twenty-four percent.

However, when the bill passed the Senate by a vote of seventy-four to nineteen, the White House denounced it. The treasury secretary called the proposal "wacky" and blamed it for a 120 point fall in the stock market. The vice president said that millions of people would lose their credit cards, and the chairman of the Federal Reserve concluded that banks would lose needed profits from interest charges. The embarrassing truth was that if rates were lowered and cards given only to people who could definitely pay, then a huge number of people would lose their credit cards. And the people who would lose their cards were exactly the group that maintained revolving balances of debt and paid the high interest rates that were saving many banks from failure. President Bush now had to threaten to veto a popular proposal for a law capping such interest rates.

Although D'Amato's bill never became law, it did help to make people more sensitive to the issue of credit card rates. Banks began to compete on the basis of their rates and the average interest rates for credit cards did ease slightly, but remained extremely high compared to rates for secured debt such as car loans or home mortgages.

So the magical power of credit cards is an illusion. If

there is any magic, it is not in the credit card but in the interest charges. The famed banker Baron de Rothschild could not name the seven wonders of the world but called compound interest the eighth wonder. Money will double in a little over six years at a twelve-percent interest rate (in part because the interest paid in the first year then earns interest in subsequent years). At twenty-percent interest, which is what the rate on credit cards has been, the money owed will double in less than four years. Looked at in another way, if a cardholder owes $2,000 and makes the minimum payment each month, it will take 22 years to pay off the $2,000 and will cost $4,919 in interest if the rate is 19.8 percent.

Especially in view of the interest costs, it is remarkable how many people pay their monthly minimums and imagine that they have no money problems. They do not consider themselves debtors. They have been solicited by a credit card issuer, filled out an application, been approved. They've earned the right to their line of credit. Who should know better than a bank whether someone's financial information justifies the issuance of a card with a credit line? It certainly seems that paying the monthly minimum meets with the bank's approval. No more is required to be considered creditworthy.

DEBTORS ANONYMOUS AND THE DISPELLING OF CREDIT CARD ILLUSIONS

The danger signs with respect to credit cards are well known. In fact, one such sign is to make only minimum payments each month. Another sign is buying food with credit cards (despite the MasterCard campaign saying their card is "smart money" when used at the supermarket). Using credit card advances to pay off other debts, combatting boredom or depression by going shopping, and having card balances at their maximum so money is unavailable for emergencies are all warning signs. So are paying for friends' purchases with a credit card and viewing the cash reimbursement from the friends as found money, regularly seeking higher credit lines on cards, repeatedly using a home equity line of credit, seeking a debt consolidation loan, not reading letters from creditors, or having wages garnished. Many people will try to ignore these warning signs, a denial made easier by the absence of programs to educate people about personal finances.

The illusion only ends when the debtor is unable to pay even the minimum balance on the credit card. A mature woman who had paid her monthly minimum for many years told of how she suddenly realized that she was deeply in debt. She sought counseling for debt and was told that based on her income-to-debt ratio she should declare bankruptcy. Instead she went to Debtors Anonymous and gave up her illusion that life could not be lived without credit cards. She cut up her cards, sought to make payment schedules with all her creditors, and eventually did pay all of her debts.

Debtors Anonymous is one of the many Twelve-Step programs that seeks to help people in recovery from an addiction. According to the Twelve Traditions of Debtors Anonymous, "The only requirement for Debtors Anonymous membership is a desire to stop incurring unsecured debt." The foundations of Debtors Anonymous are both pragmatic and spiritual. The pragmatic aspect requires a debtor to share common ground with the other members of Debtors Anonymous by admitting that "we were powerless over debt—that our lives had become unmanageable," and by making "a searching and fearless moral inventory of ourselves." The spiritual basis requires the debtor to believe "that a Power greater than ourselves could restore us to sanity," and to make "a decision to turn our will and our lives over to God as we understood him." Debtors Anonymous encourages those who feel powerless with respect to money to redirect their addictive energy toward the divine. If the adversity of debt can serve to deepen the spiritual life, then understanding debt also gives a sense of the natural abundance from which money flows.

When the woman who went to Debtors Anonymous sought freedom from debt, she met a secret and quite ugly aspect of the systematized purveying of debt through credit cards. Collection agencies called her at all hours, including late at night, early in the morning, and on weekends. She was threatened with lawsuits and a bad credit rating. For more than six months, each of ten creditors called her at least once a week. These callers usually had an angry, condescending tone and accused her of withholding money, trying to perpetrate a fraud, and lying. They sounded as if they read from scripts as they told her that she should have thought more before she had gone into debt. They repeatedly questioned whether she had savings or friends and family from whom to borrow. In response to her offers of payment schedules, they would say things like, "Even people on welfare pay more than that."

So the other side of the pleasures promised by credit cards is the pain inflicted on those who fail to pay. This pain is obviously a secret, since the companies selling credit cards hardly want us to be aware that maybe "You've earned it" and "It's smart money" are just two of the many lies used to profit from people's lack of awareness about money matters. Nor was the treatment of the woman who cut up her credit cards in any way extraordinary. It was just as much a part of the system as the initial solicitations telling college students that they can have a credit card and credit line without any requirement of a minimum income or a co-signer.

So the symbolic promise of the credit cards—a limitless credit line that need never be repaid—is, of course, not kept. The advertising with its fantasies is part of a system designed to make profits. The system entices people to get and use cards, including some who will be unable to pay. Those unable to pay are treated like statistics and turned over to professional debt collectors. In contrast to this, payment in cash is a refreshing exercise in reality. Cash symbolizes current potentials and energies, so we feel our sacrifice of cash far more intensely than we feel the promise of the future repayment that we are agreeing to make when we use a credit card. If we wish to spend less, using cash instead of credit cards definitely assists us.

BANKS SEEK THE PROFITS OF LOANS TO CONSUMERS

To gain the fullest understanding of the reason for the marketing of credit cards and the growth of debt, we have to connect the use of credit cards to the evolution of consumerism and banking in the twentieth century. At the turn of the century, banks did not seek to profit from consumers. In fact, banks did not view lending to consumers as a part of their business. If a worker had credit, it came from accounts with local merchants. A person who could not borrow from family and friends had only one remaining avenue: a loan shark who would charge usurious and often devastating rates of interest.

The very concepts of mass production and the consumerism necessary to support such production were in their infancy. Banks sought their profits through service to the business community. While workers could deposit their money with the banks for safekeeping, the banks did not circulate these deposits back to the workers in the form of loans. If the automobile is emblematic of the growth of consumerism, it is interesting to note that until 1910 cash had to be paid in full to buy an automobile.

In the difficult economic times of the 1890s, bankers viewed the credit needs of ordinary people as an issue of charity. Through the auspices of the Charity Organization Society, many of the bankers and other wealthy people subscribed money to create a pawnshop that would be able to extend small amounts of credit to people quickly. Called the Provident Loan Society of New York, it opened in 1894 as a philanthropic organization dedicated to giving people credit at a fair rate of interest (which it continues to do today). Designed to look like small Greek temples, the busy offices of the Provident revealed the hunger of people for credit.

This unmet demand for credit finally brought an entrepreneurial response from an attorney in Norfolk, Virginia, whose expertise was in banking and corporate law. Arthur J. Morris believed that eighty percent of the public did not have sufficient access to credit. In 1910, he opened the Fidelity Savings & Trust Co. in Norfolk. Lending on the basis of earning power and character at interest rates that, if high, were far better than those offered by the loan sharks, so-called Morris Banks soon spread to other cities. Morris invented the use of life insurance on borrowers to protect both the Morris Banks and co-signers of the promissory notes securing the debts. So Morris could promise, "No man's debts shall survive him."

If this were not enough, Morris also assisted in developing the concept of installment financing for the purchase of automobiles. Installment credit outstanding for automobiles rose from $304 million in 1919 to $1.384 billion in 1929. This credit expansion helped keep the factories busy turning out automobiles, which in turn stimulated the economy as the bull market of the 1920s stampeded ahead.

In fact, although the contraction of consumer credit was widespread during the 1930s, the wage earner had been shown to be a good credit risk. The banks could no longer ignore wage earners as a source of potential profit. Consumer credit soared after the end of World War Two, rising from $5.665 billion in 1945 to $38.830 billion in 1955 and to $90.314 billion in 1965. Inflation could only account for a relatively small portion of this increase.

THE SYMBOLISM OF CHANGING BANK ARCHITECTURE

Naturally banks wanted to persuade depositors that their money would be safe. The ancient treasuries at Delphi had been built for the safekeeping of the wealth of the city-states. Architects for banks in the nineteenth and early twentieth century frequently turned for models to the ancient temples of Greece and Rome. So many banks looked like temples, their magnificence imbued with the implicit power of the unseen divinities. Pillared facades, massive doors, and lofty interiors with vaulted ceilings all sought to inspire awe. To complete the sense that these buildings were large and impregnable vaults, the windows were often tiny. Even within the bank, the officers would be hidden from sight, with the give-and-take of money conducted by clerks in hushed voices.

On the reverse of the ten-dollar bill is an engraving of the United States Treasury in Washington, D.C. Its wide steps leading heavenward, handsome pillars, and vast size all give credence to its sacred and inviolable role in our lives. The Treasury building, erected in 1836, is the third oldest building in Washington and is predated only by the White House and the Capitol.

The First Bank of the United States, designed by Samuel Blodget, Jr., and built in Philadelphia between 1795 and 1797, has a white marble facade with a similar feeling: six Corinthian pillars supporting a pediment on which the arms of the United States are portrayed. Thomas Jefferson, while mistrustful of banks and credit, influenced their architecture through his love of Greek and Roman models. So the First Bank of the United States was modeled on a Roman temple at Nîmes, which Jefferson believed the most beautiful building surviving from antiquity. While architectural critics detect nonclassical influences as well, its monumental grandeur and classical sensibility made the First Bank of the United States not only the first bank to be built in such a style but also a model for later banks to follow. Until 1800, the First Bank of the United States served as the temporary seat of government for the new nation while Washington was being built.

More than a century later, in 1908, National City Bank (now Citibank) hired the famed architectural firm of McKim, Mead & White to redesign the block-long United States Customs House in New York City for use as a bank. The Customs House already had an impressive facade of one dozen Ionic pillars. Above this McKim, Mead & White added four stories fronted by one dozen Corinthian pillars arranged to balance the Ionic pillars below. Since the first row of pillars begins on a wall more than double a person's height, the overall effect is monumental. Within the building this renovation brought sunlight streaming down from the empyrean heights of the fifty-nine-foot-high ceiling.

Many more banks could be used as examples of classical influence, but the point is that this temple architecture could not survive the growth of consumerism and the banks' energetic quest for the interest profits generated by consumer debt. A new bank architecture evolved as banks reached out and sought to make the public feel welcome. The shock of the new was most dramatically realized in a bank facade designed by Skidmore, Owings & Merrill in 1953–54. The unadorned four-story building, built as a branch of Manufacturers Trust Company at Fifth Avenue and Forty-Third Street in New York City, had a facade of glass. This facade included the largest sheets of glass ever installed in a building up to that time: 9.5 feet by 22 feet.

Unlike the temple banks which projected an image of inviolable security, this modern sheath of glass invited the public into the bank. It made the interior accessible; what secrets could there be when anyone passing on the sidewalk could see into the well-illuminated interior? The architects included a striking visual proof that this bank held no secrets. Their design placed the vault, the most inner and secret precinct of earlier banks, on the level of the street. With the walls of glass, passersby have no choice but to see the vault and understand, even without thinking about it, that this bank has no pretension of being a temple. Not only was this design a public relations coup, but it set a new norm for the architecture of banks.

It is no coincidence that bank credit cards and this revolution in bank design both date to the early 1950s. They were like siblings; they belonged to the same family. This family, unlike the banks of the past, wanted company. In fact, the architecture suggested guests were welcome, and the credit cards were like an extension of this architecture. To the millions of people who received unsolicited credit cards in the mail before a federal ban on such mailings in 1970, the credit cards were an invitation to walk into one of the ever-growing number of glass banks and meet a friendly banker. As consumer credit reached $131.6 billion in 1970, $350.3 billion in 1980, and $794.4 billion in 1990, the willingness of the public to borrow complemented the glass windows through which bank officers across the nation could be seen toiling at their desks.

WHAT WE WILL LOSE IF MONEY IS REPLACED BY CREDIT CARDS AND ELECTRONIC TRANSFERS

We have explored the use of credit cards and the relationship of banks to consumer debt for several reasons. These ever-present cards function in a way which makes them a great convenience, but their purpose is to increase the amount of indebtedness among consumers. Understanding this, we can each make a more informed choice as to whether we are willing to incur this debt and contribute to the interest charges that form a significant portion of bank profits.

Beyond this, however, credit cards offer a way of seeing more deeply into the even newer phenomenon of electronic fund transfers. Whatever the motives (for both issuer and user) underlying the ever-expanding use of credit cards, these same motives could not help but affect the use of electronic transfers as well. Credit cards seem, after all, to be but a step in the direction of a cash-free society. Automatic teller machines are ubiquitous, and the next step is likely to be interactive networks that allow us to sit at home while we shop and pay bills by electronic transfers. Governments are experimenting with issuing credit cards to replace welfare payments and food stamps. The hope is to cut costs by eliminating red tape and fraud, but one effect is to deny these recipients the symbolic value inherent in exchanging money for goods or services.

If the replacement of money by electronic transfers seems remote, we should keep in mind that the largest sums of money are already moved electronically. For example, the Clearing House Interbank Payments System, owned by eleven of the largest New York banks, moves a trillion dollars each day electronically—more than the entire money supply of the United States. While cash (eighty-five percent) and checks (thirteen percent) are used in ninety-eight percent of all transactions, cash transactions account for only one percent of the total amount of all transactions. So individuals like to use cash for their transactions, but financial institutions prefer to make their far larger transfers electronically.

What would it mean if credit cards and electronic transfers completely replaced the use of paper money and coins? How would we experience this in our depths, far beneath the everyday measuring and exchanging of values in the marketplace?

We have discussed how money, despite losing the backing of gold and silver, still retains symbolic power. On one level, money speaks to us of our ability to be fruitful in the world. In this we see money as the reward for our labors and also as an invaluable mechanism of circulation and sharing. On another level money tells us of our inner richness. So Jesus Christ speaks of money in a number of his parables, but clearly he uses it because its increase can so easily symbolize spiritual growth.

Without money that passes from hand to hand, the symbolic wealth of money would vanish. We would no longer have the faces of the Founding Fathers and other national leaders portrayed on our coins and bills. The Great Seal of the United States would disappear from the reverse of the dollar. The phrase "In God We Trust" would become a relic, for that inscription and the money that bore it would have vanished to the realm of the invisible. The greenness of our paper money and the vegetative motifs that appear on both coins and bills would no longer be taken in hand with each exchange.

When cash and coins become invisible, they return to the underworld. We are no longer conscious of them. The money moved by an electronic funds transfer is no doubt going from one place to another, but that movement is utterly abstract. We do not see the movement with our eyes;

we do not use our hands to propel or receive what is moved.

Thinking not of electronic exchanges but of other exchanges that connected humankind to invisible realms, we return to the early peoples who sought some relationship with the fruitfulness of the world about them. What invisible powers made game plentiful or brought the rains to fructify the fields? Our money today offers only faint hints of the ancient origins of money in the worship of invisible forces, but at least some visual and tangible clues remain of how people first sought to forge a bond with unseen divinities. Certainly handing money back and forth is a reminder, however faint, of the connection of people to each other in the love feast and to the divine through sacrificial exchange and communion.

If money vanishes, we will, in a sense, have come full circle. Nothing will be visibly exchanged; the money that we sacrifice to receive our sustenance will vanish. We will be left, as early peoples were, with a fruitful world whose divinities and spirits conceal themselves utterly. Even the inadequate clues offered by money are signs that we can interpret, signs that offer us symbolic wealth. If money vanishes it will be the invisibility, the lack of signs, that will be our greatest challenge as we seek to understand what is fertile in our world and in ourselves.

In fact, when credit cards are examined more closely, a fundamental difference between credit cards and electronic fund transfers becomes apparent. Bank credit cards rely on the creation of debt to profit their issuers. Electronic fund transfers do not create debt. Actually, electronic fund transfers are similar to the card originally imagined by Edward Bellamy in *Looking Backward 2000–1887*. Such a card would be called a "debit card" today and can only be used to draw against an account in which the cardholder has money. Similarly, electronic transfers require that a person have a balance, presumably in a bank account, against which the instantaneous transfer of money can be processed. So until electronic fund transfers cost about the same as drawing checks, most people will prefer the old system to the new. And banks will lack strong profit incentives to change to systems of electronic transfers, because such transfers do not encourage the creation of debt and the charging of interest—the "money at once" that motivates the banks in their dealings with consumers.

HERMES AND THE INFORMATION AGE

We are told that we live in the Information Age. Certainly we are surrounded by technology that allows immense speed in the processing and moving of information. If we think of the Greek pantheon, the god ruling over the Information Age is undoubtedly Hermes (or Mercury, as he was called by the Romans). He is the swiftest of gods, the messenger. Instantaneously, he moves from Olympus to earth in aid of a hero, or to the underworld to rescue Persephone. Since Hermes is the god of commerce, we need hardly be surprised that the needs of commerce are so well served in the Information Age.

But we must remember that Hermes is the god of thieves. He is quite capable of misleading us, spinning webs of illusion and lies that make us easy victims of fraud. Vast quantities of information do not mean that each of us is receiving information of quality. The sym-

bolic wealth of money may help us maintain our equilib-
rium in a society more and more accustomed to debt and
"money at once." And in an age when so much outside of
us moves very quickly, we must still respect the speed at
which we move within.

CHAPTER NINE

BULLS AND BEARS

How the Stock Market Reflects the Renewing Cycles of Life

IN THE COURSE of writing *The Secret Life of Money*, I walked the financial district of New York City to view some of the landmarks of bank architecture. Not only did the Citicorp building with its many pillars remind me of an ancient Greek temple, but so did the facade of the New York Stock Exchange with its six Corinthian pillars rising to support a pediment surmounted by a dramatic sculptural group. As I studied this grouping, I was surprised to see that the central figure wore a winged helmet—the sign of Hermes, the god of commerce and of thieves. This figure's arms were outstretched at waist height, like a charioteer holding reins, and an infant sat at each foot while adults labored beneath the dominion of the outstretched arms.

I marveled at the wisdom of the Exchange to invoke Hermes, at once the most appropriate of gods to represent the growth of commerce, and yet an admission that human industry is sometimes accompanied by thievery and sharp practices. Curious to learn more, I inquired at the Exchange and quickly received a disclaimer. The central figure was not Hermes at all, but rather a depiction of Integrity. I could certainly understand why the Exchange would want to claim Integrity as its governing force, but in mythology the winged helmet identifies Hermes as the god who moves between the worlds. The wings on his helmet symbolize his attributes: his ability to change levels, to travel, to move quickly, to communicate over vast distances. To give these attributes to Integrity would make as much sense as saying that the symbol for a football team like the Philadelphia Eagles could equally well be used as the symbol for the Chicago Bears.

In this chapter we will seek to understand some of the symbols of the stock market, such as the sculpture of Integrity and the bulls and bears which have ancient connections to the cycles of increase and decrease in nature. To many of us, the up-and-down movements of stocks seem as arbitrary as the numbers selected to determine the winner of the state lottery. But the stock markets are, in reality, a reflection of the desire in each of us to be productive and contribute to our families and communities.

HERMES GUIDED BY INTEGRITY

The New York Stock Exchange is rooted in the formative years of our nation. Founded in 1792 under a butterwood tree on Wall Street (a street named after a wall built by the Dutch in 1653 as a defense against the English who later dismantled it), the Exchange served an agricultural nation just beginning the process of industrialization. In the colonial period there had been only half a dozen chartered companies, most of which had vanished by the Revolution. But the economic growth of the 1790s saw the formation of nearly three hundred chartered companies, many of which relied on the Exchange to raise capital by selling their stocks and bonds to the public.

The expansion and ever greater importance of the Exchange paralleled the rapid industrialization of the nineteenth century. For a long period (from 1840 to 1890), the stocks and bonds of railroad companies dominated the trading on the Exchange and reflected the crucial role of the railroad in the development of the national economy. Not only the railroad but also the telegraph (invented in 1844) and the telephone (invented in 1876 and installed in the Exchange in 1878) all suggest the increasing significance of Hermes. His attributes—speed in communication and travel—became ever more important as the Industrial Age evolved and flowed into the Information Age. This newfound and ever increasing speed transformed commerce and the daily lives of the people.

On December 15, 1886, the Exchange sold one million shares for the first time. By the end of the 1890s, trading volume soared and the Exchange readied for expanded quarters. In 1903, the Exchange moved into a newly constructed building at 18 Broad Street that is still in use today. In many ways the building was a futuristic wonder. More than 500 telephones were installed on the perimeter of the trading floor, a pioneering use of air conditioning required 247 miles of wiring, and six miles of pneumatic tubes in the walls and ceilings made trading information quickly available.

The respected sculptor John Quincy Adams Ward was

commissioned to create the pediment statuary. This grouping, titled "Integrity Protecting the Works of Man," shows Integrity as the central figure with the figures of Science, Industry, and Invention laboring to one side and the figures of Agriculture and Mining laboring to the other. For the most part, the sculpture portrays its title quite literally. The "Works of Man" flow from the muscles and minds of the nude male figures that symbolize Science, Industry, Invention, Agriculture, and Mining (except for a clothed woman who may be helping Agriculture in his tasks). What is surprising is that Integrity, the guiding force for all these works of man, is a woman attired in a flowing gown and cape.

It would be easy to dismiss this statuary as propaganda. After all, Hermes is the god of thieves. Putting his helmet on a woman and calling her Integrity could simply be a way of ignoring that thieves have often used the stock market to prey on honest investors. The rapacious manipulators of the 1980s, who made tens of millions of dollars and later served time in prison, are merely the most recent generation of wrongdoers who used the stock market without any concern for ethical conduct. In addition, women in finance were certainly a rarity at the turn of the century, when many brokers actually had separate rooms for their women customers. Only during World War Two did the Exchange allow women to work on the trading floor, and this ceased for another two decades when the returning veterans took back their jobs. It was not until 1967 that Muriel Siebert became the first woman to be a member of the Exchange. So the figure of Integrity is a woman in spite of the fact that women had almost no involvement with the Exchange at the turn of the century and for many years after.

Yet Ward's sculpture seems more than propaganda. It suggests the artist's hope of how the Exchange might serve the productive life of an evolving nation. Certainly part of this vision included the qualities of Hermes: the speed of movement and communication that within two decades would find realization in the widespread use of airplanes, automobiles, and radio. But Ward offers a new image to govern our productive efforts. He seems to want to reform the less savory aspects of Hermes, the god quite capable of stealing his brother's cattle and lying about the theft. So Ward sought to add to the world of finance what had been largely missing—the image of a woman. In this case, a handsome woman named Integrity, whose outstretched arms might bring the fair dealing of her name to every type of enterprise.

When an artist like Ward creates the figure of a woman (especially a personification such as Integrity), he may be portraying what psychologist C. G. Jung would call an image of the *anima*. Anima means soul or life (especially inner life). Through such an image a man may seek for aspects of his life which are unconscious, undiscovered by him. The image may be seen in a vision, a dream, or even be a woman whom he meets.

A man knows that he is encountering an anima figure by the great stirring of energy within him. Unknown parts of himself seek to become visible, to become part of what the man believes himself to be. To meet this woman who represents what is unknown arouses feelings of rapture and terror. At once the man feels immense possibilities open before him while the solid structure of the world he has known is shaken as if by a powerful earthquake. If the man sees his anima in a real woman, he must exercise all of his reason and restraint to understand that the anima is his fabrication, his vision of the energy of his inner possibilities. In the hands of an artist like Ward, such an anima figure may express the unknown possibility of the collective unconscious, the potential of the society for discovery and evolution.

The New York Stock Exchange and the many other exchanges around the world are the most evolved agents of the secular markets. These exchanges seek to channel money so that it will be used in ways that are productive. While the divine exchange connected people to gods and spirits through sacrifice, these secular exchanges connect people with money to people who desire money for productive purposes—whether to build railroads in the nineteenth century or automobiles and computers in the twentieth. If this view of the exchanges is simplified, it nonetheless captures the central vision and purpose of these markets. While the New York Stock Exchange handles the stocks and bonds of a limited number of the largest companies, the quest to be productive animates us all. Smaller companies may secure capital by private placements to a limited number of investors; entrepreneurs may launch their enterprises with savings or borrowings from family and friends. Employees offer the productivity of their labor, and even at leisure we often gain satisfaction from being productive.

The artist's vision in "Integrity Protecting the Works of Man" is not a reflection of history but rather a hope for the betterment of the human condition. And Integrity can only protect the "Works of Man" if first she protects the money that we use as a tool to aid us in our creations. Money's appearance can remain unchanged while its essence is transformed, as has been the case with United States currency in the twentieth century with the removal of gold and silver backing. Quite clearly, money is trust in the larger society, trust in the government, and trust in all the citizens who work to create the cornucopia of goods and services that each year give reality to a paper currency that has no intrinsic value. To protect our money, Integrity must keep us aware that money is the device by which we share our energies and exchange the fruits of our labors. Beyond this, while the frieze says nothing of the distribution of the wealth that the markets help to create, would not Integrity require a concern for the well-being of each member of the community?

On a more personal level, Hermes is the guide of souls, the god who enables us to cross boundaries within ourselves and discover what is new within us. If we apply the artist's vision to our individual psychologies, we can understand the need for Integrity to govern the search for our own natures. When we seek our inner fertility, our deepest potential whatever the form its expression may take in the world, we have no choice but to be utterly honest.

So looking at the pediment statuary of the New York Stock Exchange, we meet again with many of the themes that have been woven through *The Secret Life of Money*. We see money as a creation of the human mind, a tool that serves our desire to be productive. If we contemplate how the exchanges raise money for investment, we can't help but wonder about the spark that makes us fertile with the dreams of new ventures. Here we feel again the divine origins of the cornucopias that we create, both individually and as a society. And when we experience our fertility as flowing from an endless abundance, we can understand the importance of freeing our richness to flow into the world. That endless abundance is invisible, so both as individuals and as a society we constantly strive to know and give shape to what cannot be seen. Without the protective guidance of Integrity, we may never come to trust what is invisible and experience its richness.

The great cycles of life and death that shaped the worship of the fertility goddesses affect the stock markets as well. The very words "stock market" suggest a place for the sale of livestock. So phrases like "taking a cut" or "watered stock" have the ring of a time when livestock served as a principal form of wealth. The word "chattel," which means a movable piece of property, is closely related to the word "cattle"; and the word "pecuniary," which means of or pertaining to money, comes from the word *pecus*, which is Latin for livestock.

BULLS AND BEARS
The Psychology of the Market

The most popular words to describe the psychology of investors in the stock market are "bullish" and "bearish." To be a bull means to believe that the market (or a particular stock) will go up in value. So bulls buy. Bears, on the other hand, believe that the market or a particular stock will fall in value. So bears sell. However, the explanations offered for the origins of this usage of bulls and bears are scanty and unsatisfactory. If we could deepen our understanding of why bulls and bears symbolize different forces in the stock market and in human psychology, we might gain insight into what makes each of us and our society fertile. We might also solve a small mystery, which is the question of why such a curious phrase as "bulls and bears" has found widespread usage and feels so appropriate.

The adoption of bulls and bears goes back at least to the early 1700s when these terms were used at the London Stock Exchange. Various theories seek to explain the reasoning behind the usage. One theory, for example, is that bullish comes from the way that a bull will toss up its horns. In a bullfight the bull's powerful neck muscles must be wounded so that this tossing upward will not be so dangerous to the matador. Thus bullish refers to the belief that prices will be tossed upward. With respect to the bear, a theory is advanced that the usage comes from an old English saying about not selling the skin before the bear has been caught. Investors who are bearish on a stock often sell the stock short. This means that they sell shares that they don't own in the hope that they can later purchase the shares at a cheaper price and make a profit. But neither these nor other theories really explain the aptness of the concept of bulls and bears.

Today, of course, few of us have any contact with bulls, so we have difficulty imagining the importance of the bull for earlier generations and for many people who live in less industrialized parts of the world. For hunters, the wild cattle, called aurochs, were both a great prize and a fearsome prey. Aurochs lived in herds of cows and calves dominated by a single bull. The bull stood six feet at the shoulders and weighed over two thousand pounds. The tribe could feast on its flesh, use its bones for spear points, fishhooks, and other implements, and make its skin into clothing and tents. The last of the aurochs died in the seventeenth century in Poland.

Bullfighting appears to have grown out of the fierce bravery required to hunt the aurochs. The Spanish apparently fought bulls before their conquest by Rome and introduced the conquerors to this spectacle. The term "straw man" comes from the practice of tossing clothed figures stuffed with straw in front of the bulls to enrage them and let them exhaust some of their energy before the bullfights would begin.

We do not know exactly how cattle came to be domesticated, but this domestication forever changed the relationship of humanity to nature. No longer dependent on the hunt, the herder could follow a more settled style of life. Observing the bulls and cows, the herders may have first discovered the causal relationship between sexuality and birth. On the one hand, separating the bull from the cows meant that there would be no calves at all. On the other hand, one bull could impregnate all of the cows in the herd. So the bull symbolized not only immense strength but also boundless fertility.

Agriculture and herding began as separate activities, but ancient people imagined that the fertility of the bull could inseminate the fields which nourished the crops. When the bull pulled a plough through the fields, the furrows opened in the earth and received the life-giving force of the bull. All of the early civilizations, of the Tigris-Euphrates region and of the Nile and Indus rivers, had stockbreeding and agriculture as foundations. Each of these civilizations worshipped a bull god as one of its chief deities.

In India, the Aryans sang hymns of worship to many bull gods, including Indra, the mighty bull whose rain fertilized the earth and impregnated the herds of cattle. The ancient Sumerians worshipped the bull-god Enlil whose power over water made him the god of the storm and of fertility. Hymns to Enlil honored him with such phrases as "powerful chief of the gods," "lord of the world of life," and "exalted overpowering ox." The Sumerians believed that merely walking bulls through the fields would bring fertility. The Egyptians sang to Amen-Ra, ". . . the Bull in Heliopolis, / president of all the gods, . . . / father of the gods, / maker of men, / creator of beasts and cattle, / lord of the things which exist, / creator of the staff of life. . . ."

In both Sumeria and Egypt the king came to be closely associated with the bull. So in Sumeria both Enlil and the great king Sargon shared the honorific title of "Wild Bull." To show their divine appointment and power, kings wore bull-horned headdresses. Only kings were allowed to grow beards, which symbolized strength, and beards were also placed on the statues of the bull gods. In Egypt, the king who united Upper and Lower Egypt, Narmer-Menes, proclaimed himself a bull. Not only was the worship of the bull identified with worship of the king from a very early date but the bull cults of Apis and Mnevis each worshipped the god in the form of a living bull, which was embalmed at death and placed in a large tomb.

Bull worship spanned the Mediterranean. Earlier we discussed how the Phoenicians spread the worship of the bull-god Ba'al to such places as Carthage. The god Dionysus, whose wanderings and connection to the fertility goddess Cybele we also explored, was worshipped as a bull. In Crete, the bull again symbolized fertility and was also linked with the roar and destructive force of the earthquakes that rocked the island. The Cretans held a spring festival in which they sought to make the divine fertility of the bull serve humankind. Young men and women would "dance" with the bull by waiting for the charge, grasping the horns, and, as the bull gave its powerful upward thrust of the head, somersaulting to safety over its back. The immense danger of this ritual was redeemed by the belief that touching the horns conveyed a fertility that would benefit the entire community. The masculine prowess of the bull found a reflection in the numerous images of bulls with erect phalli, and also in the fact that the women bull dancers dressed with their clothing bunched in such a way that they, too, seemed to possess male sexual organs.

In the centuries following the death of Christ, many of the soldiers of the Roman Empire worshipped the god Mithra, and the Mithraic religion competed with the Christian religion for adherents and eventual dominance. Mithra served as a divine mediator between the ultimate, unknowable god and the human race. Mithra's most famous feat was to slay the wild bull, the first living creature created by the god. When Mithra found this immense bull grazing on the mountain side, he boldly grasped its horns and leapt on its back. The struggling bull unseated him, but Mithra kept his grip on the horns until the bull surrendered in exhaustion.

Then Mithra lifted the bull by its hind hoofs and dragged it on a road that had many obstacles. This painful journey symbolized the suffering of humanity. Mithra left the bull in a cave, but the bull escaped, and Mithra, against his own will, had to obey the decree of heaven and kill it. When the bull returned to the entrance of the cave, Mithra grasped its nostrils to pull back its head and struck a deadly blow with his hunting knife.

A miracle followed this slaughter. The body of the dead bull sprouted with the useful vegetation that covers the earth—its spine gave forth wheat, its blood engendered the vine—and its semen brought forth all of the animals useful to humanity. So the death of the bull was, in fact, a sacrifice of cosmic consequence. After other feats, Mithra partook of a last supper, commemorated in the Mithraic rituals of communion, and ascended to heaven where he watched over and helped humanity.

Mithraic doctrine posited a life after death in which the good would be rewarded and the evil punished. At a predestined time, when the world would be destroyed, a marvelous bull would again be sent by the god to the earth. Mithra would return to the earth and select the dead to be awakened to life. Mithra would then sacrifice this divine bull. Eating of its flesh mixed with consecrated wine would give immortality to those awakened. Yielding to the prayers of these new immortals, the god would destroy all of the wicked and bring eternal joy to the universe.

If we step back from this religious imagery, we see why the bull serves so excellently as the symbol of hoped-for increase in the stock market. Cattle played a key role in the evolution of economies and, therefore, of civilization. The great strength and fertility of the bull made it worthy of veneration and sacrifice. To worship the bull was to worship the abundance and fertility of the divine. Not only were people thankful, but by their own efforts they tried to augment these divine gifts.

When we are bullish on a stock or on the stock market, we are hoping that our human endeavors will be fertile and manifest the richness which is divine. To be bullish is to become like the bull, to be the inseminating agent of fertility. To buy is to sacrifice life energy (in the form of money) in the hope that a certain company will grow. If we are investing in ourselves, perhaps paying for education or training, we are showing how we believe that we will be more productive in the future. Whether investing in a company or in ourselves, we are circulating energy into the realm of the invisible in the hope that we will free the richness that is boundless.

Investors who scrutinize the bottom line may not recognize in themselves the energy of the divine bull whose sacrifice brought all that is useful in nature into being. Trend lines, price/earnings ratios, and asset liquidation values are useful tools that may nonetheless obscure the larger efforts of the community to produce and nourish. Beyond this, the bullish investor may have great difficulty in valuing anything other than growth. Yet there are other values—necessary values—that we must also honor if we are to receive a vision that is whole.

THE BEAR AS SPIRIT HELPER

Worship of the bear is also ancient and widespread. Neanderthal peoples set bear skulls on what may have been altars, although we will never be certain that the purpose was for worship. As discussed earlier, many hunting tribes had rituals to ensure that a slain bear would wish to return from the spirit world and be hunted again. In the myths of the American Indians, the bear often acts as a spirit helper for a hero. Because bears dig for roots, many Indian tribes considered them to be shamans and healers. A number of superstitions in Europe and America revolve around the curative powers of bear grease (for baldness and to cure aches), bear teeth (for toothache and to aid teething children to have strong teeth), riding on a bear's back (to cure whooping cough), sleeping on a bearskin (to cure backache), and fur taken from a living bear (which, when mixed with alcohol, was thought to cure fits). In fact, the phrase "lick into shape" comes from the superstition that bear cubs, which look small and shapeless when first born, were licked by their mothers into the shape of a bear.

Today we possess far more accurate information about the bear, especially about the biochemistry of the bear during hibernation. The bear does not lower its body temperature in hibernation, the way that deep hibernators like the woodchuck and squirrel do. Instead the bear burns nearly 4,000 calories a day and maintains a state that might be described as meditation-like. While the woodchuck and squirrel are defenseless, the bear is quite capable of waking and defending itself from intruders. During the five months of hibernation, the bear can even be pregnant or nurse a cub.

The bear seems to defy the rules that would govern other mammals, such as humans, were they to attempt to match the feat of hibernation. Living off accumulated body fat and taking no nourishment, the bear's bones do not become thin despite five months of inactivity; the bear's lean body mass actually increases despite the lack of exercise; and there is no toxic buildup of urea despite the bear's failure to eliminate waste during the entire period of hibernation. Scientists studying the bear are finding that these apparent miracles are due to a unique system of recycling in which calcium from bone loss is apparently captured for new bone growth and urea that would become toxic is absorbed by the bladder and synthesized into useful proteins and neurotransmitters. The hope of scientists is that study of the bear may offer insights into the creation of medicines to aid humans suffering from osteoporosis or kidney failure.

There are a number of fascinating differences between

the bear and the bull. The bull walks on four legs, the bear can walk on two like a person. The bull is a herding animal, the bear is not. The bull has been domesticated, the bear never has been. The bull is constant in its fertile powers, the bear withdraws from life for the months of winter. The bull lives on the sunlit surface of the earth, while the bear enters the darkness of its den beneath that surface.

In terms of mythology, the bear offers a striking image of descent to the underworld, self-nurturing in the womb of the earth, and rebirth with each wakening for the spring. So the bear is like the human hero who dares to venture into the underworld, the world of the unknown and the unconscious. The worship of the bull brings renewal of the land through the sacrifice of the bull. However, the bear emerges from the womb of the earth to be reborn each spring—without sacrifice.

So the bull and bear exist in symbolic counterpoint. The bull is ever fertile, ever active in its inseminating power. Thus the bull lives in the world of time, of life and death. Only sacrifice can bring new energy into this world and nurture new life. The bear lives much of its life in the underworld, in the timeless realm of the spirits. Here it lives on its own flesh and is self-devouring. Like Persephone, it eats of its own nature and becomes more and more the essence of what it is. By this mysterious process, this biochemical miracle of conservation, the bear exists without the ordinary functions of life. It does not eat; it does not eliminate waste. When it rises with the spring, it leaves the underworld and is reborn to the everyday world that we know. It returns to the flux of nature until the coming of the next winter when it will again withdraw to the timeless realm of hibernation.

To imagine that the bearish investor merely believes that a stock or the stock market will fall in value is to diminish the deeper significance of being a bear. In symbolic terms, the bearish investor is truly focused on the world of nature, the world that cannot be domesticated and made to serve us through cultivation. To be bearish is to know that we must have time for conservation, we must have time to recycle what we have gained from the sacrifice of the bull. In a sense, the bear is the healer and wise being within us who demands that we contain our boundless desires to acquire and, instead, seek for the riches that we carry within. So we may withdraw like the bear and wait patiently, meditative and yet alert, until the season comes for us to be reborn in the world of time. In this rebirth we will be licked into a new shape.

Since all investors seek to know the cycles of the stock market, becoming bulls and bears in turn, we might seek a synthesis, an image of ever-changing wholeness, that would be the bull/bear. There is a hint of such a synthesis in the story of Mithra slaying the bull, for Mithra takes the captured bull to a cave. Although the bull escapes, it returns to the cave where Mithra slays it at the entrance. But if Mithra had let the bull return to the darkness of the cave, would the bull have become like the bear? This is really the question of the balance in human nature. Can we be both expansive like the bull and contractive like the bear? Can we both develop our economies and conserve the natural resources of the world? Can we both strive for money and strive to learn more deeply of ourselves?

IN THE LABYRINTH

One of the most famous myths of antiquity, that of the Minotaur in the maze, may offer insights to help us. Zeus, the principal god of the Greeks, had the sex drive of a bull and would often take animal form if this helped him satisfy his sexual urges. When he became enamored of the beautiful maiden Europa, he changed into a bull and carried her off to the island of Crete. The perversity of this shape-shifting was to have monstrous consequences for the generations that followed.

Zeus and Europa had a son, Minos, who became king of Crete. Poseidon, the god of the oceans, gave Minos a white bull to offer as a sacrifice. Minos coveted the bull and refused to sacrifice it. In retribution, Minos's wife, Pasiphaë, was made to fall in love with this bull. Her son by the bull was the dreaded Minotaur, who had the head of a bull and the body of a man. King Minos imprisoned the Minotaur in a maze built beneath his palace at Knossos in Crete.

Because one of his sons had been killed helping the Athenians fight the bull that fathered the Minotaur, every nine years King Minos received from Athens a tribute of seven maidens and seven youths. Minos then sacrificed this living tribute to the Minotaur. At last an Athenian hero, Theseus, dared to enter the labyrinth and kill the Minotaur with his bare hands. Theseus escaped from the darkness by following the thread of a clew of yarn given to him by Ariadne, the daughter of Minos, who later became the bride of the bull-god Dionysus.

The myth of the Minotaur contains the image of the bull in the cave of the bear. The Minotaur is the union of beast and human; it is also the union of human and god. If Theseus had been a more clever hero, he might have sat and communed with this marvelous being. He might have learned the darker secrets of his own nature, secrets that would soon lead him to abandon Ariadne and cause the death of his own father.

The Minotaur, alone in the timeless dark of the maze, might have yearned to speak. If he had been able, if a human ear would have heard him, how might he have been transformed? For the name of the Minotaur was Asterion, which means "of the stars." So the Minotaur possessed the starry light of his celestial grandfather Zeus. Indeed, the labyrinth may not originally have been a maze but rather a spiral. So the person who journeyed downward to the center could return in safety to the light.

The spiral is a good image to conclude our discussion of the bull and the bear. If we think of the cycles of the stock market, we imagine an undulating curve that moves from left to right on a graph. The height of the curve measures the market's value and the movement to the right measures the passage of time.

But let us imagine that the cycles of the stock market are like a rising spiral. This would be an image of the ascending spiral of consciousness. On one level we might feel that our only purpose in playing the market was to gain or lose money. On another level we might see the usefulness of sacrificing money in service to others. And on yet a different level we might see the value of struggling with the paradoxes of our natures. So we might face in ourselves the images of the bull and bear, of Integrity and Hermes, as we become more fully what we are capable of being.

EPILOGUE

To CONFRONT THE PARADOXES of our natures requires information about ourselves, about our depths. It requires the facing of so many illusions. It is not one journey, but a lifetime of journeys. How slowly, if ever, do we accumulate the wisdom that brings us awareness of what once we could not have imagined. How long it takes to become what we are, to discover in ourselves the rich potential that for so long remained invisible.

THEIR EYES WERE WATCHING GOD

The interplay of money with this inner unfoldment forms a core of *Their Eyes Were Watching God* by Zora Neale Hurston. Published in 1937, this novel tells the story of Janie, an African-American girl who grows to be a woman through her experiences in three marriages. Deserted by her mother, Janie is raised by her grandmother, who had been a slave and the mistress of the plantation master.

Money plays a crucial role in Janie's life, which certainly has as much pain as joy. She starts by accepting the values of her grandmother. There is no doubt that her grandmother cares for Janie and wants the best for her. Her grandmother insists that Janie marry Logan Killicks, an older, well-to-do farmer. Janie has no liking for Logan, whom she says looks like "some ole skull head in de grave yard," but she marries him to please her grandmother.

Three months later Janie comes to tell her grandmother that she has not grown to love Logan. Submitting to her grandmother's wishes and marrying for money has violated Janie's girlhood dreams of love. Rather than submit to abuse by Killicks, she runs away with Joe Starks, who has big dreams about achieving position and power in the world. When Joe succeeds, Janie finds herself relegated to playing the role of wife to a rich man. She feels the pain of not knowing her own heart and not living the natural flow of her own life. She is only slowly learning of herself, of her interior life. Estranged from her rich husband, she is finally freed after twenty years of marriage by Joe's death.

Janie is wealthy now in her own right but lonely. She realizes how she hates her dead grandmother "who had twisted her in the name of love." When Janie had been sixteen and "getting ready for her great journey to the horizon in search of people," her grandmother had undermined her and made her seek for "things." Janie laughs at the many men who tell her that a woman cannot stand alone and needs a man. She even likes being lonesome, for it means being free as well.

Six months after Joe Starks's death, Janie meets a man who makes her laugh. He is ten years her junior and his life isn't measured by money. When, for example, he wants to ride a train he "rides anyway—money or no money." His name is Vergible Woods, but he's called by his nickname, Tea Cake. At their first meeting Janie feels "as if she had known him all her life."

To love Tea Cake she has to overcome her suspicion that he is trading on his youth and ignore the friends who tell her that she is too important to be with someone like him. It is with Tea Cake that her interior life at last finds expression in the world. Here is a companion who assigns her no role, who cares for her as she is. Money is not a force for domination in their relationship. She is a rich woman; she has her money in the bank. With Tea Cake she is willing to do what she would refuse or resent with another man. She is joyous to share with him, to labor with him.

The novel ends with a terrible death, as Tea Cake saves Janie's life only to die himself from the bite of a rabid dog. Yet even as Janie grieves to lose him, she becomes ever more herself. She is both a part of the people and the events around her and an observer of them. She loves Tea Cake, but her view of reality has grown. She has reached deeply within herself and touched the invisible source that is within us all. From this inner discovery she is then able to live to the fullest in the world by being true to her own beliefs and desires. And at the same time, she understands that the events and people, even Tea Cake and her love for him, are not the only or the final reality. She has observed the invisible richness within herself; she has brought her soul into her life. If money at first held her captive, she has grown through this captivity and transformed herself and her relationship to money and to other people.

Janie, who has narrated her story to a friend, ends by saying that "you got tuh go there tuh know there." No one can make the life journey for us. "Two things everybody's got tuh do fuh theyselves. They got tuh go tuh God, and they got tuh find out about livin' fuh theyselves." Alone, she feels that Tea Cake will never die as long as she is alive. Thinking of all the events of her life, she feels how richly she has lived. She is both a part of this rich life experience and also the observer of it, for the novel ends with the sentence: "She called in her soul to come and see."

Janie makes of her life a journey. She moves through different relationships to men and money as her self-awareness deepens. To our everyday thinking, money would hardly seem a useful tool for this journey to greater awareness of ourselves and our relationships to others. Yet in so many ways, the symbolic richness of money can open a path to the richness that we carry within.

THE WIZARD OF OZ

This journey to awareness is archetypal, a pattern of initiation and growth that has taken many forms in many different cultures. This journey is not for everyone. The risks are great, the rewards uncertain. Yet those who take the journey find new depths and potentials that were once invisible to them. One of the most famous tales of this archetypal journey is a story written for children: *The Wizard of Oz*.

In 1896, when the Democrats held their convention in Chicago and heard William Jennings Bryan cry out against crucifixion on a Cross of Gold, one of the residents of Chicago was L. Frank Baum, author of *The Wizard of Oz*. Having had a play on Broadway in his early twenties and then having failed as a newspaper publisher in South Dakota before moving to Chicago in 1890, he frequented the Chicago Press Club and certainly heard many discussions of the silver issue. While Baum never said that one level of his story dealt with the great national debate over gold and silver, the book was mostly written in 1899 and published in 1900, the year William Jennings Bryan failed in his second attempt for the presidency. Could money, in fact, play an important role in *The Wizard of Oz?* If so, the story may be an allegory about the power and illusions generated by money.

The story begins as Dorothy, an orphan girl who lives with her aunt and uncle in drought-ravaged Kansas (the western states were parched by drought before the election of 1896), and her dog Toto are swept away by a cyclone that carries their house to the land of Oz. The house falls on and kills the Wicked Witch of the East. The kindly Munchkins, who inhabit Oz, give the witch's silver shoes to Dorothy. (The wonderful movie, with Judy Garland and Bert Lahr, changed Baum's story in a number of ways and made the shoes ruby instead of silver.) When Dorothy says that she wants to go home, a message comes that to do so she must go to the Emerald City at the very center of Oz. To travel to this place, she must follow the yellow brick road (the yellow brick strongly suggesting the ingots of gold that we would have expected to find stored in bank vaults at the end of the nineteenth century).

Why is the land called Oz? Baum said that he looked at a drawer in his filing cabinet and saw the letters O–Z, which became Oz. But Oz has another meaning as well: ounces, which is a measuring unit for both silver and gold. And Dorothy, who comes from Bryan's "hardy pioneers . . . who have made the desert to blossom as the rose," is quickly drawn into matters of which she understands very little. She is a pioneer in a fabulous land, and she must involve herself with gold (yellow brick) and silver (the silver shoes) if she is ever to find her way home to Kansas. And who was the Wicked Witch of the East? President Grover Cleveland hailed from the East, where he had been Governor of New York before winning his first term as president. When the cyclone of the silver movement swept out of the west, the Democratic Convention failed to nominate Cleveland (who backed the gold standard). So the house had fallen on him, killing him before the story (the campaign) really got underway.

Putting on her silver shoes, Dorothy starts on her journey and soon meets her companions: the Scarecrow, who feels himself a fool and yearns to have brains; the Tin Woodman, who wants to love and yearns for a heart; and the Lion, who yearns for courage. After many adventures, these four seekers come to the Guardian of the Gates of the Emerald City. This gatekeeper is hardly as terrible as Kerberos, the many-headed snake-dog that guards the gates of the underworld. The Guardian merely makes Dorothy and her friends (even Toto) put on emerald spectacles locked in place by two bands of gold.

Using a golden key, the Guardian unlocks the gates of the Emerald City. The newcomers are dazzled by its brilliance: "The streets were lined with beautiful houses all built of green marble and studded everywhere with sparkling emeralds. They walked over a pavement of the same green marble . . . The window panes were of green glass; even the sky above the City had a green tint, and the rays of the sun were green." Needless to say, the people, too, are green as are the shops and everything in them. No doubt the spectacles create much of what is spectacular in the Emerald City by making everyone see in the way that the Wizard wishes. This pervasive greenness brings to mind both the vegetative world and the greenback dollars that had figured in the gold and silver debates.

No living person has seen the Wizard, the Great Oz, "who can take on any form he wishes . . . who the real Oz is, when he is in his own form, no living person can tell." Dorothy and each of her band are ushered alone into the throne room of the Wizard. Each sees a different sight: Dorothy sees a giant head; the Scarecrow sees a beautiful woman; the Tin Woodman sees a terrible beast; and the Lion sees a ball of fire. The Wizard says he will only grant their wishes if Dorothy kills the Wicked Witch of the West and the others help her.

Many adventures later, Dorothy throws a bucket of water on the Wicked Witch of the West and, to her surprise, the Wicked Witch melts away. So the rainfalls after the election of 1896 brought good harvests to the western states and melted away the witch of drought. Returning to the throne room to have the Wizard grant them their wishes, Toto upsets a screen and reveals the Wizard—"a little old man, with a bald head and wrinkled face," just, in his own words, "a common man" and "a humbug." So the illusions by which he terrified Dorothy and the others were mere tricks.

Even knowing that the Wizard has no magical powers, they all still believe that he can grant their wishes and insist that he do so. The Wizard gives the Scarecrow a brain of bran, the Tin Woodman a heart of sawdust and silk, and the Lion a drink of courage. When they have left him alone, he laments and wonders, "How can I help being a humbug, when all these people make me do things that everybody knows can't be done?"

Yet the Scarecrow, the Tin Woodman, and the Lion have already shown that they possess what they are seeking. The obstacles on the yellow brick road have allowed them to discover in themselves what they seek to be given by the Wizard. Since they have become what they wish, the

Wizard can truly perform magic by giving them the outer symbol that confirms what they already are. Receiving this symbol is like a ritual that allows them to take the final step in their process of transformation, the step of knowing what they have become.

While the Wizard cannot help Dorothy, she, too, eventually learns that she has always possessed the power to grant her own wish. What she has lacked is awareness of her power. As the Good Witch of the South tells her, the silver shoes "can carry you wherever you wish to go." And with three clicks of her heels, Dorothy and Toto fly to the Kansas prairie and the embrace of her beloved Aunt Em.

We will never know if L. Frank Baum intended his story to be a monetary allegory. Yet the creative journey, to write a story or learn about ourselves, is often so much more than we intend. Whether the land of Oz is simply the letters O–Z from a cabinet drawer or is the symbol for gold and silver ounces, it is certainly a land of magical adventures. It lies outside the realms we know; it is the place awaiting our discovery.

Early in the story Dorothy tells the Good Witch of the North that Aunt Em said all the witches were dead. The Good Witch asks if Kansas is a civilized country. Dorothy says that it is.

"That accounts for it," says the Good Witch of the North. "In the civilized countries I believe there are no witches left, nor wizards, nor sorceresses, nor magicians. But, you see, the Land of Oz has never been civilized, for we are cut off from all the rest of the world. Therefore, we still have witches and wizards among us."

The challenge with such a place in us—"cut off from all the rest of the world"—is to make our journey and pass the Guardian of the Gates so that we may bring back its riches to the civilized world, the world of our everyday awareness. We may call this place Oz, the maze, the underworld, or the unconscious, but its challenge is to make us eat of our own natures. From this process we bring back the Scarecrow's wisdom, the Tin Woodman's love, and the Lion's courage; and we may return to the place from which we started, be it Kansas or anywhere else, with a newfound self-awareness.

Sometimes we may feel that our journeys seem to waste so much of our lives. Why must we be like the Scarecrow, the Tin Woodman, or the Lion? Why must each of us face the yellow brick road with its terrors and wonders? That we are not born like gods, fully knowledgeable about ourselves and our fate, is our human condition—a condition that we struggle to understand. We are part of the vast cycles of death and rebirth, part of the interplay in which sacrifice may at last bring us the riches of the invisible world.

The Secret Life of Money began with the story of the man who prayed to a wooden idol to give him money and make him prosper. We have traveled a long way on the yellow brick road since we met that man and his idol. We have seen how money can take innumerable forms without diminishing the symbolic power that allows it to obsess us. We have seen the radiance of Moneta, the face of the fertility goddess from whom money flows. We have learned how money challenges each of us and our society to be productive.

The quest for fertility—which assures our sustenance and, in more contemporary terms, our productivity—connects money to earlier rituals in which gifts were offered to the spirit world. The ease with which we worship money is more comprehensible when we look at these offerings that sought divine favor and attempted to initiate an exchange with the divine. That these rituals might require human or animal sacrifice helps us understand why money issues can make us feel our very lives are at stake.

The power of money to symbolize our life energy confuses us; we imagine that our self-worth and value depend on possessing money instead of using money as a tool to look more deeply within ourselves. Misers build their sense of self-worth and security around the hoarding of their life energy. Yet this hoarding defeats the very purpose of having money, since circulation is crucial if money is to serve its purpose of exchange among people. To circulate money, especially in service to our community, allows us to contact the natural wealth that we have within, energy that is augmented by giving to others.

Yet money that is given—for example, as an inheritance—can be weighted with emotional issues. Only by a careful evaluation of what is truly ours can we choose what to keep from the inheritance of money, property, love, education, and values that our parents have offered us. In its own way, debt, too, involves a giving and a receiving. If we are not to be imprisoned by debt, we must understand how debt is a statement about our future, how we will develop, and what our capacity will be to repay the energies that others offer to us.

The Secret Life of Money has focused on some of the images that are likely to confuse us. For example, United States money looks much the same as it always has, but it is no longer backed by gold or silver. Credit cards suggest that we can borrow without ever having to repay, but this illusion simply leads to the imprisonment that is always a potential of debt. And banks, in the last hundred years, have changed from temples serving the few to merchandisers of consumer debt that profit from the many. Even the stock market, which ideally channels the energy of society toward those enterprises that will be most productive, offers a symbolism of bulls and bears, of the flux of increase and decline that come one after another in never-ending cycles. So we see that the stock market bulls are but shadows of the divine bulls whose seminal fluids fructified the earth.

Dispelling illusions about money guides us toward the values that are most true for us. Each of us must find the nature of our own abundance. Each of us must decide how willing we are to share our money, our productivity, and our energy. So our relationship to money can deepen our understanding of our connection to other people and to our community.

Our consumer culture seems to value money and possessions, but our explorations tell us that the secret life of money may speak of inner richness. Understanding money can actually help us call in our souls to come and see. For the fertility of Moneta is not only found in the fields, the factory, or the office, but also in the creativity and love of our minds and hearts.

NOTES

No numbering is used for the Notes. Rather, the Notes are connected to the appropriate passage in the text by reference to the
page number in the text and the quotation of a brief phrase
from the page to locate the passage. Once a source is fully an-
notated in the Notes, additional references to that source are
abbreviated by giving only the title. References to the Bible are
to the Revised Standard Version unless noted otherwise.

INTRODUCTION

Page xi. "... **prosperity eluded him.**" "A Man and a Wooden
God," *Fables of Aesop According to Sir Roger L'Estrange* (New
York: Dover Publications, 1967), pp. 91–2.

CHAPTER ONE. THE MANY FORMS OF MONEY:
UNDERSTANDING ITS SYMBOLIC VALUE

Page 4. "... **poles and carried.**" Norman Angell, *The Story of
Money* (Garden City, New York: Garden City Publishing Com-
pany, 1929), pp. 88–9. This account is based on William Henry
Furness, *The Island of Stone Money* (Philadelphia and London:
J. P. Lippincott Co., 1910).

Pages 7–10. As to the many forms of early money, *see* A. Hingston Quiggin, *A Survey of Primitive Money* (London: Methuen

& Co. Ltd., 1949); Paul Einzig, *Primitive Money* (Oxford and New York: Pergamon Press, 1966); J. P. Jones, *The Money Story* (New York: Drake Publishers Inc., 1973), pp. 11–22; and *The Story of Money*, pp. 72–90.

Page 11. "... **the minds of its inventors.**" *The Story of Money*, pp. 85–7.

Page 13. "... **it is archetypal.**" This theory of archetypes has been developed by psychologist C. G. Jung. "On a personal level, archetypal motifs are patterns of thought or behavior that are common to humanity at all times and in all places." Daryl Sharp, *Jung Lexicon* (Toronto: Inner City Books, 1991), p. 29.

Page 14. "... **English word 'mint.'** " Eric Partridge, *Origins: A Short Etymological Dictionary of Modern English* (New York: Greenwich House, 1983), p. 405.

Page 15. "... **as Juno** *Matronalia.*" Joël Schmidt, *Larousse Greek and Roman Mythology*, Seth Benadete, ed. (New York: McGraw-Hill Book Company, 1980), p. 152.

Page 15. "... **rich beyond measure or imagining.**" The image of Juno Moneta is a composite drawn in part from Demeter, the Greek goddess, and in part from Lakshmi, the Hindu goddess. Some pictures of Lakshmi show coins pouring from one of her four hands. She is a fertility goddess who brings abundance and luck to those who worship her. *See* David Kinsley, *The Goddesses' Mirror* (Albany: State University of New York Press, 1989), pp. 53–70.

Page 16. "... **mind or think.**" *Origins: A Short Etymological Dictionary of Modern English*, pp. 390–2, 403–5.

Page 16. "... **his rabbi for advice.**" "One Big Worry," *A Treasury of Jewish Folklore*, Nathan Ausubel, ed. (New York: Crown Publishers, 1948), p. 5.

CHAPTER TWO. THE ALMIGHTY DOLLAR: WHY MONEY IS SO EASILY WORSHIPPED

Page 19. "... **root of all evils** ..." 1 Tim. 6:10.

Page 20. "... **one religion over another.**" *Everson* v. *Board of Education*, 330 U.S.1 at p. 15.

Page 22. "... **game that nourished them.**" Joseph H. Wherry, *Indian Masks and Myths of the West* (New York: Bonanza Books, 1969), pp. 167–74.

Page 23. "... **as a knife and skis.**" *New Larousse Encyclopedia of Mythology* (London: Hamlyn Publishing Group, 1959), p. 307.

Page 23. "... **the Ainu of Japan.**" *Man, Myth and Magic*, Richard Cavendish, ed. (New York and London: Marshall Cavendish, 1985), vol. 2, p. 246.

Page 24. "... **mesas of Arizona in August.**" *The World of the American Indian*, Jules B. Billard, ed. (Washington, D.C.: National Geographic Society, 1974), pp. 163–9.

Page 24. "... **year-round procession of rituals.**" Frank Waters, *Book of the Hopi* (New York: Ballentine Books, 1963), pp. 123–247, and, particularly with respect to the mystic marriage, pp. 222–3.

Page 25. "... **the Greater Mysteries (held in September).**" Katherine G. Kanta, *Eleusis* (Athens: Kanta, 1979), pp. 10–17.

Page 26. "... **the rice harvest with a feast.**" James George Fraser, *The Golden Bough*, abridged paperback edition (New York: Macmillan Publishing Company, 1963), pp. 558–9.

Page 28. "... **love and familial responsibilities.**" William H. Desmonde, *Magic, Myth, and Money* (New York: The Free Press of Glencoe, Inc., 1962), pp. 29–36.

Page 28. " '. . . **upon himself alone.**' " *The Rig-Veda*, Wendy Doniger O'Flaherty, trans. (New York and London: Penguin Books, 1981), p. 69.

Page 28. " '. . . **to be of darkness.**' " *The Bhagavad Gita*, Annie Besant, trans. (Adyar, Madras: The Theosophical Publishing House, 1895), xvii.13, p. 178.

Page 28. " '. . . **out of action.**' " *The Bhagavad Gita*, iii.14, p. 54.

Page 29. ". . . **the hiring of mourners.**" *Fables of Aesop According to Sir Roger L'Estrange*, p. 31.

Page 29. ". . . **distort our view of the world.**" "The Veneer of Silver," *A Treasury of Jewish Folklore*, p. 60.

Page 30. ". . . **impetus to the creation of money.**" *Magic, Myth, and Money*, pp. 171–4; *see also The Illustrated Encyclopedia of Mankind* (New York and London: Marshall Cavendish, 1990), vol. 3, p. 2058.

Page 32. ". . . **that represented immense wealth.**" John S. Bowman, *Treasures of Ancient Greece* (New York: W. H. Smith Publishers, Inc., 1986), p. 68.

Page 32. ". . . **treasures as security for borrowing.**" *The Horizon Book of Ancient Greece* (New York: American Heritage Publishing Co., Inc., 1965), p. 318.

Page 32. ". . . **treasure moved into the world of trade.**" *The Story of Money*, p. 96.

Page 33. ". . . **most of these coins clearly do.**" *Magic, Myth, and Money*, pp. 111–14 (especially notes 4 and 5); cf. George Macdonald, *Coin Types: Their Origin and Development* (Glasgow: James Maclehose & Sons, 1905; reprint ed., Chicago: Argonaut Inc., Publishers, 1969).

Page 33. "... **goddess of fertility as well.**" George Dontas, *The Acropolis and Its Museum* (Athens: Clio Editions, 1979), pp. 8–9.

Page 34. "... **godlike portrayals of themselves on coins.**" *Coin Types: Their Origin and Development*, pp. 151–2.

Page 35. "... **the words 'God, liberty, law.'** " Leon Lindheim, *Facts and Fictions about Coins* (Cleveland and New York: The World Publishing Company, 1967), pp. 190–1.

Page 35. "... **all coins of the United States.**" *Facts and Fictions about Coins*, pp. 200–1.

Page 36. "... **bills as well as coins.**" *Coin World Almanac*, P. Bradley Reed, ed. (New York: World Almanac, 1990), p. 271.

Page 36. " '... **has approved our undertaking.'** " *Coin World Almanac*, p. 271.

Page 37. "... **later St. Joachim.**" Norman M. Davis, *The Complete Book of United States Coin Collecting* (New York: Macmillan, 1971), pp. 265–69; Adrian Room, *Dictionary of Coin Names* (London: Routledge and Kegan Paul, 1987), pp. 215–16.

Page 38. "... **to pay 'ten thousand dollars.'** " *Macbeth*, I, ii, line 64.

Page 38. " '... **adopted from south to north.'** " Thomas Jefferson, "Notes on a Money Unit for the United States," 1782, quoted in *Dictionary of Coin Names*, pp. 215–16. See also Merrill D. Peterson, *Thomas Jefferson and the New Nation*, (London and New York: Oxford University Press, 1970), pp. 275–8, indicating that Jefferson first made this proposal in 1776.

Page 38. "... **of the sign for pesos.**" *The Complete Book of United States Coin Collecting*, pp. 264–5.

Page 39. ". . . **roots of the taler itself.**" *The Money Story*, pp. 45–6. Cf. *The Complete Book of United States Coin Collecting*, pp. 264–5.

CHAPTER THREE. MONEY AND SACRIFICE: WHEN MONEY FEELS MORE IMPORTANT THAN LIFE

Page 43. ". . . **caused by the love of money.**" D. H. Lawrence, "The Rocking-Horse Winner," *The Portable D. H. Lawrence*, Diana Trilling, ed. (New York: The Viking Press, 1947), pp. 147–66.

Page 45. ". . . **gold and his daughter, Marygold.**" Nathaniel Hawthorne, "The Golden Touch," *A Wonder Book* (New York: Lancer Books Inc., 1968), pp. 51–81.

Page 48. ". . . **in *The Metamorphoses.***" Ovid, *The Metamorphoses*, trans. Horace Gregory (New York: The Viking Press, 1958), pp. 301–5.

Page 49. ". . . **the goddess herself must sacrifice.**" *The Golden Bough*, pp. 403–10.

Page 50. " '. . . **before the people of Israel.**' " 2 Chron. 28:1–3; 2 Kings 16:2–3.

Page 51. ". . . **even the prophet Elijah.**" 1 Kings 16:34; Judg. 11:30–30; 1 Kings 18:20–46; cf. Jer. 7:31 which expresses the later revulsion against human sacrifice.

Page 51. ". . . **children were offered as sacrifices.**" *The Golden Bough*, p. 327; Patrick Tierney, *The Highest Altar* (London, Bloomsbury Publishing Limited, 1989), pp. 396–7.

Page 51. ". . . **the fertility of the land.**" *The Golden Bough*, pp. 757–63.

Page 51. ". . . **that of the Aztecs.**" Brian M. Fagan, *The Aztecs* (New York, W. H. Freeman and Company, 1984), pp. 228–33, 245–6.

Page 52. "... **feeds the growth of the corn.**" Erich Neumann, *The Great Mother*, Ralph Manheim, trans., Bollingen Series XLVII (Princeton, N.J.: Princeton University Press, 1955), pp. 195, 322–3.

Page 52. "... **the Maize Goddess Chicomecohuatl.**" *The Golden Bough*, pp. 682–6.

Page 53. "... **but for money.**" *The Highest Altar*, pp. 322, 354. *See also* M. J. Sallnow, "Precious Metals in the Andean Moral Economy," *Money and the Morality of Exchange*, J. Parry and M. Bloch, ed. (New York and Cambridge: Cambridge University Press, 1989), pp. 209–31.

Page 57. "... **of the culture as well.**" The collective unconscious is a key aspect of the theories of psychologist C. G. Jung. It is collective because it contains "psychic contents that belong not to one individual but to a society, a people or the human race in general." *Jung Lexicon*, p. 35.

Page 62. "... **prevailed before the Civil War.**" For a discussion of issues pertaining to gold and silver, *see* Milton Friedman, *Money Mischief* (New York: Harcourt Brace Jovanovich, 1992).

Page 63. "... **they had cost in 1869.**" Hugh Rockoff, "The 'Wizard of Oz' as a Monetary Allegory," *Journal of Political Economy*, vol. 98, no. 4, 1990, pp. 742–4.

Page 63. "... **with striking religious metaphors.**" William Jennings Bryan, "The Cross of Gold," July 8, 1896. This speech appears in *Documentary History of Banking and Currency in the United States*, Herman E. Krooss, ed. (New York: McGraw-Hill Book Co., 1969), vol. 3, pp. 2009–15.

Page 67. " '... **have been vindicated?**' " William Jennings Bryan and Mary Baird Bryan, *The Memoirs of William Jennings Bryan* (Chicago: Winston, 1925), p. 471.

CHAPTER FOUR. HOARDING MONEY: WHY THE LIFE
ENERGY OF MISERS IS STOLEN

Page 69. "... **a miller who loved gold.**" "A Miller Burying His Gold," *Fables of Aesop According to Sir Roger L'Estrange*, p. 10.

Page 71. " '... **Punishment of the Stingy.**' " George Bird Grinnell, "The Punishment of the Stingy," *The Punishment of the Stingy and Other Indian Stories* (New York: Harper and Brothers, 1901; reprint ed., Lincoln, Nebraska and London: University of Nebraska Press, 1982), pp. 3–15.

Page 77. "... **by Charles Dickens.**" Charles Dickens, *A Christmas Carol*, in *The Christmas Books* (London and New York: Penguin Books, 1985), vol. 1, pp. 45–133.

Page 87. "... **worries that it imposes.**" Henry D. Thoreau, *Walden*, J. Lyndon Shanley, ed. (Princeton, N.J.: Princeton University Press, 1971), p. 32.

Page 87. "... **learned the reward of hard work.**" Peter Baida, *Poor Richard's Legacy* (New York: William Morrow and Company, Inc., 1990), pp. 80–3.

Page 87. "... **one rich and one poor.**" "Money Makes Cares," *Folktales of China*, Wolfram Eberhard, ed. (Chicago and London: The University of Chicago Press, 1965), pp. 180–2.

Page 92. "... **ruled a vast empire in India.**" Swami Muktananda, *Play of Consciousness* (South Fallsburg, New York: Syda Foundation. 1978), pp. 219–32. The original story appears in the *Yoga Vasishtha*.

Page 98. "... **of Alcoholics Anonymous.**" *C. G. Jung Letters*, vol. 2, 1951–61 (Princeton, N.J.: Princeton University Press, 1975), pp. 623–4.

CHAPTER FIVE. THE SOURCE OF RICHES: GAINING A NEW UNDERSTANDING OF SUPPLY

Page 101. ". . . **as a boy of eight or nine.**" C. G. Jung, *Memories, Dreams, Reflections*, Aniela Jaffé, ed., and Richard and Clara Winston, trans., rev. ed. (New York: Vintage Books, 1965), p. 20.

Page 102. ". . . **of a man named James Kidd.**" John G. Fuller, *The Great Soul Trial* (New York: The Macmillan Company, 1969).

Page 104. ". . . **richness of the Self.**" According to Jung's theories, the Self is "the archetype of wholeness and the regulating center of the psyche; a transpersonal power that transcends the ego. . . . Like any archetype, the essential nature of the self is unknowable, but its manifestations are the content of myth and legend." *Jung Lexicon*, p. 119.

Page 104. " '. . . **inherit eternal life.**' " Mark 10:17–26; Matt. 19:16–22.

Page 105. " '. . . **to receive kingly power.**' " Luke 19:11–26.

Page 106. " '. . . **serve God and mammon.**' " Luke 16:13.

Page 106. " '. . . **and buys that field.**' " Matt. 13:44.

Page 107. " '. . . **come to this house . . .**' " Luke 19:1–10.

Page 107. " '. . . **be yours as well.**' " Matt. 7:25–33; Luke 12:22–31.

Page 107. " '. . . **is within you.**' " Luke 17:21 (King James Version).

Page 108. " '. . . **is not rich toward God.**' " Luke 12:21.

Page 108. ". . . **and become homeless.**" *Grimms' Tales for Young and Old*, Ralph Manheim, trans. (Garden City, New York: Anchor Press/Doubleday, 1977), p. 494.

Page 109. "... **in service to others.**" Annette Lieberman and Vicki Lindner, *Unbalanced Accounts* (New York: Atlantic Monthly Press, 1987), pp. 18–20.

Page 110. " '... **in your experience.**' " Joel Goldsmith, *The Infinite Way* (Marina del Rey, California: DeVorss and Co., 1947), pp. 133–7

Page 111. " '... **that supply to escape.**' " Joel Goldsmith, *The Art of Spiritual Healing* (New York: Harper and Row, 1959), p. 142–4.

Page 112. "... **value to him when he dies.**" "Only the Dead Are Without Hope," *A Treasury of Jewish Folklore*, pp. 125–6.

Page 113. "... **of the wealthy man.**" "The Father of the Poor," *A Treasury of Jewish Folklore*, pp. 127–30.

Page 115. "... **the Golden Ladder of Charity.**" "The Golden Ladder of Charity," *A Treasury of Jewish Folklore*, pp. 124–5.

Page 116. " '... **for the forgiveness of sins.**' " Matt. 26:26–8.

Page 117. "... *dana* **or pure gifts ...**" J. Parry, "On the Moral Perils of Exchange," *Money and the Morality of Exchange*, pp. 64–93.

Page 119. "... **whose friars lived by begging.**" *The Encyclopedia of Religion*, Mircea Eliade, ed. (New York: Macmillan Publishing Company, 1987), vol. 9, pp. 371–3.

CHAPTER SIX. INHERITANCE: THE ACTUAL AND SYMBOLIC WEALTH OF OUR PARENTS

Page 124. " '... **as cocaine is to morality.**' " Quoted in Lewis H. Lapham, *Money and Class in America* (New York: Ballantine Books, 1988), p. 13, n. 8.

Page 129. "... **the fertility goddess Demeter.**" "To Demeter," *Hesiod, the Homeric Hymns and Homerica*, Hugh G. Evelyn-

White, trans., Loeb Classical Library (Cambridge, Massachusetts: Harvard University Press, 1907), vol. 57, pp. 289–325.

Page 131. " '. . . **giver of good things!**' " "To Hermes," *Hesiod, the Homeric Hymns and Homerica*, p. 443.

Page 134. ". . . **be used as a contraceptive.**" John M. Riddle, J. Worth Estes, and Josiah C. Russell, "Birth Control in the Ancient World," *Archeology*, vol. 47, no. 2 (March/April, 1994), p. 31.

Page 135. ". . . **as an offering to Persephone.**" Vergil, *The Aeneid*, Patric Dickinson, trans. (New York: New American Library, 1961), Book VI, pp. 120–46.

Page 137. " '. . . **he'll dig it up again!**' " T. S. Eliot, *The Waste Land and Other Poems* (New York: Harcourt, Brace and World, Inc., 1930), p. 32.

Page 138. " '. . . **to be crowned again.**' " *The Portable D. H. Lawrence*, p. 481–4.

Page 140. " '. . . **abundance of his possessions.**' " Luke 12:13–15.

Page 140. ". . . **a treasure in the vineyard.**" "A Father and His Sons," *Fables of Aesop According to Sir Roger L'Estrange*, p. 68.

Page 141. ". . . **losing his ax in the river.**" "Mercury and a Carpenter," *Fables of Aesop According to Sir Roger L'Estrange*, p. 52.

Page 142. ". . . **from *Grimms' Fairy Tales*.**" "The Spirit in the Bottle," *Grimms' Tales for Young and Old*, pp. 346–9.

Page 148. ". . . **to it on his birthday.**" Lewis Hyde, *The Gift* (New York: Vintage Books, 1979), pp. 53–4. For a wonderful play in which a guardian spirit is portrayed, *see* Plautus, *The Pot* *of Gold and Other Plays*, E. F. Watling, trans. (New York and London: Penguin Books, 1965), pp. 7–49.

Page 151. "**. . . who was this thief?**" "To Hermes," *Hesiod, the Homeric Hymns and the Homerica*, pp. 362–405.

CHAPTER SEVEN. INDEBTEDNESS: HOW THE DEBTORS' TOWER CONNECTS EARTH TO HEAVEN

Page 155. " '**. . . crushed in my breast.**' " Quoted in Peter Ackroyd, *Dickens* (New York: HarperCollins Publishers, 1990), p. 68.

Page 156. " '**. . . and so say I.**' " Quoted in Peter J. Coleman, *Debtors and Creditors in America* (Madison, Wisconsin: The State Historical Society of Wisconsin, 1974), p. 5.

Page 158. "**. . . clothing and dismissed him.**" Edgar Johnson, *Charles Dickens: His Tragedy and Triumph* (New York: Simon and Schuster, 1952), p. 37.

Page 158. "**. . . in Massachusetts prisons.**" *Debtors and Creditors in America*, p. 42.

Page 158. "**. . . fear for a great many people.**" *Dickens*, p. 69.

Page 159. "**. . . especially from England.**" *Debtors and Creditors in America*, pp. 6–8.

Page 159. " '**. . . be given their freedom.**' " Quoted in Lewis Mandell, *The Credit Card Industry: A History* (Boston: Twayne Publishers, 1990), p. 6. *See* pp. 6–8 as to the early development of credit.

Page 160. "**. . . a debt too large to pay.**" Matt. 18:23–35.

Page 162. "**. . . become slaves.**" *New York Times*, 23 May 1993, p. 3.

Page 162. "**. . . meals, and rent.**" *New York Times*, 9 June 1993, pp. A1, A8.

Page 162. "... **hands with a boy.**" *New York Times*, 23 July 1993, p. B1.

Page 162. "... **the failure to repay debt.**" U.S. Bureau of the Census, *Statistical Abstract of the United States: 1992*, 112th ed. (Washington, D.C., 1992), chart no. 849; U.S. Bureau of the Census, *Statistical Abstract of the United States: 1989*, 109th ed. (Washington, D.C., 1989), chart no. 867; *New York Times*, 28 June 1993, pp. D1, D3; *New York Times*, 7 November 1992, p. 33.

Page 163. " '... **would make him wretched.**' " Quoted in *Charles Dickens: His Tragedy and Triumph*, p. 35.

Page 163. " '... **slave of the lender.**' " Prov. 22:7.

Page 163. " '... **not exact interest from him.**' " Exod. 22:25–27.

Page 164. " '... **to repay the loan.**' " Deut. 24:6, 12–13.

Page 164. " '... **from the hand of the fowler.**' " Prov. 6:1–5.

Page 165. "... **of Ghana in West Africa.**" Harold Courlander, "How Debt Came to Ashanti," *A Treasury of African Folklore* (New York: Crown Publishers, 1975), pp. 145–6.

Page 170. " '... **be nourished and multiply.**' " Gen. 1:27–30.

Page 170. " '... **man became a living being.**' " Gen. 2:7.

Page 171. " '... **to dust you shall return.**' " Gen. 3:19.

Page 171. "... **of eating forbidden fruit.**" "Rapunzel," *Grimms' Tales for Young and Old*, pp. 46–49.

Page 175. " '... **pays all debts.**' " William Shakespeare, *The Tempest*, III, ii, line 136.

Page 175. " '... **they are in their minds.**' " William Thackeray, *Vanity Fair* (New York and London: Penguin Books, 1985), p. 265.

Page 176. "... **an heir and not a debtor.**" *Charles Dickens: His Triumph and Tragedy*, p. 42.

Page 176. " '... **that time of my life.**' " *Charles Dickens: His Triumph and Tragedy*, p. 34.

Page 176. "... **between debt and inheritance.**" "The Bridge of Ch'üan-chou," *Folktales of China*, pp. 103–10.

Page 182. "... *Alcestis* **by Euripides.**" Euripides, *Alcestis*, Arthur S. Way, trans., *Greek Dramas* (New York: Appleton and Company, 1900), pp. 195–238.

Page 185. " '... **to love one another.**' " Rom. 13:8.

Page 186. "... **their taxes are lower.**" *New York Times*, 9 February 1994, p. A17.

Page 186. "... **to give the organ.**" *New York Times*, 30 June 1993, p. C14.

Page 187. " '... **render life of little value.**' " Letter from Thomas Jefferson to Nicholas Lewis, July 29, 1787, Thomas Jefferson Papers, Micro Film edition, reel 7, Manuscript Library of Congress, Washington, D.C.

Page 188. " '... **the best of his abilities.**' " Saul K. Padover, *Jefferson* (New York: The New American Library, 1942), p. 160.

Page 188. " '... **laws we cannot repeal.**' " Jack McLaughlin, *Jefferson and Monticello* (New York: Henry Holt and Company, 1988), pp. 4, 269.

Page 188. " '... **would devour his estate . . .**' " *Jefferson*, p. 174, 175.

Page 189. "... **declared bankruptcy in 1819.**" *Thomas Jefferson and the New Nation*, p. 991.

Page 189. " '... **line I am writing . . .**' " *Jefferson*, p. 182.

Page 190. "... **daughter and grandchildren.**" *Thomas Jefferson and the New Nation*, p. 1007.

Page 191. "... **the law of hospitality.**" *Jefferson and Monticello*, p. 269.

Page 191. " '... **that God is just. ...**' " *Thomas Jefferson and the New Nation*, p. 260.

Page 192. " '... **is incalculable.**' " C. G. Jung, *Psychological Types, Collected Works of C. G. Jung*, H. G. Baynes, trans., revised by R. F. C. Hull (Princeton, N.J.: Princeton University Press, 1971), vol. 6, p. 63.

CHAPTER EIGHT. CHANGING SYMBOLS: MONEY, CREDIT CARDS, AND BANKS

Page 194. "... **sale in the market.**" "The Image-Seller," *Aesop's Fables*, V.S. Vernon Jones, trans. (New York: Gramercy Books, reprint of 1912 ed.), p. 88.

Page 195. "... **our day-to-day lives.**" Bureau of Economic Analysis, *The Economic Report of the President* (Washington, D.C.: Federal Reserve Board, 1992).

Page 197. " '... **value with this standard.**' " *Documentary History of Banking and Currency in the United States*, p. 2016.

Page 197. "... **issue Federal Reserve Notes.**" For the history leading to the creation of the Federal Reserve System, *see Documentary History of Banking and Currency in the United States*, pp. 2083–416.

Page 198. "... **or using gold as money.**" James Grant, *Money of the Mind* (New York: Farrar Straus Giroux, 1992), pp. 154, 227, 233–4, 275; Glenn G. Munn and F. L. Garcia, *Encyclopedia of Banking and Finance*, 8th ed. (Boston: Bankers Publishing Company, 1983), p. 432.

Page 198. ". . . **defended at thirty-five dollars per ounce.**" *Money of the Mind*, pp. 271, 285.

Page 200. ". . . **of sacred obligations.**" "Message by President Rutherford B. Hayes Vetoing the Bland-Allison Act, February 28, 1878," *Documentary History of Banking and Currency in the United States*, p. 1922.

Page 201. ". . . **by Edward Bellamy.**" Edward Bellamy, *Looking Backward 2000–1887* (Boston and New York: Houghton, Mifflin and Company, 1888), pp. 118–20.

Page 202. ". . . **by Diners Club in 1950.**" *See*, for a history of the development of credit cards, *The Credit Card Industry: A History*.

Page 204. ". . . **$15.73 billion for that year.**" *New York Times*, 18 November 1991, pp. A1, D9.

Page 208. ". . . **three Visa cards).**" *New York Times*, 26 August 1991, pp. A1, A17.

Page 208. ". . . **two-thirds of them did.**" *New York Times*, 29 March 1993, pp. A1, D7.

Page 209. ". . . **awareness of credit card holders.**" *New York Times*, 16 November 1991, pp. 33, 45; *New York Times*, 19 November 1991, pp. A1, D9.

Page 210. ". . . **is 19.8 percent.**" *New York Times*, 12 December 1993, p. B1.

Page 211. " '. . . **stop incurring unsecured debt.**' " Debtors Anonymous, *Spending Plan* (P.O. Box 20322, New York, New York 10025–9992: Debtors Anonymous General Service Board, Inc., 1989), pp. 10–11.

Page 213. ". . . **banking in the twentieth century.**" *Money of the Mind*, pp. 76–95, 161–3.

Page 215. "... **to $1.384 billion in 1929.**" *Historical Abstract of the United States, Colonial Times to 1970* (Washington, D.C.: U.S. Government Printing Office), series X, pp. 551–60. This also shows total consumer credit outstanding from 1919 through 1970.

Page 217. "... **the public feel welcome.**" *Money Matters: A Critical Look at Bank Architecture*, Joel Stein and Caroline Levine, eds. (New York: McGraw-Hill, 1990). This offers a pictorial review of the changing styles of bank architectures.

Page 218. "... **toiling at their desks.**" *Statistical Abstract of the United States: 1992*, chart no. 796.

Page 219. "... **for goods and services.**" *New York Times*, 14 March 1993, p. 26; *New York Times*, 5 March 1994, p. 30.

Page 220. ". . . **of all transactions.**" Peter Passell, "Fast Money," *New York Times Magazine*, 18 October 1992, pp. 42, 66.

CHAPTER NINE. BULLS AND BEARS: HOW THE STOCK MARKET REFLECTS THE RENEWING CYCLES OF LIFE

Page 225. "... **formative years of our nation.**" *The New York Stock Exchange: The First 200 Years*, James E. Buck, ed. (Essex, Connecticut: Greenwich Publishing Group, Inc.), 1992. This history includes a photograph of "Integrity Protecting the Works of Man" on pp. 106–7.

Page 232. "... **toss up its horns.**" William and Mary Morris, *Dictionary of Word and Phrase Origins* (New York: Harper and Row, 1962), p. 56.

Page 233. "... **and agriculture as foundations.**" *Man, Myth and Magic*, vol. 2, pp. 363–7. This gives background with respect to the bull and includes portions of the hymns to Enlil and Amen-Ra.

NOTES

Page 235. "... and eventual dominance." Franz Cumont, *The Mysteries of Mithra* (New York: Dover Publications, Inc., 1956).

Page 237. "... ancient and widespread." *Man, Myth and Magic*, vol. 1, pp. 243–46. This gives background for the bear.

EPILOGUE

Page 243. "... by Zora Neale Hurston." Zora Neale Hurston, *Their Eyes Were Watching God* (Chicago and London: University of Illinois Press, 1978).

Page 246. "... for children: *The Wizard of Oz*." L. Frank Baum, *The Wizard of Oz* (London: Puffin Books, 1982).

Page 247. "... and illusions generated by money." *Journal of Political Economy*, pp. 739–60.

SELECTED BIBLIOGRAPHY

Anderson, Quentin. *Making Americans: An Essay on Individualism and Money*. New York: Harcourt Brace Jovanovich, Publishers, 1992.

Angell, Norman. *The Story of Money*. Garden City: Garden City Publishing Company, Inc., 1929.

Bornemann, Ernest, comp. *The Psychoanalysis of Money*. New York: Urizen Books, Inc., 1976.

Breton, Denise, and Christopher Largent. *The Soul of Economies: Spiritual Evolution Goes to the Marketplace*. Wilmington: Idea House Publishing Company, 1991.

Brown, Norman O. *Life Against Death: The Psychoanalytical Meaning of History*. 2d ed. Hanover: Wesleyan University Press, 1985.

Buck, James E., ed. *The New York Stock Exchange: The First 200 Years*. Essex: Greenwich Publishing Group, Inc., 1992.

Bush, Lawrence, and Jeffery Dekro. *Jews, Money & Social Responsibility: Developing a "Torah of Money" for Contemporary Life*. Philadelphia: The Shefa Fund, 1993.

Butterworth, Eric. *Spiritual Economics: You Deserve Abundance; Reshaping Your Attitudes About Money, Spirituality, and Personal Prosperity*, rev. ed. Unity Village: Unity Books, 1993.

Coleman, Peter J. *Debtors and Creditors in America: Insol-*

vency, Imprisonment for Debt, and Bankruptcy, 1607–1900. Madison: The State Historical Society of Wisconsin, 1974.

Desmonde, William H. *Magic, Myth, and Money: The Origins of Money in Religious Ritual.* New York: The Free Press of Glencoe, Inc., 1962.

Einzig, Paul. *Primitive Money.* Oxford and New York: Pergamon Press, 1960.

Fitch, Alger. *What the Bible Says about Money.* What the Bible Says Series. Joplin: College Press Publishing Company, 1987.

Friedman, Milton. *Money Mischief: Episodes in Monetary History.* New York: Harcourt Brace Jovanovich, 1992.

Fromm, Erich. *To Have or to Be?* 2d ed. New York: Bantam Books, 1981.

Grant, James. *Money of the Mind: Borrowing and Lending in America from the Civil War to Michael Milken.* New York: Farrar Straus Giroux, 1992.

Greider, William. *Secrets of the Temple.* New York: Simon and Schuster, 1987.

Hyde, Lewis. *The Gift: Imagination and the Erotic Life of Property.* New York: Vintage Books, 1979.

Jones, J. P. *The Money Story.* New York: Drake Publishers Inc., 1973.

Kurtzman, Joel. *The Death of Money: How the Electronic Economy Has Destabilized the World's Markets and Created Financial Chaos.* New York: Simon and Schuster, 1993.

Lapham, Lewis H. *Money and Class in America: Notes and Observations on the Civil Religion.* New York: Ballantine Books, 1988.

Lindgren, Henry Clay. *Great Expectations: The Psychology of Money.* Los Altos: William Kaufmann, Inc., 1980.

Lockhart, Russell A., James Hillman, Arwind Vasavada, John Weir Perry, Joel Covitz, Adolf Guggenbuhl-Craig. *Soul and Money.* Dallas: Spring Publications, Inc., 1982.

Mandell, Lewis. *The Credit Card Industry: A History.*

Twayne's Evolution of American Business Series, edited by Edwin J. Perkins. Boston: Twayne Publishers, 1990.

Millman, Marcia. *Warm Hearts and Cold Cash: The Intimate Dynamics of Families and Money.* New York: The Free Press, 1991.

"Money," *Parabola: The Magazine of Myth and Tradition,* Spring 1991.

Needleman, Jacob. *Money and the Meaning of Life.* New York: Doubleday Currency, 1991.

Parry, Jonathan, and Maurice Bloch, eds. *Money and the Morality of Exchange.* Cambridge and New York: Cambridge University Press, 1989.

Quiggin, A. Hingston. *A Survey of Primitive Money: The Beginnings of Currency.* London: Methuen and Co. Ltd., 1949.

Rockoff, Hugh. "The 'Wizard of Oz' as a Monetary Allegory," *Journal of Political Economy,* vol. 98, no. 4, pp. 739–60.

Sardello, Robert J., and Randolf Severson. *Money and the Soul of the World.* Dallas: The Pegasus Foundation, 1983.

Seidman, L. William. *Full Faith and Credit.* New York: Times Books, 1993.

Simmel, Georg. *The Philosophy of Money.* Edited by David Frisby. Translated by Tom Bottomore and David Frisby. 2d ed. London and New York: Routledge, 1990.

Stein, Joel, and Caroline Levine, eds. The Museum of Fine Arts, Houston, and Parnassus Foundation. *Money Matters: A Critical Look at Bank Architecture.* New York: McGraw-Hill Publishing Company, 1990.

Tierney, Patrick. *The Highest Altar: The Story of Human Sacrifice.* London: Bloomsbury, 1989.

Wixen, Burton N. *Children of the Rich.* New York: Crown Publishers, Inc., 1973.

Yablonsky, Lewis. *The Emotional Meaning of Money.* New York and London: The Gardner Press, Inc., 1991.

INDEX

ABOUT THE AUTHOR

TAD CRAWFORD studied economics at Tufts University and is a graduate of Columbia Law School. Author of six books and co-author of three, his articles have appeared in *Art in America, Glamour, Harper's Bazaar, Self,* and *The Nation.* He is the president of Allworth Press in New York City.